ART DECO
AND MODERNIST
CERAMICS

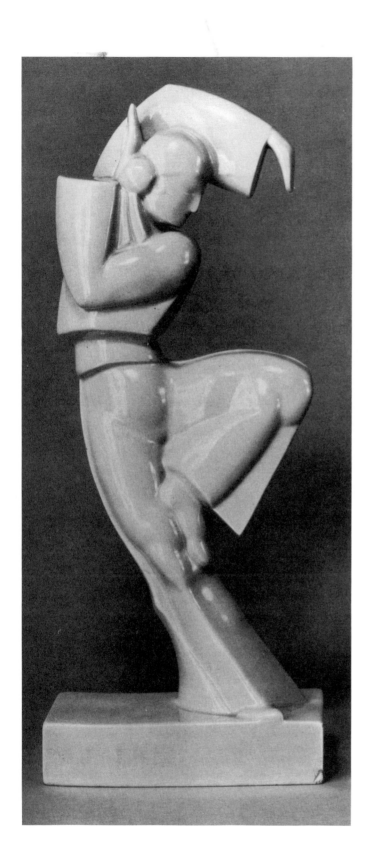

ART DECO AND MODERNIST CERAMICS

KAREN McCREADY

Introduction by Garth Clark

with 287 illustrations, 201 in color

THAMES AND HUDSON

For my lovely husband, Jean-Yves Noblet,
whose patience and understanding saw me
through the process of writing this book, which
is also dedicated to the memory of two dear
friends, Kevin and Len.

Frontispiece, p. 2: *Spanish Dancer*, glazed figurine
by Marjerie for Robj, 1929.

© 1995 Thames and Hudson Ltd, London
First paperback edition

First published in the United States of America in 1995 by Thames
and Hudson Inc., 500 Fifth Avenue, New York, New York 10110

Library of Congress Catalog Card Number 94-61467

ISBN 0-500-27825-3

Printed and bound in Singapore

CONTENTS

ACKNOWLEDGMENTS

My greatest debt of gratitude goes to my friend and mentor Garth Clark, who suggested this project to me some four years ago and made the recommendation to Thames and Hudson on my behalf. His introduction provides the historical background to the individual potters and factories whose work is featured in the text and illustrations. His generosity in providing photographs from the Ceramic Arts Foundation (formerly the Institute for Ceramic History [ICH]) and the Garth Clark Gallery was invaluable. I also wish to express my thanks to the ceramics historian Christina Corsiglia, who freely shared her knowledge of and enthusiasm for modern ceramics with me, generously helping with information (notably biographical details concerning Dr Hermann Gretsch and A. Drexel Jacobson and the proper attribution of a plate by Thelma Frazier Winter) and in multifarious other ways.

John White and Billy Cunningham photographed many of the pieces illustrated, and special thanks are due to both of them for their generosity in contributing their time and skills to the visual realization of the book. Thanks are also due to Sandy Gellis, who helped with its design, and Miguel Cardenas, who provided the line drawings of marks. Collectors were an important resource of rich illustrative material and information: John Loring opened his own collection and that of John Innes and provided the photography session with Billy Cunningham; Joseph Maresca, a delightful connoisseur of Art Deco ceramics, became a special friend; Jerome and Patricia Shaw allowed pieces from their encyclopedic ceramics collection to be photo-graphed; and in the early stages of my research Edward Thorp and Robert Ellison gave me access to their respective collections. Todd Marks generously shared his knowledge of German ceramics with me, and special thanks are also due to Lisha and Robert Sherman, Dawn Bennett and Martin Davidson, Judith and Martin Schwartz, and Susan and Arnold Wechsler.

Many museum professionals came to my aid in gathering information and photographs, including: David McFadden, Deborah Shinn, and Tim Sullivan at the Cooper-Hewitt, National Design Museum, Smithsonian Institution; David Burnhauser, Wolfsonian Foundation; Ulysses G. Dietz and Margaret Di Salvi, Newark Art Museum; Victoria Peltz, Cowan Pottery Museum, Rocky River Public Library; Dr Ingeborg Becker, Bröhan-Museum; Yvònne G.J.M. Joris and Thea Sterken of the Museum Het Kruithuis; and Mary Hujsak, the American Crafts Council Library. I am also grateful to Professor Cheryl Buckley and Nina Lobanov-Rostovsky, both of whom inspired me through their own writing and research. Elisabeth Cameron's *Encyclopedia of Porcelain and Pottery: 1880 to 1960* was an invaluable resource. A lecture by and the writings of Milena Lamarová provided valuable information about Czech Cubism. Sources of all photographs reproduced are listed separately.

I am also indebted to numerous galleries, auction houses, museums, and manufacturers for help. Galleries and their representatives include: Arlie Sulka, Lillian Nassau Ltd; Deborah Pesci and Jonathan Hallam, Barry Friedman Ltd; Mark Waller, Galerié Moderne; Martine de Crevens, Le Pavillon de Sèvres; Georg Kargl, Galerie Metropol; Carole Berk, Carole Berk Ltd; Edward Johnson, Nancy Ltd; and Liz O'Brien, 41 Gallery; Nancy McClelland and Lars Rachen of Christie's, New York, offered their expertise and photo archive, and Philippe Garner of Sotheby's, London, also provided valuable assistance.

I would also like to thank: Lynn Miller of Josiah Wedgwood & Sons Ltd, who was extremely helpful; David Ryan of Norwest Corporation, who kindly lent transparencies and acted as a sounding board for ideas about the period under consideration; Dr Berndt Fritz, Rosenthal AG; Joan Jones, Minton Museum; Ubaldo Grazia, Maioliche Grazia; and Marjory Exton, Lenox China and Crystal.

Missy McHugh provided excellent editorial support and advice as did Ray Fournier, while Jan Axel offered critical suggestions about the glossary. I also wish to thank Dawn Bennett, Stephanie Bleecher, Lisa Goldberg, Meg Malloy, Nancy McCain, Dana McCucci, Mary O'Hearn, Laura Rabhan, Kim Schmidt, Lara Schoeberlein, Keith Seward, Carleen Sheehan, and Vesela Strenovic for research, editorial, and clerical assistance. Susan Gilgore and Natalie Danford helped me with trans-lations from Italian, and Peter Daferner, Margarete Roeder, and Heidi Singer from German. Friends and colleagues who were supportive throughout the writing process include Bonnie Wyper, Maria Friedrich, Dorothy Hafner, and Mort Abromson, and I thank them too.

K.M.   December 1994
New York City

PREFACE

I N THE COURSE OF THE TWO decades between the World Wars, a vast array of arresting ceramic objects—functional and sculptural, manufactured, and hand-made—was produced in styles that reflect not only traditional influences, but also contemporary avant-garde aesthetics, as well as new trends in architecture and engineering. The rich confluence of sources reflected in the ceramics of the era make it an exciting one for investigation. Unlike significant work produced in previous centuries, many fine and historically important pieces dating from 1919–39 have not yet found their way into museums or private collections: hence they are available to be studied and enjoyed, and possibly to be acquired. The aim of this book is not only to stimulate interest in the objects discussed and illustrated, but also to illuminate them in the context of their time and place.

The generic term "ceramics" embraces the entire range of domestic and technical wares made from various clay bodies, including earthenware, stoneware, bone china, terra cotta, and porcelain. (Sometimes less durable ceramic wares such as earthenware are incorrectly referred to as "pottery," which in the vernacular often seems to encompass all types except porcelain, and in some older books on the subject of ceramics a general distinction is made between the categories "pottery" and "porcelain.")

Although dozens of books have been written about the decorative and applied arts of the interwar years, few to date have dealt exclusively with ceramics. The legacy of this explosively creative period includes a rich profusion of ornamental, utilitarian, and sculptural ceramics, which, when viewed together, evoke a colorful picture of the cultures from which they came. The interwar years were characterized not by any single quality, but by contradictions that manifested themselves in the decorative and applied arts in contrasts such as purism vs. ornamentation, tectonic vs. fluid, cube vs. sphere, and ziggurat vs. streamline. Society at large can also be characterized by extremes: prosperity vs. deprivation, and Paradise vs. Utopia come immediately to mind. Within a short space of time the world would become a very different place: people shifted from country to city in large numbers, the middle class grew to become a powerful force and, with it, the "consumer age" was born, effectively democratizing the decorative and applied arts.

Earlier, the fine arts had taken a radical turn with the advent of Cubism (1907) and abstraction in painting. By breaking the conventional "picture plane," Cubism had freed canvas painting for new forms of artistic invention. The new styles in the fine and applied arts found an audience beyond the *cognoscenti* through, for example, Picasso's designs for the ballet *Parade*, which effectively brought avant-garde art to the attention of the theater-going public. Around the same time (1909), Diaghilev's Ballets Russes took Paris by storm: Léon Bakst's exotic sets and costume designs startled audiences and, in effect, liberated color and introduced Oriental motifs to the West. For designers generally, this resulted in greater public acceptance of new, sometimes exotic, idioms. Dozens of other avant-garde movements in art (Futurism, Constructivism, De Stijl, Purism, etc.) and design (Czech Cubism, the Wiener Werkstätte, the Bauhaus, etc.) were emerging in Europe, and created a new visual language evident in all the applied and decorative arts. These rapidly became part of the vocabulary of ceramic form and decoration. At this time, perhaps uncharacteristically, the applied arts absorbed many of the creative inventions of the fine arts. Designers also borrowed concepts such as streamlining from modern engineering, while some architects also designed household objects.

The World at Large: Aesthetic Growing Pains

Prior to the great Exposition Internationale des Arts Décoratifs et Industriels Modernes (originally planned for 1914), held in Paris in 1925, the modern ferment had been boosted by the founding of the Wiener Werkstätte, a craft collaborative that produced a wide range of handsomely designed household objects, fashions, and fabrics. From 1913 to 1932, the Wiener Keramik executed ceramic designs by Wiener Werkstätte artists and architects. During these years, the Bauhaus, the Italian Futurists, and the Russian avant-garde also became involved in the design and production of ceramics, and in Russia after the Revolution of 1917, precious porcelain was employed as a means of conveying the political ideals of the new Communist order to the proletariat.

The Paris Exposition of 1925 as symbol of the era

Today, the Paris Exposition is known to everyone interested in modern decorative art and industrial design. This seminal event, held from April to October, was both heterogeneous, reflecting the visions of many different nations, and homogeneous, exposing a zeitgeist of sorts, articulated by the design of interiors and objects. Viewing the styles of 1925, Robert Pincus-Witten noted in 1970 that "one is forced to observe the interconnections of ultimately highly differentiated extremes," which pivoted around the central theme of "modern design," as specified in the official invitation to participating nations.

Two highly differentiated viewpoints represented at the Exposition can be readily observed by comparing *L'Esprit Nouveau*, the forward-looking plan for a house designed by Le Corbusier and Pierre Jeanneret, with the *Hôtel d'un Collectionneur* (town-house for a collector), created by the leading cabinetmaker of the day, Jacques-Emile Ruhlmann. The first surprise is that such extremes of Modernism were gathered together under the same auspices. On the one hand, there was the sparely articulated "International Style" vision of an architect who stated forthrightly in his writings that "Modern decorative art is not decorated" (the phrase "decorative art" was used by Le Corbusier in reference to the design of objects, including ceramics, below the scale of architecture); on the other hand, the work of Ruhlmann drew unashamedly on the past, borrowing specifically from Louis XVI and eighteenth-century styles, to create masterpieces of Art Deco furniture "fit for a king." Despite their polarized viewpoints, both men are considered Modernists, each having his own cohesive design plan, synthesizing art, craft, and architecture for the creation of a "total" environment, albeit one created using very different materials. This concept of the total work of art, known in German as *Gesamtkunstwerk*, is central to most modern design.

The style now familiarly known as Art Deco followed closely on the heels of Art Nouveau. It was created in France from *c.* 1910 to 1925 and in its own time was called Art Moderne or Style Moderne. An object or piece of furniture in this style was characteristically extremely luxuriant, sumptuously decorated, and precious, something that would fit perfectly into the concept of a totally styled room, perhaps created by the popular design team Louis Süe and André Mare, or by Ruhlmann. In this context a ceramic object modelled by an artisan might be painted by a well-known artist such as Raoul Dufy. Such interdisciplinary cross-fertilization was commonplace and contributed to the enduring excitement of the ceramics of the time, as many leading architects and artists made their contributions in this field.

French Art Deco ceramics are, however, only a part of the story. This study is concerned with not only unique works and those by known designers, but also more common mass-produced examples of modern ceramics in styles ranging from Bauhaus and De Stijl to Streamlined Modern and Machine Age. Many of these ceramics were conceived using only simple combinations of geometric shapes: in the case of one manufactured vase (illustrated in pl. 197), a radical approach to form is evident, representing a startling break from past models. The vase interior, normally a single chamber, is here divided into seven angled compartments; in conjunction with its lozenge-shaped base, this object has a dynamic quality that bespeaks the idea of a modern metropolis, while simultaneously alluding to a sunburst. The piece is glazed in yellow, which reinforces the notion of a sunburst, while eschewing traditional floral decoration and anticipating the future trend of decoration using a single color. In other examples, such as a pitcher made by the Hall China Company (pl. 162), an appreciation of the principles of aerodynamics is obvious in the conception of form, and with it the acknowledgment of the importance of the machine, manufacturing, and speed in the modern age. In addition, many ceramists of the period relied on neoclassical, Asian, or ancient Egyptian examples as models, thereby amalgamating historical precedent and the results of new ethnographic research and archaeological discoveries, especially the opening of Tutankhamen's tomb in 1922. This powerful mix of elements created a surprising new aesthetic that expressed modern ideas.

The style of a ceramic object, like that of a painting or sculpture, offers a point of departure for its appreciation. But, unlike the creation of a painting or a sculpture, the making of functional objects calls for a successful mediation by the designer between utilitarian and aesthetic considerations—to produce work that at its best bespeaks the myths, manners, and ideals of its creator in the context of time and place. The ceramics considered here proclaim the modern era in a variety of ways: some are beautiful, some witty, austere, or purely kitsch; in their diversity of purpose, they utilize a vocabulary which is identifiable and coherent, though sometimes difficult to quantify. Despite varying *raisons d'être* for individual pieces, one discovers many characteristics in common, including an inherent formal sophistication, often rooted in geometry, and a break with historical and folk traditions.

Art Deco and Modernist ceramics, whether handcrafted or factory-made, utilitarian or ornamental, present a glorious microcosm of stylistic currents, with both "high" and "low" examples sharing many common traits. Although seminal ideas have rarely originated in ceramics, some of these objects speak with as much authority as some of the sculpture and architecture of the interwar era. We can thus experience directly the effects upon design of the explosive aesthetic and technological changes that helped to shape the modern world. The lasting force of their aesthetic realization is confirmed by the large number of stylistic conventions which are derived from the design vocabulary of the period. Quite possibly, this was the one time in the history of ceramics that genuinely avant-garde work was produced, a striking example being the tea set by Kasimir Malevich (see p. 16).

The excitement in investigating ceramics of the interwar years is derived much less from the materials or the techniques used (in fact, studies of technical aspects constitute a major field of research in their own right), than from an exploration of their place in a period of exceptional creative activity worldwide—one which engendered an unusual conjunction of avant-garde art and innovative design with modern industrial methods and new marketing techniques.

*   *   *

Following a historical overview of the period by the noted ceramics historian Garth Clark, this compendium of interwar ceramics includes 200 color plates arranged country by country, and a reference section, organized alphabetically, with over 240 entries. The color plates, together with 86 black-and-white photographs and a selection of makers' marks, cover the work of most of the principal artist-potters, designers, and factories active in the 1920s and 1930s, although for reasons of copyright pieces by a few well-known artists (including Jean Dupas, Emile Lenoble, and Edouard-Marcel Sandoz) could not be included. This book thus allows the reader easy access to information about the ceramics of the period that may lead to further research and enjoyment via the extensive Bibliography.

INTRODUCTION

A SURVEY OF CERAMIC ART AND DESIGN, 1919–1939
by Garth Clark

THE PERIOD SURVEYED IN THIS BOOK, embracing the years between the two World Wars, was a time of remarkable creativity for the potter, the ceramic sculptor, and those who designed for industry. Also, it was unparalleled in terms of the collaborative energy between ceramics and the fine arts. Out of the workshops, studios, and factories of this era poured a dazzling stream of ceramic objects of every conceivable color, texture, form, and style. Art Deco, Art Moderne (or Modern), and the various derivations, combinations, and mutations of Modernism produced everything from restrained and unadorned minimalism—with all the integrity and intellectual power of abstract art—to eclectic, jazzy decoration, and luscious, rich glazes that were unashamedly frivolous and hedonistic.

Three major style philosophies dominated this period: Art Deco, Modernism, and Art Moderne. The terms are confusing because they are applied very loosely, are sometimes employed as virtual synonyms, and their usage has changed over time. The situation is further complicated by the fact that the terms are sometimes used to describe periods as well as styles. Historians will frequently talk of the time from 1910 to 1940 as the Modernist era, but this does not of course mean that all the work produced within that period is Modernist in style.

The most popular term today, Art Deco, only gained general currency in the 1960s. The name was derived from the influential Exposition Internationale des Arts Décoratifs et Industriels Modernes held in Paris in 1925. In a purist sense, the phrase "Art Deco style" is applied only to French decorative arts of the years between 1910 and the late 1920s. In this book it is applied in its more populist usage to describe a lively, stylized, and eclectic style of decorative art that began around 1910 and found expression internationally during the 1920s. By 1925 it had already begun its decline.

Modernism was an aesthetic movement that has largely dictated the direction of the more progressive manifestations of art, design, and architecture during this century. Although the simpler, more geometric aspects of Art Deco often resembled or mimicked the stern Modernist ethos, it will be shown that these two aesthetic movements are in fact polar opposites of each other in terms of their design ideologies. Modernism as a style has had a long life and remained the dominant influence until the 1960s, after which it began to be overtaken by the more permissive Post-Modernism.

Art Deco embraced decoration, while Modernism, which rejected embellishment as decadent and bourgeois, was more concerned with issues of utility and social value. Modernism also rejected the highly crafted objects which Art Deco celebrated. Modernists were by and large committed to a vision of a Socialist Utopia and argued that the practice of handcrafting would produce costly bibelots for an elitist market and that in the twentieth century industrial mass production was the only acceptable method of making inexpensive objects.

Art Moderne could be viewed as the illegitimate offspring of Art Deco and Modernism. Denounced as too cold and machine-like by adherents of the softer Art Deco style, it was considered too playful and lacking in ideological purpose by the more cerebral Modernists. However, it celebrated elements of both, and as a result reached and satisfied a larger audience than either of its polarized parents. It was less decorative than Art Deco, less obviously eclectic, and strove harder to appear modern and reductive. The style emerged in the second decade of the century and lasted into the 1950s. (To complicate the nomenclature, the term Art Moderne or Style Moderne was used during the 1920s to describe French Art Deco.)

In addition, the inter-war period saw the emergence of a traditionalist movement amongst studio potters which Karen McCready has wisely decided does not belong within the visual parameters of this compendium. Although some readers may be astounded to find that the single most influential potter of this era, Bernard Leach, does not feature in the book, I feel certain that Leach would have endorsed this omission, for his work has nothing in common with the Art Deco/Moderne/Modernism axis that is the core of Karen McCready's study. Nonetheless, the role played by the more traditional studio potters needs to be suitably acknowledged.

As those acquainted with this period are well aware, the labels Modernism, Art Deco, Art Moderne can be very confusing. A Modernist shape may be emblazoned with decoration that is distinctly Art Deco in character. How then do we label the resulting object? Moreover, the exponents of ceramics—always pragmatic— responded to these often warring protagonists of style in their own way. Some ceramists took up a fundamentalist stance in one camp or another. Others mixed-and-matched styles or simply moved from one to another as the mood took them. Ceramists also produced hybrid styles unique to the medium. Hence readers are advised to adopt a less academic reading of stylistic definitions and to see Art Deco, Modernism, and Art Moderne merely as beacon points to assist them.

This introduction seeks to reveal a selective chronology of events that are keys to the development of ceramics between the World Wars. The emphasis and focus may differ from a broader history of this period, because they are seen in the specific context of pottery and the potter. Also, because it is only an overview of an immensely complex period, many events, workshops, designers, and artists are of necessity omitted from the discussion or only mentioned in passing. A fuller

Monumental vase, glazed earthenware, William D. Gates, American Terra Cotta and Ceramic Company, c.1905–10. H. 18 in. (45.8 cm). An unusual form with strong vertical emphasis represents a proto-modern design, while the use of a green mat glaze links the piece to American art pottery.

Vase, glazed earthenware, Max Laeuger, c.1900. H. 8½ in. (21.2 cm). This piece, shown at the Exposition Universelle in Paris in 1900, utilizes the curvaceous forms typical of Art Nouveau while projecting a distinctly modern presence.

chronology would demand a book unto itself. Many of the factories and individuals not featured in this introduction can be explored in depth in the reference section of this fascinating study.

1850–1910: Proto Art Deco and Modernism

Although adherents of Art Deco and Modernism had become diametrically opposed forces by the early 1920s, they shared common roots. The tap root, in a sense, was the British reform movement which first began to voice its discontent with industrial design in the 1840s. The flashpoint was the Great Exhibition of 1851 held in London—the first major international event of its kind. This event aroused the ire of a small but vociferous group who denounced the adverse effect of industry on the quality of design in daily life.

The most influential of these activists was William Morris (1834–96), who established his workshops in an attempt to restore the values of craftsmanship, and launched a crusade to thwart what he saw as the evils of industrial design. This led eventually to the founding in 1888 of the Arts and Crafts Exhibiting Society, which gave the movement its title. Morris's rabidly anti-industrial views and his refusal to accept the reality of mass production placed him out of step with his times, greatly impairing his effectiveness as a missionary of reform. Interestingly, it was during a lecture to an audience of potters that he revealed a rare moment of compromise with the machine: if they must employ a machine in their work, he cautioned, then the process should be "mechanical with a vengeance." ("Art and the beauty of the Earth," London, 1898, p. 22).

The greatly undervalued Christopher Dresser (1834–1904) provides an interesting contrast to Morris. The two men shared similar political beliefs, as well as a desire to improve design for the home. For both of them the Great Exhibition of 1851 was a clarion call to action, but Dresser saw the machine as the friend of the masses and accepted that only through industry could his designs reach a large public at a low cost. In this he was arguably more consistent with his Socialist beliefs than Morris, and Dresser's thinking would be echoed by the Modernist movement in the twentieth century, though perhaps more puritanically than he had advocated.

Dresser's work in metal was startlingly proto-Modern. If one had come upon one of his kettles or metal teapots in the workshops of the Bauhaus in 1920, its design would not have seemed at all out of place. His ceramics were also prophetic, some of them having a slightly Art Deco edge in their geometric construction, but these designs—and particularly those produced while he was art director of Linthorpe Pottery from 1879 to 1882—spoke more of the coming of Art Nouveau's exploration of organic abstraction in the decorative arts. For Dresser, as well as others who contributed to the Aesthetic and Art Nouveau movements, inspiration came from a serious study of Japanese art and craft.

The ideals of the British Arts and Crafts Movement were soon transported across the Channel. Many important early proto-Modernists, from Hermann

Vase with underglaze decoration in blue, black, and green with crackle finish, Edmond Lachenal, c.1900–10. This example of the style known as Japonisme is decorated overall with naturalistic bamboo shoots. H. 14 in. (35.5 cm).

Porcelain cup with solid handle and contrasting geometrical decorative motifs, Josef Böck, Vienna, c.1901–2.

Porcelain tea set with stencilled red-orange decoration on a white ground, Jutta Sika, Josef Böck, Vienna, c.1901–2. H. of teapot 10¾ in. (27.3 cm). Here the use of avant-garde shapes and spare decoration presages the reductive trends of later Modernist designs.

Muthesius to Henry van de Velde and Josef Hoffmann, found ideological excitement and challenge in the articles of faith proposed by Morris and the Arts and Crafts Movement. The accent on functionality, on simple forms, on truth to materials, and, in the case of Morris, an underlying commitment to Socialism, created the foundation for a new, intellectually rigorous approach to design and art.

However, the Europeans were little impressed with the aesthetic models of the British movement (except for some of the architecture), and progressive European designers proceeded to create the vibrant, but short-lived style, variously known as Art Nouveau, *Jugendstil* and *Sezessionsstil*, that emerged in the 1890s and was all but over by 1900. French and Belgian Art Nouveau was erotic and sensual, while the German *Jugendstil* and Austria's *Sezessionsstil* took a more objective, structural, approach to form, seeking out the geometric soul of the natural world.

For ceramics in particular, it was in the domains of the Austro-Hungarian Empire that the mood of clean, stylish, and indisputably "modern" design was first and most effectively struck. The designs of the architect Josef Hoffmann and of the Wiener Werkstätte are of particular interest. One of several architects active in the movement, Hoffmann worked primarily in a palette of black and white (because he believed that color had too many historicist overtones). Hoffmann created startlingly modern ceramic designs, using simple decoration consisting of borders of black-and-white squares, reflecting his admiration for similar decorative motifs employed by the Glaswegian, Charles Rennie Mackintosh.

Koloman Moser, who taught with Hoffmann at the Kunstgewerbeschule in Vienna, encouraged his students to develop new designs for ceramics which were produced in 1903–4 by the porcelain firm of Josef Böck. Again, just like the metalware of Dresser which could be transposed easily into another era, these designs would still have looked aggressively modern in the mid-1920s. At that time too, one would not have been surprised to find these objects—with their fecund motifs of rising bubbles (similar to the leitmotif of effervescent champagne in the Jazz Age), their stylized geometric decorations and solid triangular handles—in a chic, decorative-art boutique of a Paris department store.

Other Secession designers, such as Michael Powolny, founder of the Wiener Keramik, were more playful and consciously decorative. His figurines in the form of fat putti are conventional enough, but a modern styling is evident in garlands of flowers that have been slightly geometricized and abstracted and either painted in rich polychrome or presented in the *Sezessionsstil* look of black and white. He also used the latter palette to create superb vases with geometric designs, although he would sometimes offset their simplicity with a lick of gold around the rim, revealing a taste for the traditional and the bourgeois that later overcame and erased his Modernist leanings.

While the Viennese creations often betrayed this underlying taste for sugar and cream, the designs coming out of Prague between 1908 and 1914 were tougher and more Modernist. This tendency expressed itself in what is now called Czech Cubism, in which the spirit of Cubist painting was applied with great ingenuity and clarity in the Czech decorative arts. The ceramics of the Artěl Cooperative (an organization founded in 1908 by a group of architects and designers to mirror the aims of the Wiener Werkstätte) was particularly prescient. Their vessels were stark assemblies of volume, decoration was essentially there to expose the structure of a vase, and Artěl often adopted Hoffmann's black-and-white motif to render these forms even more powerful and startling.

The vases of, for example, Vlastislav Hofman and Pavel Janák are remarkable examples of proto-Modernism—sometimes playing with the disjunctive, bold angularity of Cubism and at other times combining serene, powerfully rational assemblies of black-and-white geometric elements. Equally intriguing in an examination of Czech Cubism in the decorative arts are the drawings for unrealized ceramic designs. One of the most dramatic of these was Bedrich Feuerstein's *Design for a tea set* (1919), which combines decoration, form, handles, and spout into a unity so intimately intertwined that one cannot conceive of any one part without the others (see *Czech Cubism: Architecture, Furniture and Decorative Arts 1910–1925*, New York, 1992; fig. 196). Moreover, in an act of sophistry the surface decoration actually mimics and reveals the interior volumetric rhythms of the teapot.

1917–1925: Russian Revolutionary Porcelains

The first Revolutionary porcelains were produced in Russia soon after the October Revolution of 1917, when the Imperial Porcelain Factory was taken over. The Imperial factory was renamed first the State Porcelain Factory and then in 1925 the Lomonosov State Porcelain Factory, producing some of the most impressive and fascinating ceramics of this period. These objects were not destined for the tables of the common man, but were instruments of *agitprop* designed to carry political and moral messages, created in limited editions as inspirational showpieces that were taken to international fairs and presented to the public in special patriotic window displays at the State Telegraph Agency in Moscow and other cities. Costly to produce, they were somewhat out of line with Socialist values, despite their

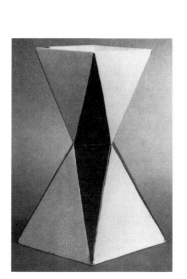

Vase featuring contrasting geometric elements, Vlastislav Hofman, 1914. H. 12 in. (30.5 cm).

Mug, hand-painted porcelain, Mikhail Mikhailovich Adamovich, State Porcelain Factory, c.1924. The design, *The Shift is Coming*, dates from 1919.

Porcelain cup and teapot, designed by Kasimir Malevich, State Porcelain Factory, 1922. H. of cup 2⅜ in. (6.0 cm); of teapot 6½ in. (16.5 cm).

moralistic and propagandist slogans and drawings of valiant workers and the hammer and sickle wreathed in flowers.

The ceramics have an art world glamour due to the direct involvement of seminal figures in early Modern art, such as Vassily Kandinsky, Alexander Rodchenko, Vladimir Tatlin (founder of Constructivism), and Kasimir Malevich (founder of Suprematism). Tatlin taught ceramics at the Moscow Art School (Vkhutein), while Malevich was responsible for perhaps one of the most important ceramic objects of the era, the Suprematist teapot (discussed below).

Russian Revolutionary ceramics were not well known even in specialist circles until recently, but those who did know of this work have tended to revere it as one of the great achievements of modern ceramic art. A recent flurry of exhibitions and publications has provided ample opportunity for the initial celebrity status of this material to dull and for a more objective assessment to emerge. After viewing the work in successive exhibitions, one is able to distance oneself somewhat from the intimidating pedigree and its romantic "brave new world" aura, and to see more clearly what it did and did not contribute to ceramic art and design. Firstly, the achievement of the bulk of the Revolutionary porcelains is, with a handful of exceptions, attributable to the world of graphic design, and it comes as no surprise to discover how many of the decorators of these wares had a background of book illustration or graphic design.

This point is not made in order to demean the importance of the work, which in fact encompasses some of the most inspired and accomplished surface decoration of ceramics in this century. What is surprising, however, is that the underpinning for most of the painting, particularly on plates, is a classical sensibility which—if one sets aside the freshness of style, imagery, and subject—obeys quite closely the compositional rules of the traditional decoration used at the Imperial Porcelain Factory, rather than attempting any radical new approach to surface ornament. However, this body of work lacked a parallel exploration of new forms. Indeed, most of the best Revolutionary platters had their decoration painted on porcelain blanks left over from the reign of the Tsar, conveying proletarian messages on wares that had previously been destined to reach the tables of the aristocracy. Ian Wardropper of the Art Institute of Chicago has wittily characterized this seeming contradiction as "Red Stars on White Plates" (*News from a Radiant Future: Soviet Porcelain from the Collection of Craig H. and Kay A. Tuber*, exhibition catalogue, Chicago, 1992, p. 14).

Only a handful of forms were created that matched the kind of innovation that was evident at that time in sculpture or architecture. An attempt under Tatlin's guidance to create double-walled vessels (to help reduce heat loss), while at the same time doing away with the need for a handle, was perhaps the most radical experiment in utilitarian terms. The most impressive design, however, was a set of three cups and a teapot by Malevich, the teapot in particular being one of the most important pieces of twentieth-century ceramic art. Apart from its startling beauty, this teapot—made up of a brutal, confrontational assemblage of geometric volumes—represents a watershed for the conceptual freedom of ceramics. Malevich

Suprematist half-cup, experimental design by Kasimir Malevich, porcelain decorated with a Suprematist painting, State Porcelain Factory, 1923. H. 2 ⅜ in. (6.0 cm).

set out to play with the idea of a teapot, ignoring its utilitarian imperatives, endorsing the notion that such a vessel could provide a format for the expression of art. Instead of simply making a teapot, he created an object that was *about* being a teapot. The half-cup is another important work by Malevich, with a Suprematist design by Ilya Chasnik painted on the surface. The decoration and the form are not entirely at ease with each other, but the tension is dynamic and forces one to try to marry the energy of the painting and its specific and active notions of space with the physical reality of the oddly shaped half-cup.

These objects were seen by other designers and ceramists when shown at the Paris Exposition in 1925 and had a considerable impact: firstly, because they showed ceramics imbued with a serious message—political education; secondly, because they represented the fruits of a collaboration with two of the most seminal avant-garde art movements of the century; and lastly, due to the startling graphic bravura and heroic qualities of the work itself. Amongst those touched by the porcelains was Tullio d'Albisola, as a result of which he was inspired to found the Futurist ceramics movement in Italy.

1918: The Bauhaus and Modernism

Modernism was from the outset an ideological movement, with its manifestos, clearly articulated social goals, and critical intellectual stance. Art Deco was by comparison less a movement *per se* than a spontaneous flowering of fashion. Modernist thinking was at odds with the spirit of Art Deco: its search for the new, combined with edicts that form should follow function, and its blanket rejection of decoration for decoration's sake, meant that it could never be at ease with the permissive eclectic nature of Art Deco.

The crucible for Modernism's identity, at least in reference to design, was the Bauhaus school, founded in 1919 in Weimar. In its first year the school was sympathetic to the crafts. Indeed, its founder, Walter Gropius, an admirer of the British Arts and Crafts movement, wrote in the first manifesto of wanting to tear down the "arrogant barrier between craftsman and artist" created by class distinctions. The cover of the manifesto carried a wood-engraving of a cathedral by Lyonel Feininger, intended to underscore the fact that the Bauhaus was a modern-day attempt to recreate the spirit of the craft guilds which had collaborated in the construction of the great medieval cathedrals of Europe.

Within a few years, as more radical thinkers began to take over the faculty, the approach of the Bauhaus to art, crafts, and design began to alter. This change was signaled in 1922 with a new slogan, "Art and Technics," replacing the original liaison of art and craft. Craft as an end in itself was deemed too bourgeois by the new guard made up of László Moholy-Nagy, Marcel Breuer, and others. The Bauhaus masters saw the making of objects by hand as inefficient and costly. Reformers feared that the market for crafts would inevitably be restricted to the more affluent middle and upper classes and would be, as a result, decadent and regressive.

Craft was considered acceptable as a means of learning about materials and processes, provided that the end-result was a design that could be used for mass production, placing the product within reach of the majority. This thinking was fundamentally accurate. Morris found to his dismay that the cost of hand production limited him to the role of maker of elaborately ornamented baubles for the rich. However, the Bauhaus view of crafts was simplistic, predicated upon the belief that the *only* role of the crafts was to make and sell wares, whereas the progressive wing of the modern crafts movement was more concerned (as it is today) with opening up a dialogue about processes and materials, an experimental direction unlikely to flourish in an industrial setting and equally unlikely to appeal to conventional bourgeois taste.

The rejection of decoration is similarly based upon a spurious theory about its inherent decadence, but whether or not the dislike of decoration was rational, this attitude suited Modernism's puritanism, with its back-to-basics approach to design, and certainly was a refreshing contrast to some of the decorative excesses of the recent past. However, the assumption that the average man and woman would appreciate and desire the spare, undecorated Modernist designs proved to be incorrect. Indeed, the working class found Bauhaus design alien, cold and unappealing, and instead it attracted the cognoscenti of modern design, a small group of affluent, cultured, and privileged followers—exactly the opposite of its intended audience.

The pottery produced by the Bauhaus reflects the early ideological bent of the school. Led by joint-masters, the sculptor Gerhard Marcks (Master of Form) and the Thuringian folk potter Max Krehan (Master of Craft), the school focused on design for industry. The talented group of ceramics students included Otto Lindig, Lucia Moholy, Theodor Bogler, Marguerite Friedlaender, and her future husband Frans Wildenhain. Their prototypes, which reflected the sturdy influence of German folk pottery, featuring full-bodied forms with generous handles and spouts, had some influence on contemporary commercial design. Friedlaender was one of the most prolific designers and, after leaving the school, she worked for the Staatliche Porzellan-Manufaktur in Berlin, creating rather pure designs featuring tea- and coffee-pots with intrusively large spouts that were a distinctive feature of the Bauhaus Pottery Workshop aesthetic (see plate 2). Both Lindig and Bogler designed ceramics for factories such as Staatliche Majolika-Manufaktur Karlsruhe and Velten-Vordamm.

However, Bauhaus ceramics did not make a dramatic impact on a par with the Bauhaus influence on furniture design, architecture, graphics, and even photography. In part this might have been because the pottery was situated in Dornburg-an-der-Saale, some distance from the main school, hence collaboration between the pottery and the other workshops was limited. In any event, the ceramics workshop closed in 1925, when the Bauhaus moved to Dessau. Another, more likely, reason lies in the nature of ceramics. Whereas new technologies and new materials could be adopted in designing furniture or buildings, thereby

Stoneware pitcher with banded decoration, Otto Lindig, *c*.1930. H. (approx.) 12 in. (30.5 cm).

producing dramatic advances in design, "new" ceramics had still to grapple with the same long-established, traditional processes and basic materials that had been used for centuries.

Equally, the forms could not be reinvented to suit the taste of the twentieth century. Even today, the most modern teapot designs are essentially similar to the form of the first teapots made in China in the late Ming period five hundred years ago (excluding the addition in the nineteenth century of the small inner sieve to trap tea-leaves when pouring). A simple, unadorned, straight-cylinder Empire-style cup from the early nineteenth century was almost as modern in appearance and as utilitarian as anything the Bauhaus pottery workshop could design. Most ceramic forms had been perfected by the time of the Bauhaus, hence all the designers could do was strip pottery of its ornament and offer a new style that was more pared down and fundamentalist in appearance.

1925: Art Deco and the Paris Exposition

The French Art Deco style was popularized internationally by the Exposition Internationale des Arts Décoratifs et Industriels Modernes (which drew over 28 million visitors). Art Deco style dates from around 1910, though it was only after World War I that it began to develop momentum. By 1925 it had begun to peak and by 1928 was already in decline. Amongst the earliest Art Deco ceramists was André Metthey, whose work reflected exotic influences from the Middle East; it features rich glazes with crackled golds and jewel-like overglazes, thus setting exactly the hedonistic approach to decorative art that was to become the rage of the 1920s. It should be understood, however, that the Art Deco artists saw themselves as Modern, even though they were not adherents of orthodox Modernism. This outlook was expressed in "modernizing" elements—a sense of abstraction and geometricizing of form and ornament which were vaguely Cubist in appearance, but more usually drawn from older influences such as Aztec design. Even when Art Deco was pursued with a reductive panache, as in the stylish and spare designs of Jean Luce, this tendency must not be mistaken for Modernism proper.

Art Deco design derived from a simplifying of historical design sources, rather than from a real search for the new. For the greater part, Art Deco design is a promiscuous pastiche, albeit a glorious one, of classic decorative art of the past: Chinese, Persian, Japanese, Egyptian, Pre-Columbian, and other cultures. The original source of inspiration was revised, restyled, and revamped with superb taste and an eye for fashionable drama. However, while borrowing generously from the past, Art Deco designers were generally able to avoid the pitfalls of the overwrought nineteenth-century historicism and, while what they made was not new in the strictest sense of the word, it was at least theatrically innovative.

The stars of the Art Deco ceramics are unquestionably the French studio potters. First André Metthey, then Emile Lenoble, Emile Decœur, Jean Mayodon, René Buthaud, Henri Simmen, Séraphin Soudbinine, and many others, brought extraordinary skill and vitality to the ceramic arts. In the 1920s, Paris was the center of the ceramic art world. Purists of the day objected to the whiff of decadence in this work, but that was part of a deliberate statement of excess and affluence. While one may quibble over ideological issues, the pots themselves were undeniably beautiful and seductive. In terms of truth to materials, the potters did not deny the nature of ceramics, but simply sought to extract from clays and glazes the most opulent effects that the medium could produce.

French designers who worked for the ceramics industry enjoyed the same spirit and high-craft ethics as the studio potters, adapted to the realities of industrial processes. In particular, they excelled at high-quality wares in porcelain. Edouard-Marcel Sandoz's sublime lidded bird vessels for Théodore Haviland of Limoges are amongst the best of a seemingly endless array of high-quality manufactured decorative ceramics. The variety of decorative and functional ceramics was as breathtaking in its diversity as in its stylishness—from Robj's amusing jazz-musician figurines to the elegant dinnerware of Jean Luce. Soon other countries began to explore the potential of Art Deco Ceramics, with varying degrees of success and quality. Czechoslovakia and other Central European countries produced quantities of cheaply made wares in lively designs. Denmark and Sweden, on the other hand, concentrated on the high end of the market, making finely crafted objects that revealed a sobriety of design and seriousness of purpose.

Among the finest expressions of Art Deco outside France were the Italian architect Gio Ponti's designs from 1923 to 1930 for the porcelain factory Richard-Ginori. Ponti merged the influence of Giorgio de Chirico's surreal landscapes with translations of painted decoration on Renaissance maiolica, creating a body of designs that were witty, vibrantly colored, and impressively literate in their references to the ceramic and decorative arts. Ginori executed a large number of these designs, which collectively comprise one of the most important and accomplished groups of industrially produced decorative ceramic wares in the twentieth century. They capture what is best and most intelligent in the Art Deco spirit, combined with a uniquely Italianate sensibility and vitality.

Scandinavia's role was important, although its approach was not as playful as that of the French. Art Deco pottery from Denmark, Norway, Sweden, and Finland tended to be a touch heroic, heavier in appearance, and less colorful. The key to the success of Scandinavian ceramic art lay in the liberal-minded approach of factory managements—Arabia, Gustavsberg, Royal Copenhagen Porcelain, Bing & Grøndahl—who encouraged imaginative designers, but also provided workshops, stipends, and other support for studio potters to encourage experiment and innovation. Ebbe Sadolin, Jais Nielsen, Knud Kyhn, Nils Thorson, Ewald Dahlskog, Arthur Percy, and the legendary Wilhelm Kåge were amongst the galaxy of designers and artists who worked for the factories. Due to the support that the artists received, Scandinavian ceramics, unlike those of France and England, did not lose momentum after World War II, remaining at the forefront both of modern design and of fine studio-pottery production into the 1960s.

Group of jazz musicians, glazed porcelain figures, Robj, c.1925. H. of standing figure 10 in. (25.4 cm).

Group of vases, glazed earthenware, Ewald Dahlskog, Bo Fajans, c.1930. H. of middle vase 7 in. (17.7 cm). The use of molded ribbing (left and right) and painted ribbing (centre) lends the pieces a strong modern presence. The effect is similar to that of banding, a popular technique used by designers such as Susie Cooper.

1928: British Art Deco

By contrast with the Continent, the Art Deco of British manufacturers was much more populist, for economic rather than social reasons. Britain's middle and upper classes lacked the sense of fashion and experiment that their counterparts across the Channel seemed to savor so greatly. The market for costly, high-fashion, decorative ceramics was limited, and so Art Deco was redesigned for the larger working-class and lower-middle-class audience. The wares were manufactured as cheaply as possible, often with an earthenware body, though some exceptional bone china was produced. British designers took the elegance of French Art Deco and, by vulgarizing it for a less discriminating market, scored a commercial success.

Although a case could be made to justify excluding such populist material from this study, for it is after all a pastiche of a pastiche, the cheap, novelty end of the Art Deco market does possess a real charm. It is very much the folk art of the machine age and it is therefore appropriate for it to be featured because it represents a mainstream taste that counterbalances the more esoteric and elitist elements of the Art Deco marketplace. One thinks most readily of the novelty teapots (cars with licence plates reading "T42," tanks, women in crinoline skirts, cottages, Humpty Dumpty, and other equally amusing forms), and the flashy wares of Clarice Cliff. However, one must acknowledge that even though British industry was very sluggish in responding to this market and did not begin to offer interesting Art Deco designs until 1928–32, some creations of consequence were produced. Perhaps not surprisingly, it was the British love of tea that brought out the best. The finest tea-service designs of Carlton Ware, Shelley Potteries, A.E. Gray, Foley Potteries, and others are, aside from a slight crudeness in their execution, the stylistic peers of their French counterparts; in particular, the work of Susie Cooper is amongst the best of all British Art Deco design.

Women played a crucial role. Apart from Susie Cooper, Clarice Cliff designed for Wilkinson Pottery, Charlotte Rhead for Wood & Sons, and Millicent Taplin for Wedgwood. They created some of the most lively and commercially successful designs. The attraction of these wares was that they were all hand-painted, the work of an army of anonymous but talented decorators. Cliff's "Bizarre" and other pottery designs became so popular that by 1939 she employed over 200 paintresses to hand-paint her wares.

Painters from the fine arts were attracted to the 1930s rage for painted decorative ceramic ware, such as the distinguished Royal Academician Sir Frank Brangwyn, who designed a bucolic "Harvest" pattern for Royal Doulton. In 1934, the involvement of artists in china decoration was given a new focus in an "Exhibition of Contemporary Art for the Table," held in London at Harrod's department store. Organized by E. Brain & Co. and Wilkinson Pottery, this show attracted an interesting group of artists, each of whom was paid a fee of £10 plus the promise of royalties. In addition to some of the leading ceramic designers, such as Gordon Forsyth and Clarice Cliff, the project included the Bloomsbury figures

Vase with stepped profile and turned grooves designed by Keith Murray, glazed earthenware, Josiah Wedgwood & Sons Ltd, c.1935. H. 9 in. (22.9 cm).

Duncan Grant and Vanessa Bell and other well-known painters of the day—Paul Nash, Graham Sutherland, Dame Laura Knight, John Armstrong, and Ben Nicholson. The sculptress Barbara Hepworth also submitted designs. The designs were meant to find a popular audience, but in fact the wares ended up being sold at a relatively high price, as much as £35 for a dinner service for twelve (more than three times the cost of an equivalent service by Susie Cooper). Interestingly, the most popular of all the designs proved to be "Circus" by Dame Laura Knight, arguably the most old-fashioned and least stylish of the services on display.

The British pottery industry produced very little that could be termed true Modernism. The British taste seemed to be for whimsy and pattern. The one important exception is found in the work of the architect and designer Keith Murray, one of the best exponents of Modernist design in ceramics. His vase designs for Wedgwood in the 1930s are amongst the purest explorations of ceramic form of this era. Undecorated except for lines incised or stepped into the clay, these vases are simple and elegant. Wedgwood developed a dense, mat, "Moonstone" glaze (in green, white, blue, and straw) that was the perfect match for the generous volumes. The lines were not simply decorative, but revealed the structure of the vessel and the finishing process of hand-turning. Furthermore, the work was a witty nod to the past, in particular the "engine-turned" wares introduced by Josiah Wedgwood in the late eighteenth century, engraved with lines using an ingenious eccentric lathe.

Futurist Ceramics: Fine Arts and Clay

The Art Deco period was a busy time of collaboration between art and industry, brought about by a mixture of goals—aesthetic, social, economic, and political. A belief in Socialism was almost *de rigueur* amongst the more progressive art community of the time, and artists were seeking a more proletarian outlet for their talents. However, in the impoverished 1930s the motivation was more often one of financial survival. During the Depression the art market slumped, and in order to earn a living artists turned to designing tableware, fabrics, and furniture, as well as to working in other areas of the applied arts.

Aeroceramica, the Futurist ceramics movement, was propelled by a mixture of commercial optimism and aesthetic ambition. While the artists hoped to derive some income from their works, their overwhelming desire was to create a new body of important limited-edition ceramics in the Futurist idiom. Tullio d'Albisola (Tullio Mazzotti), the founder of the movement, was inspired by the visit he made to the 1925 Exposition in Paris, where he saw examples of the Revolutionary porcelains from Russia. He returned to his father's pottery in Albisola Mare on the Italian Riviera and, together with F.T. Marinetti (1876–1944), the founder of Futurism and a frequent visitor to the pottery, wrote and published a manifesto for Futurist ceramics entitled *Ceramica e Aeroceramica* (1930).

The ceramics produced between 1928 and 1939 were imaginative, witty, satirical, and saturated with color and light. Amongst those who participated were painters, sculptors, and "poets" (a Futurist term for multi-media artists), including Giuseppe Anselmo, Nicolaj Diulgheroff, Farfa, Fillia, Alfredo Gaudenzi, Bruno Munari (b.1907), Enrico Prampolini (1894–1956), and Nino Strada. The painter Lucio Fontana also worked at the factory in the 1930s, but his works were not within the general stylistic parameters of the "Aeroceramisti."

Apart from a single exhibition held in 1982 at the Museo Internazionale delle Ceramiche in Faenza, the achievements of Futuristic ceramics have only been superficially explored. It is fascinating on several levels, for this was one of the few ceramic experiments of its kind (other than the Soviet Revolutionary porcelains) which deliberately set out to locate ceramics within a major fine arts movement (albeit somewhat late in its influence). The resulting work was often powerful and prophetic, particularly of the direction that some American pottery was to take in the decades ahead.

1930s: The USA and Art Moderne

Art Moderne, less decorative than Art Deco, was aggressively modern in appearance, although in its approach to function it could be just as self-indulgent as Art Deco. It was known by several names, including the "Machine Art Modern" style and "streamline" style. It was consumer-oriented and promised (though it did not always deliver) the speed, efficiency, and optimism associated with a brave, new technological world.

America excelled at this style, though less so in ceramics than in other materials. The style is at its best in adventurous, Futurist-seeming designs such as Norman Bel Geddes's proposed cruise ships and Raymond Loewy's powerful, streamlined steam locomotives which, even while stationary, give the impression of a bullet racing to some exciting future destiny. Interestingly, these massive ship and locomotive forms, simplified, miniaturized and abstracted, found their way into every element of the design vocabulary—from architecture to toasters—and they were even mimicked in ceramics, particularly in the "locomotive" teapots of Hall China Company.

In part Art Moderne was the result of a new-found romance with the machine. The notion of "Machine Art" started to become popular in exhibitions held at the ground-breaking Museum of Modern Art in New York, where industrial objects were put on show and accorded the same reverence as sculpture and painting. The notion that machines could be aesthetically attractive was not new; Marinetti had made this claim for the machine in his Futurist manifesto of 1909, but this romance with the Machine Age was picked up by the media and the machine aesthetic became a fad of the 1930s.

The weakness of American Art Moderne is that unlike Modernism it lacked the cold steel of idealistic commitment comparable to that of Modernism's intellectual resolve and as a result was dedicated less to reinventing than to restyling—clothing old designs in sleek modern camouflage. When Yvònne Joris of the Kruithuis

Museum at 's Hertogenbosch in the Netherlands came up with the title "Functional Glamour" to describe an exhibition of American utilitarian pottery, albeit works from the 1980s, she hit on the core difference between European Modernism and American Art Moderne.

To the Europeans the very notion of glamour was antithetical to Modern Functionalism, but to American designers, living under the cultural shadow of Hollywood, this kind of allure was essential to seduce the consumer. American Art Moderne was consumer-driven, and thus was socially responsive without necessarily being socially activist. The style was shrewdly calculated to sell. Yet, even given the pragmatism of Art Moderne, it was sometimes too progressive for the taste of the average consumer.

Curiously, America was never an important player in the field of ceramic design and manufacture (in contrast to its virtually unchallenged dominance in ceramic art since the 1950s), but it did produce a few Art Moderne designs that deserve comment. The "refrigerator wares" of Hall China Company (so named because they were water pitchers, butter containers, and other useful items, often created as premiums for the refrigerator manufacturers to encourage potential buyers during the Great Depression) are a perfect example of populist Art Moderne. The simple shapes required only the most basic two-part moulds and the wares were cheap to manufacture. Individual pieces were usually glazed in a single color chosen from a very appealing palette: acid green, vivid orange, crisp blues, and a startling fire-engine red. The forms were often inspired by the sleek pressed-metal shapes of contemporary refrigerators, while others slyly suggested abstracted renderings of automobiles or locomotives.

These wares have stood the test of time remarkably well and are still actively collected and enjoyed today. Indeed, interest in these designs has been so great that some of the better examples are being remanufactured today. Many present-day ceramists have been strongly influenced by the obvious economy of means in their production, as well as by the persistent cheerfulness of the pieces. They would seem to meet Morris's admonition that industrially produced pots be made "mechanical with a vengeance."

Another important example is the 1938 "American Modern" dinnerware by Russel Wright, one of America's leading modern designers. This was the first truly modern tableware to be both designed and manufactured in the United States. (One might cite the gimmicky "Fiesta Ware" of Frederick H. Rhead that had been released earlier, but this was more a pastiche drawn from Californian art pottery and did not have the originality and design integrity of "American Modern.") Surprisingly, when "American Modern" was released, it became an instant rage amongst American housewives starved for good modern design. The success of this single design was to turn the small, struggling Steubenville Pottery into a highly successful and profitable company.

Today, devotees of Wright (including this writer) still collect the service, which retains considerable visual charm, with its unusual glaze colors and sensual organic styling. However, it also summarizes the failing of American ceramic design. The real issues of functionalism received less careful attention from Wright than did the styling. The service has a myriad design problems, beginning with the clay and the glaze, which tends to chip relatively easily. Quality control was inconsistent and colors varied from firing to firing. Many of the forms have design flaws: the cup is too wide and shallow, hence hot beverages cool within minutes; the sugar bowl has a small constricted opening that makes access and cleaning difficult; the plate has no collar and a low rim, making spillage likely when serving foods with sauces. Worst of all, the wide-mouthed spouts on the coffee-pots and teapots, though attractive and consistent with the overall style of the wares, allow the contents to gush rather than pour.

Despite this, there are successes: the water pitcher is one of the finest designs of the era and is very practical. Aside from the slightly disturbing fact that the salad bowls look a little like bedpans, the incurving sides do serve a useful purpose by keeping the salad in when it is being tossed. For the purist, "function-determines-form," European school of Modernists the interesting lesson to be learned from the continued popularity of Wright's "American Modern"—despite some glaring utilitarian failings—is that in functional ceramics efficiency is not necessarily the ultimate virtue.

The affection that one feels for these objects is the sum of a number of factors. Convenience of use is important, but equally significant is the ability of the ware to arouse the senses by its tactile quality, its sensuality, and its charm. If an object provides enjoyment, the user will often come to terms with and accept some design flaws. All of these elements came together in Wright's "American Modern," which captured (and has retained) the heart of the American consumer.

The work of Eva Zeisel, the only other Modern ceramics designer of consequence during this period, brought a greater unity of function and style to American dinnerware. Zeisel had been designing ceramics since 1926 in Eastern Europe and then in Russia, where she was appointed art director of the China and Glass Industry of the Russian Republic. She was ousted in a purge of foreign experts, fled to Vienna, and then traveled via England to settle in the United States. Her style was remarkably fluid and elegant and sought to embody the spirit of Modernism. For instance, one of her first commissions was a dinner service for the retail and mail order firm Sears, Roebuck. She named the design "Stratoware" in honor of Trans World Airlines' new Stratoliner, thus associating the humble dinner plate with a product of the latest technology.

However, it was her commission for the Castleton China Company of New Castle, Pennsylvania, that rocketed her to national prominence. The resulting design, named "Museum," was launched in 1946 at a special exhibition held at the Museum of Modern Art, New York; this was only the fourth modern service of any quality to be made and marketed in the United States. (The first three were Wright's "American Modern," Frederick H. Rhead's "Fiesta Ware" for Homer Laughlin, and Viktor Schreckengost's "Manhattan" for American Limoges.) She then went on to her own design for Red Wing, Riverside, and many other leading potteries, creating a distinctive formal language—a marriage of soft lyrical biomorphism with a structure that was pure and classical, usually unadorned or with only sparse decoration. In her work, Zeisel brought a pure Modernist distinction to the field of ceramics that has yet to be equaled.

Traditionalism and the Studio Pottery Movement

While the Bauhaus Pottery Workshop was trying to introduce designs for the ceramic industry, another revolution of sorts was taking place in the years following World War I—the emergence of the studio potter. Although some pioneering studio potters were already active at the turn of the century, the movement in its more cohesive sense was very much a post-World War I phenomenon. In the late nineteenth and the early twentieth century, unique ceramic objects were created by the artist-potter—an altogether different kind of maker—and produced by hand. The artist-potter was in effect a white-collar supervisor presiding over a workshop, designing on paper and delving into glaze science, but leaving the handling of the clay and the decoration of the pottery to a team of craftspeople and skilled workers. Arguably, the first of such artist-potters were French, Théodore Deck being one of the pioneers. The idea of small workshops producing unique decorative wares quickly spread to other parts of Europe, to England, and then to the United States. Art pottery became a popular rage for some time and was one of the most commercially successful "products" of the reform movement, with independent potteries as well as art pottery departments being opened within ceramic factories and flourishing throughout the West.

Although there were rare individuals working at the turn of the century who can be termed studio potters (Adelaide Alsop Robineau and George Ohr in America, and Sir Edmund Elton and the Martin brothers in Britain), the emergence of a studio-pottery movement begins around 1920 and is tied to the energies and writings of a charismatic English polymath, Bernard Leach (1887–1979).

The stricter studio potters believed that the individual maker should not only be solely responsible for throwing, glazing, and decorating his or her wares, but should even dig and process the clay and create the glazes from raw materials, or as Leach put it, "A potter is one of the few people left who uses his natural faculties of heart, head and hand in balance—the whole man." ("Belief and Hope" in *Bernard Leach: Fifty Years a Potter*, Arts Council exhibition catalogue, London, 1961, p. 16.) The pots should ideally be made for everyday use and, if not, should at least be inspired by classical periods in the history of ceramics (mainly early Korean, Song Dynasty and English Medieval).

Leach was born in the Far East, returned briefly to Britain for his education, and then headed back with an etching press in his luggage to teach art to the Japanese. To his surprise, the roles were reversed, and instead Leach became the student learning the subtleties of Asian ceramic techniques. In 1920, he returned to England

Double vessel with lids, stoneware with wax-resist decoration, Shoji Hamada, c.1931-32.

accompanied by an apprentice, Shoji Hamada, who was himself destined to become one of Japan's "living treasures," and set up a pottery in St Ives on the Cornish coast. At about the same time, William Staite Murray (1881–1962) had begun experimenting with Chinese stonewares. Leach and Murray met at an exhibition and briefly became allies, but their accord soon crumbled as their ideological differences in respect of ceramics as art became apparent. Both were inspired by Eastern philosophy and art. Leach preached a strictly functionalist line, while Murray saw the pot as an object of contemplation. "Pottery", stated Murray, "is practical theology." (quoted in Malcolm Haslam's *William Staite Murray*, Cleveland County Museum exhibition catalogue, 1984, p. 69). Although his work was traditionalist in style, Murray eschewed contact with the craft world with which Leach had allied himself, preferring the company of artists, in particular the group around Ben Nicholson with whom he exhibited. Murray became the professor of ceramics at the Royal College of Art in London, attracting talented students, including the brilliant Surrealist potter, Sam Haile. The third and crucial figure in this emerging movement was Michael Cardew, Leach's first Western apprentice, who arrived on the scene with a very clear mind as to the direction he wished to follow, working in the tradition of British slip-decorated earthenware rather than the high-fired glazed pottery of the East. Cardew was even more a functionalist than Leach, making his work in quantity and selling it cheaply as dinnerware, while Leach rather enjoyed the glamour and prestige of the world of art galleries.

Leach, Cardew, and Murray (with occasional assistance from Hamada, who would make visits to England from time to time) were the dynamic forces in developing the movement. Murray and Leach became bitter rivals in their fight to represent the soul of British studio pottery. Murray was arguably a finer potter than Leach, but Leach's skills as a crafts evangelist were superior. In 1939, Murray was stranded in Rhodesia by the outbreak of war and never returned to pottery, leaving Leach as the undisputed *éminence grise* of his field. A year later, Leach's *A Potter's Book* was published and was instantly seized upon internationally as the holy writ of the studio potter.

Leach's beliefs and dogmas were adopted unquestioningly, and look-alike potters sprouted everywhere (except in Europe, where the accent on use and process, rather than on art, was felt to be too idiosyncratically English for Continental tastes). Cardew's book *Pioneer Pottery* was also popular amongst the stricter functionalists. After World War II, these two potters became the most influential figures in the world of ceramics. The effect of their influence was mixed, but certainly it brought higher standards to the craft, thanks to an insistence on the primacy of form. This was a lesson that was all too often lost on Continental potters, with their tendency to become obsessed by surface above all else. Also, the Leach school linked contemporary potters with their utilitarian past.

Leach's writing gave the field an analytical and ideological voice that it had hitherto lacked. However, on the negative side it can be said that neither Leach nor Cardew was fully in touch with the times. Their aesthetic was somewhat regressive,

Vase, stoneware with sgraffito decoration revealing the brownish body color beneath overall black slip, Michael Cardew. H. 13½ in. (34.3cm).

relying too closely on the examples of historical models. Cardew, and occasionally Leach, were able to overcome this limitation and find a powerful voice through the universality of their pots. However, their followers rarely managed to achieve the same vitality. The Leach school dominated British studio pottery into the 1960s. Tiresomely conservative, it was eventually supplanted by younger potters in search of a greater aesthetic legitimacy, and by the 1970s an aggressively Post-Modern style free of Leachian shackles had emerged. Despite the fact that Leach and his school outlasted their welcome, their fundamentalism did serve to build a solid, classical, foundation for the explosive postwar growth of the studio-pottery movement.

Architectural Ceramics

Although a discussion of decorative architectural ceramics does not feature in this study, it seems fitting to acknowledge briefly a topic which, in the context of ceramic history, warrants its own separate detailed assessment. Briefly, Art Deco offered great potential for colorful decoration, ranging from sculptured terra cotta glazed bricks to tile murals and tile-clad exteriors. Most exciting of all, however, were the custom-designed buildings clad in glazed terra cotta that were created in ceramic factories. These elaborate exteriors could be carved, molded, glazed, and fired in factories, the sections then loaded onto freight wagons and assembled on arrival at the destination. Terra cotta had many advantages, for it could mimic stone and marble, yet was much lighter and more economical than the more costly materials it imitated. This resulted in some interesting architectural work in Europe (particularly the colorful majolica-clad pubs that sprouted throughout Britain in the late nineteenth century), but it was in America that this method of building was adopted with particular enthusiasm.

The first American buildings of this type emerged around 1870, and these became increasingly elaborate and ambitious in scale. New York City's 23-storey Flatiron Building (1903) by Daniel Burnham was clad in decorative terra cotta, as was the Woolworth Building and other examples of Manhattan's first true skyscrapers. The technique allowed for elaborate relief decoration, as well as a limitless palette of color, although the latter was not exploited with any sense of adventure in cities on the East Coast. The arrival of the Jazz Age inspired architects to create particularly dazzling buildings, introducing metallic glazes in gold, silver, and copper, so adding a new feeling of excitement and hedonism to architecture. The glazed surface provided for ease of maintenance and a distinctive solidness and grandeur. These rather lavish-looking buildings began to spring up all over the United States. Chicago was another of the centers for glazed architectural terra cotta, the black-and-gold Wrigley Building being a masterpiece of this genre.

However, California was the home for some of the finest Art Deco ceramic architecture. The West Coast's pre-eminence in this aspect of architecture was due to the founding in 1875 of the Gladding McBean Company in Lincoln, California. The company became one of the most adventurous, skilled, stylish, and ambitious producers of polychrome ceramic "curtain-walling" (a building technique of creating a non-load bearing shell around metal-framed structures) in the United States, and decorative buildings—ranging from modest single-storied shops to huge skyscrapers—began to be erected all over the West Coast, with particular concentrations in Oakland and Los Angeles. By the time of the Great Depression the Gladding McBean factory had produced ceramic facings for over 1,500 buildings, turning the downtown areas of many cities into a glazed sea of color and ornament. While the bulk of the company's business was on the West Coast, its products were used as far afield as Chicago (the Wrigley Building) and New York (the Carnegie Hall).

The booming city of Los Angeles, with some of the most elaborate examples of Art Deco ceramic architecture, could boast the gigantic City Hall, the Bullocks Wilshire, Atlantic Richfield and Eastern Columbia Buildings, among others. The Eastern Building, a glowing combination of gold, silver, and turquoise, still stands in downtown Los Angeles, but the Richfield Building, perhaps the most magnificent and extravagant example of Art Deco architecture, with its surround of stylized gold-glazed goddesses, was demolished in 1968 to make way for the current headquarters of this oil company.

In Conclusion

The last celebration of the decorative arts for some time came with the World's Fair in New York, which opened in 1939. Its theme was "The World of Tomorrow" and it presented a message of hope and prosperity after a period of grinding depression. The event, which continued into 1940, attracted over 45 million visitors, but it took place against the ever-darkening shadow created by the outbreak of war in Europe.

The decorative arts adapted to these changes and the 1940s saw the emergence of a new stripped-down style known as "Austerity Ware." This was obviously not a stylistic preference, but a sensibility forged out of tough times when most raw materials had to be reserved for the war effort. Even after the war, it took time for the decorative industries to return to normal. In Britain the ceramics industry was restricted to making undecorated wares in order to conserve resources, and it was not until 1952 that these restrictions were lifted and a new look for the decade began to emerge.

In retrospect, one cannot but be astounded by the diversity, skill and artistic energy displayed by the ceramics made between the two World Wars. It was a time of productivity and invention which, for many reasons, is unlikely to be experienced again in industry and architecture. The studio-pottery movement happily went on the become even livelier and more aesthetically powerful after 1950.

For industrially made wares, however, the road has been difficult and the options have gradually but remorselessly narrowed. Several factors forced this simplification of the marketplace. Firstly, potteries began to merge (in order to remain viable), combine their operations, and manufacture only the most profitable of their lines

Souvenir plate made for the New York World's Fair, Homer Laughlin Company, 1939.

(mainly traditional in design), hence there are fewer large-scale producers of dinnerware and decorative wares today. Secondly, lifestyles began to alter and become less formal. As a result, most dinner services today are sold as sets of plates, soup bowls, cups and saucers, but with none of the outmoded extras such as soup tureens, dessert dishes, butter dishes, candlesticks, and centerpieces that were formerly considered *de rigueur* at well-set tables. Indeed, ceramic coffee-pots have all but disappeared, and teapots designed as part of a matching service are becoming an endangered species.

The way in which industrial wares are made today has also resulted in fewer and fewer new forms being introduced. These wares are now pressure-molded in a machine using a dry clay. This innovation did away with the drying stage, as the pottery goes directly by conveyor belt from the form-making machines to the kiln. This entire process for producing ceramics takes a mere six hours in contrast to the conventional process which took days to complete. The system is highly efficient and can produce vast quantities of standard ware, but the machines can only be used for simple, uncomplicated shapes and the tooling costs for setting up new forms are massive. To become successful, any new design has to sell millions of units to justify the capital investment, and this requirement has put a damper on experiment and risk-taking.

Architecture is also unable to return to the halcyon days of the 1920s and 1930s, when ceramic-clad buildings were springing up in cities all over the United States. The technology involved is now simply too expensive and labor-intensive. In addition, the skills necessary to design and fabricate these remarkable buildings have become almost extinct. In America only one of the great decorative terra cotta factories, Gladding McBean, remains in business, having been able to survive by offering restoration services for existing buildings which have been damaged either by the urban air pollution or by brutalizing "modernization" of store fronts and other aspects of the buildings' facades.

More and more, we are coming to understand and appreciate that the period surveyed in this book is unique—truly a golden period, a time when the possibilities for new designers, architects, and potters with ambition and talent were endless. All of this only serves to make the collecting of the wares of this time the more satisfying. Happily, collecting Art Deco or Modernist pottery is so broad a field (and so much work was produced in its day) that it covers every taste, ideological bent, and personal budget.

What makes this assemblage of pots, figures, and other *objets* so enjoyable is that the author is herself a collector with a highly evolved sensibility for the period and its many styles. Her approach has not been to treat this book as an academic guide. Instead she has, in common with the best of collectors, trusted and shared her eye for the best of every category—be it low, middle, or high art—and in so doing she has provided a carefully selected and unusually sensual view of ceramic culture in an age that arrived with a feeling of unrestrained hedonism and was destined to depart in a mood of harsh austerity.

THE PLATES

The objects illustrated in the color plates are presented country by country as follows:

For a list of subjects illustrated in color (with dimensions where available) see pp. 184, 185.

Facing page
1 Floor vase (*Bodenvase*) with abstract painted decoration in the manner of De Stijl by Gustav Heinkel, Staatliche Majolika-Manufaktur, Karlsruhe, 1930.

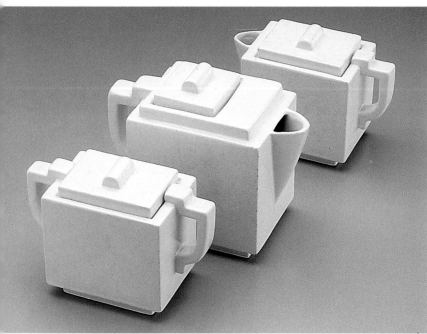

Opposite, above
2 Teapot, glazed hard-paste porcelain, designed by Margarete Friedländer-Wildenhain, made at the Staatliche Porzellan-Manufaktur, Berlin, 1930; the form exemplifies the rational design methods practiced at the Bauhaus, where Friedländer-Wildenhain had worked 1919–25.

Opposite, below left
3 Teapot with covered sugar bowl and creamer from a glazed earthenware tea set designed by Eva Stricker (later Zeisel), Schramberger Majolika Fabrik, late 1920s. The forms, based on a combination of rectangular surface areas and applied handles similar in shape to those found in contemporary metalwork, present the austere side of Modernist design.

Opposite, below right
4 Porcelain teapot designed by Grete Heymann-Marks, Haël-Werkstätten, 1930. With its simple geometric design features—the body in the form of an inverted truncated cone, triangular spout, and handles made from circular flat press-molded discs—this object of everyday use represents a remarkable Modernist icon, breaking with historical precedents through its overall shape and lack of surface decoration. In terms of practical use, however, the solid handle may be less easy to grip than the traditional loop handle.

Left
5 *Korean Dancer*, glazed porcelain figure with gilt decoration, Constantin Holzer-Defanti, Rosenthal, 1919.

Above
6 "Madeleine" coffee service, glazed porcelain with fanciful floral decoration by Friedrich Fleischmann, Rosenthal, *c*. 1927–34.

Below
7 Coffee service, an example of wares exhibiting Modernist tendencies such as abstract decoration and a cup with a solid handle, while also revealing the historical influence of German folk pottery; maker and date unknown.

Opposite, top left
8 Tea caddy in glazed earthenware by Paul Speck, Staatliche Majolika-Manufaktur, Karlsruhe, *c.* 1926. The striped decoration and pencil banding emphasize the overall rectilinear form; an inner tight-fitting ceramic plug acts as a seal to help keep the contents fresh.

Opposite, below left
9 Collared cylindrical vessel by Grete Heymann-Marks, Haël-Werkstätten, 1920s. The painted bands create a harmonious surface decoration, with the form enhanced by the use of yellow glaze on the inside of the collar.

Opposite, above right
10 Small glazed earthenware plate with abstract painted decoration suggestive of sea and sky, Willi Ohler, Worpswede, *c.* 1920s.

Opposite, below right
11 Footed box with abstract painted decoration by Hermann Volmar, 1920s/1930s; the unusual trapezoidal shape features conforming lid, handle, and feet.

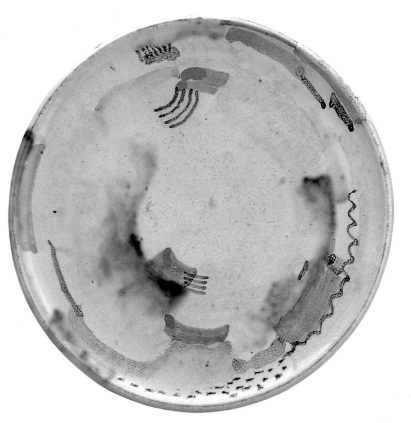

Below
12 Bottle vase with banded decoration emphasizing the "telescopic" shape of the neck, 1930s; maker unknown.

Right
13 Pitcher in glazed earthenware by Werner Burri, Velten-Vordamm, *c*. 1927–30.

14 Small pitcher in glazed earthenware
with banded decoration by Theodor
Bogler, Staatliche Porzellan-Manufaktur,
Berlin, 1925–26.

15 Tea caddy, glazed earthenware,
by Paul Speck, probably made at
the Staatliche Majolika-Manufaktur,
Karlsruhe, c. 1926.

Opposite
16 Coffee pot, glazed earthenware, by Ursula Fesca, Wächtersbacher Steingutfabrik, 1935.

Above
17 Tea set, slip-cast whiteware, Rosenthal, 1930s; the Modernist form of the individual pieces is enlivened by airbrushed banding emphasizing the contoured edges.

Left
18 Flared vase with abstract air-brushed decoration, attributed to Carstens, 1920s/1930s; this style of decoration was often used on ceramic wares of the Weimar Republic period.

Above
19 Small Weimar vase, glazed porcelain, 1920s; the appearance of traditional form is brought up to date by the use of bright orange luster (similar luster decoration is found on contemporary wares produced in the USA, Czechoslovakia, and Japan).

Above, right
20 Vase, glazed earthenware, by Gustav Heinkel, Staatliche Majolika-Manufaktur, Karlsruhe, c. 1925–30.

Right
21 Head by Gerhard Marcks, c. 1923.

Left
22 Vases, stoneware with aerographed decoration, Feinsteinzeugfabrik Reinhold & Co., Bunzlau, 1930.

Below
23 Bread box, wooden frame with glazed ceramic inserts, Villeroy & Boch, *c.* 1930.

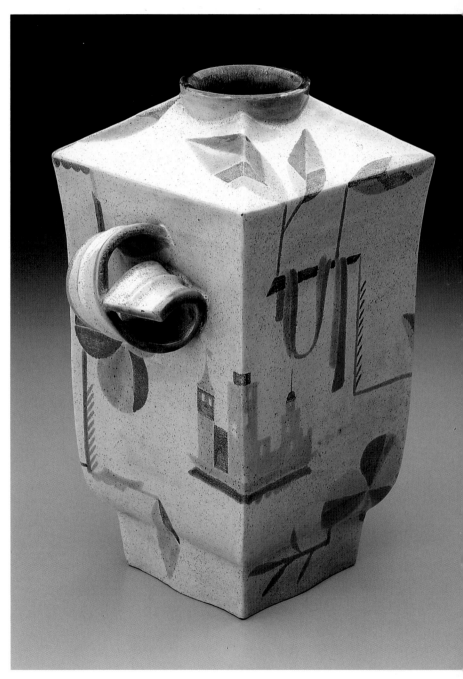

Below
27 Tea service designed by Josef Hoffmann, glazed porcelain with decoration in black, Wiener Porzellan-Manufaktur Augarten, *c.* 1928.

Opposite, above
28 Design for a coffee pot by Vally Wieselthier, before 1929; the lid with finial in the form of a human head exemplifies Modernism as interpreted with wit by members of the Wiener Werkstätte.

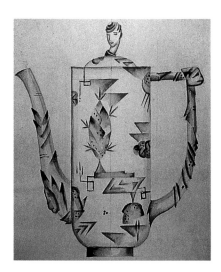

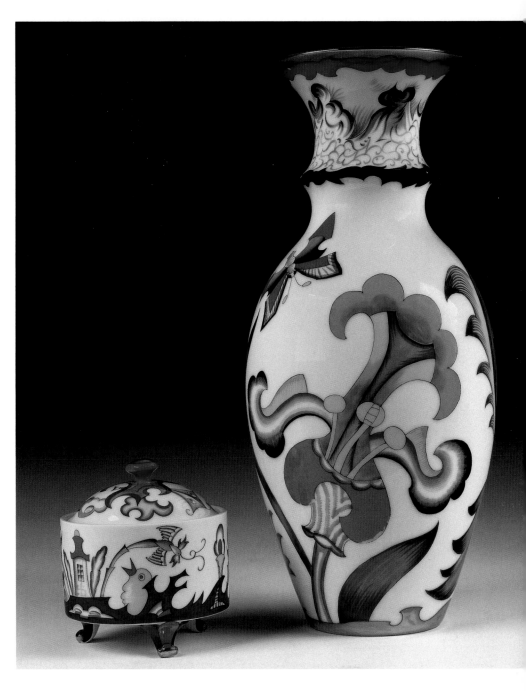

Below
29 Box with lid and vase, porcelain with
chinoiserie-style painting in a distinctively
Austrian manner, Franz von Zülow, produced at
Wiener Porzellan-Manufaktur Augarten, 1925.

Above
30, 31 Figures of orange-bearded gnome and
dwarf, hand-painted by Berthold Löffler,
Wiener Keramik, *c.* 1905.

Right
32 Bookend (one of a pair), glazed
earthenware, Bimini Werkstätten, 1930s.

33, 34 Seated female figure and kneeling figure, Susi Singer, 1920s; the artist's expressive modelling and use of audacious colors—taken to the limit of acceptable "good taste"—prefigure developments in American ceramics of the late 20th century, which sometimes reflect the influence of members of the Wiener Werkstätte.

35 Tall bottle vase with luster decoration inspired by Egyptian and Islamic wares, Zsolnay, 1920s; the extraordinary skill of decorators at this factory is demonstrated in the intricate overall pattern.

Above left
36 Porcelain plate with painted decoration including a portrait of Lenin, after Altman, design by Mikhail Mikhailovich Adamovich, State Porcelain Factory, 1919.

Above right
37 Porcelain plate decorated with the Red Star and other motifs associated with the Soviet regime, designed by Mikhail Mikhailovich Adamovich, State Porcelain Factory, 1922.

Right
38 Plate, decorated with a political slogan "The land is for the workers," after a banner designed by Natan Isaevich Altman, 1919; porcelain, probably State Porcelain Factory.

39 Vase, glazed slip-cast earthenware; date and maker unknown. The exaggerated elliptical shape and graduated applied handles evoke a certain Art Deco elegance, though the piece may be of later date.

40 Coffee set, after 1918; maker unknown. Thanks to the imaginative forms of the lidded creamer, coffee pot and sugar bowl, no additional decoration is required.

Above
41 Coffee set, porcelain with subtle colored banding emphasizing the elegance of the functional forms, after 1922; maker unknown.

Below left
42 Fish, glazed earthenware, *c.* 1930; maker unknown. The rounded body is suggestive of a globefish when inflated, maker unknown.

Below right
43 Covered hexagonal box, glazed earthenware, designed by Pavel Janák and decorated in a manner derived from folk art by František Kysela, 1914.

44 Cup and saucer, porcelain decorated with a combination of printed and hand-painted designs, Shelley Potteries, c. 1925–40.

45 "Tea-for-two" set, porcelain decorated with a stylized sunburst (a popular Art Deco motif), Shelley Potteries, c. 1930. The bold design is accentuated by the distinctive triangular handles of individual pieces, thus producing a perfect unity of form and decoration.

46 Demitasse set, hand-painted glazed earthenware marked "Bizarre by Clarice Cliff," *c*. 1929–39; made for the leading London retailer, Lawleys of Regent Street.

47 Globular jug, glazed earthenware, Jewel Ware, 1930s.

Top and above
48, 50 Kangaroo, Monkey, Deer, and
Polar Bear, from the set of fourteen
animal figures modelled by John
Skeaping, black basalt and creamware,
Wedgwood, 1927 and after.

Left
49 "Toucans," figural group by Adrian
Paul Allinson, *c.* 1930.

Right
51 Drawing for a Cubistic ceramic cat by Louis Wain, inscribed "Hold on to me and fortune will smile on thee."

Below
52 Pig, Robot, and Cat, glazed ceramic figures based on designs by Louis Wain; date and maker unknown.

Left
53 Vase forms designed for Wedgwood by Keith Murray in the 1930s: "Moonstone Ridge," "Yellow Ridge," and "Green Shoulder." The simple shapes are suggestive of the Orient, while engine-turned ridges indicate products of the machine age; the subtly colored mat glazes were specially developed to enhance Murray's designs.

Below left
54 Plate, creamer, and teapot, A.J. Wilkinson Ltd, c. 1930; the forms—unmistakably associated with the jazz era—are accentuated by the use of an orange "tango" glaze and white banding.

Below right
55 Cup and saucer and matching plate, Shelley Potteries, 1930.

56, 57 "Kestrel" coffee set with mahogany-colored band, *c.* 1932, and "Kestrel" teapot with polka-dot decoration, Susie Cooper, 1930s

58 Group of glazed earthenware "Fantasque" objects hand-painted by Clarice Cliff: (left) Ziggurat candle holder and, in foreground, small sugar bowl in Stanford, both *Gardenia* pattern; (back row, left to right) vase, Alpine pattern, pair of candlesticks, *Orange Roof Cottage* pattern, and vase, *Orange House* pattern; blue-roof cottage vase; (center foreground) plate, Windbells pattern. A.J. Wilkinson Ltd, c. 1930.

Opposite, below
60 "Toadstool house" teapot, painted earthenware, from a set of nursery ware designed by Mabel Lucie Attwell for Shelley Potteries, 1926.

Below
59 "Fantasque" milk jug, glazed earthenware,
from the *Bizarre* line by Clarice Cliff,
c. 1925–35; the use of a rustic subject (an
English country cottage) as painted decoration
conveys the visual complexity and expressive
quality of some avant-garde painting of the
period.

Above
61 Vase with flanged handles, slip-cast
earthenware with hand-painted floral
decoration on a sponged background imitating
the style of many contemporary Japanese wares,
Royal Art Pottery, 1930s.

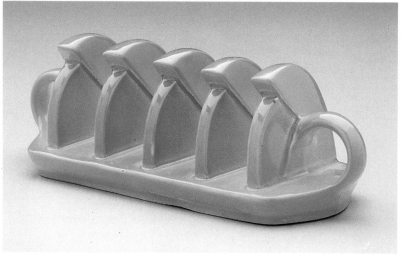

Above
62 "Moon and Mountain" tea set (including hot-water jug), hand-painted earthenware, Susie Cooper, A.E. Gray & Co., *c.* 1930.

Left
63 "Machine Age" toast rack, an unusual slip-cast version of an object designed for everyday use, Carlton Ware, *c.* 1925 or later.

Below
64 "Casino" casserole, from the range of tableware introduced by Royal Doulton in 1932.

Above
65 Jug in stepped pyramidal form, glazed earthenware, Royal Winton Pottery, Grimwades Ltd, *c.* 1934–50.

Left
66 Cube tea set, glazed earthenware, designed 1916, R.C. Johnson, George Clews & Co. The Cunard Steamship Company, as well as other shipowners, favored such flat-bottomed wares for use on ocean liners.

Above
67 Items by Charlotte Rhead (including, right, "Persian Rose" jug for the *Crown Ducal* line), A.E. Richardson & Co., 1930s.

Right
68 "Tulip" charger, Charlotte Rhead, 1930s; the style of the complex tube-lined decoration reveals the influence both of Persian wares and of William Morris and the Arts and Crafts movement.

Left
69 "Circus" plate, glazed earthenware, design by Dame Laura Knight for E. Brain & Co., produced by A.J. Wilkinson Ltd, *c.* 1932–34.

Below left
70 "Harvest" vase, buff-colored earthenware with painted decoration after Frank Brangwyn, Royal Doulton, *c.* 1935. Brangwyn created several impressionistic patterns in the 1930s, but the wares on which they featured were not commercially successful.

Below right
71 Vases, in forms inspired by Oriental models, relying on random glazing "accidents" for decorative effects, William Howson Taylor, Ruskin Pottery Workshop, 1924 and 1933.

72 Shallow footed bowl, Claude Lévy, Atelier Primavera, 1920s; the turquoise glaze is deliberately puddled for decorative effect, while the simple design is enhanced by the use of platinum overglaze luster.

Opposite
73 Bulbous bottle with vestigial handles, glazed earthenware with gilding and painted decoration depicting a mythological archer and stylized birds, Jean Mayodon; date unknown.

74 Melon-shaped vase, hand-painted cobalt-blue glaze and gold luster, Raoul Lachenal, 1920s; the decoration, with its allusion to the sun's energy, is an example of a popular Art Deco theme.

75 Tapering vase, glazed stoneware, Félix Massoul, *c.* 1920–25.

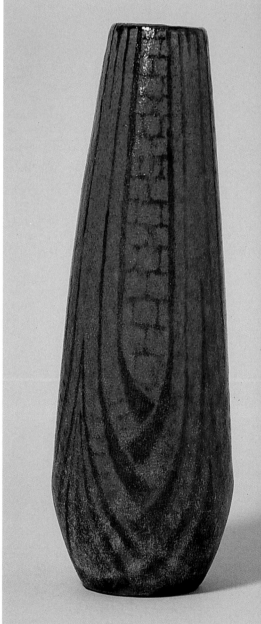

76 Teapot, Raoul Lachenal, 1920s/1930s; the form of a traditional object of everyday use is adapted to resemble an Aladdin's lamp, animated by the distinctive shape of the spout, finial, and handle.

77 Group of vases glazed in primary colors, Raoul Lachenal, 1920s/1940s.

Opposite
78 Charger, hand-painted interlocking
stylized floral decoration, Raoul Lachenal,
1920s/1930s.

79, 80 Design for a porcelain bowl,
watercolor on paper, Jacques-Emile
Ruhlmann 1931; and glazed porcelain bowl
based on this design, with decoration by
Maurice Herbillon, Manufacture Nationale
de Sèvres, 1925.

Below
81 Monumental vase, hand-painted *pâte
nouvelle* with decoration depicting Adam and
Eve, Manufacture Nationale de Sèvres, 1929
(form by Mme Bethmont, decoration by Jean
Beaumont painted by L. Trager).

Above
82 Footed bowl, hand-thrown glazed
porcelain with gilding and painted decoration
depicting figures in silhouette, Jean Mayodon,
Manufacture Nationale de Sèvres; date
unknown. The effect of a type of "moving
picture" unique in ceramic decoration is a
masterpiece of Art Deco design derived from
ancient Greek sources.

Below
83 Vase, glazed stoneware decorated with painted imbricated figures mingled with organic forms, Edouard Cazaux, *c.* 1925; the use of *sang-de-bœuf* glaze, allowed to "run" during high-temperature firing, was part of the artist's sophisticated treatment.

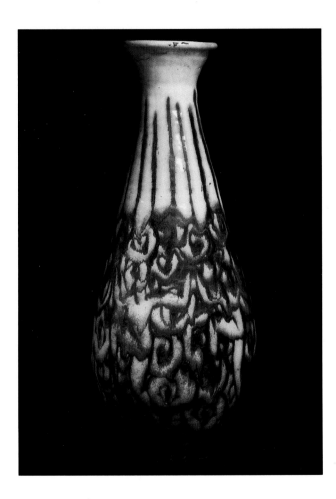

Above right
84 Bottle, earthenware with painted decoration showing one of two odalisque figures on the bulbous body, René Buthaud, *c.* 1918–25.

Right
85 Vase with lug handles, earthenware with painted decoration depicting an odalisque, René Buthaud, 1925.

Opposite
86 *L'Adieu au voyageur*, glazed slip-cast porcelain, from a design of 1930 by Jean Debarre, Manufacture Nationale de Sèvres, 1933.

Right
87 Candelabrum (one of a pair), faience with crackle glaze, Robert Lallemant, 1920s. The design, with its rectangular base and abstract pierced motifs, suggests that recently discovered archeological remains, such as Aztec temples, may have been a source of inspiration.

Below
88 *St George and the Dragon*, glazed earthenware group designed by Willy Wuilleumier, Fau & Gaillard, *c.* 1924.

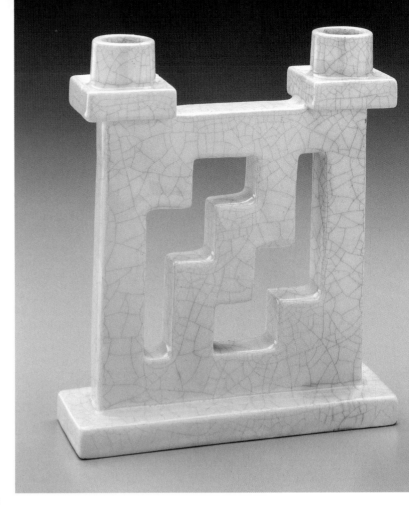

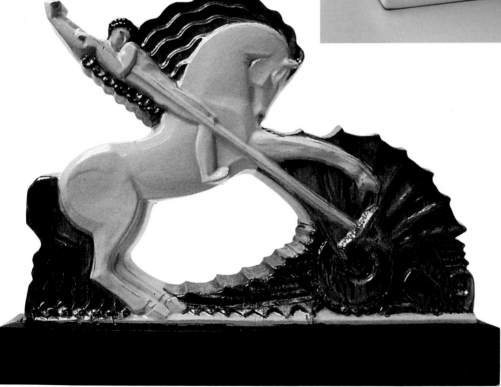

Left
89 Group of plates (from a set of twelve), glazed porcelain with painted decoration highlighted with gilding and silvering, designed by Jean Luce, *c.* 1935, and decorated by Charles Ahrenfeldt, 1937.

Below
90 Vase, glazed earthenware with abstract decoration, Robert Lallemant, *c.* 1925–30. The angular outline of the molded body is enhanced by the graphic painted decoration reflecting the influence of Cubism.

91 Charger, *pâte nouvelle* porcelain with painted decoration, Anne-Marie Fontaine, Manufacture Nationale de Sèvres, 1927.

92 Large charger, earthenware with crackle glaze and colored enamel decoration, R. Chevallier, Société des Faïenceries, Longwy, 1920s; the sophisticated handling of the surface decoration featuring a mythical bird is a superb technical achievement.

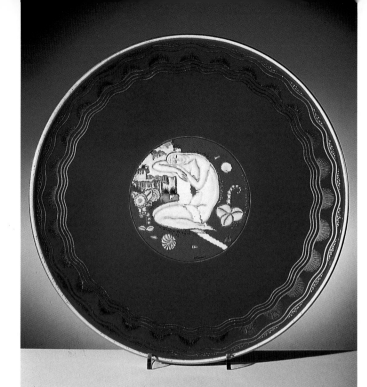

93 Plates, porcelain with painted decoration embellished with gilding, Jean Luce, 1923.

94 Large charger, stoneware with *pâte-sur-pâte* glaze (a complicated procedure using a succession of layers to produce surface decoration in relief), André Metthey, *c.* 1917–19. The spear of the mythological hunter (Orion?) is curved to fit the shape of the piece, suggesting the appearance of a bow, while the disposition of the stag and deer create a feeling of movement.

Opposite
95 Footed vase, porcellaneous stoneware with *sang-de-bœuf* glaze, Frédéric Kiefer, 1930s. In this piece, the form and color of which are suggestive of an aubergine, Kiefer incorporates a carved foot reminiscent of an Oriental wooden pot-stand, together with a fluted and patterned neck echoing the foot.

96 Plate, hand-thrown glazed porcellaneous stoneware, Emile Decœur, 1920s/1930s; subtle use of glazes produces the effect of a rosette or patera.

97 Globular vessel, stoneware with high-fired glaze, Auguste Delaherche; date unknown.

98 Small vase, stoneware with relief decoration, Georges Serré, 1932.

Below left
99 Bowl, glazed stoneware, Maurice Gensoli; date unknown.

Below
100 Globular vase, glazed stoneware, Odetta, Quimper, date unknown. In addition to traditional wares, Quimper potteries also produced modern designs under the name "Odetta."

Bottom
101 Shallow bowl, wheel-thrown glazed stoneware, Séraphin Soudbinine, 1930s; the incised decoration includes leaves around the rim and in the central medallion.

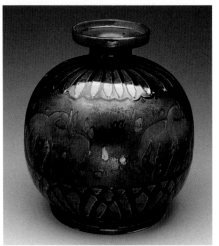

Left
102 Lidded box designed as a sphere within a cube, glazed stoneware, Marcel Guillemard, *c*. 1930; an example of a Modernist design based on simple geometric forms.

Below
103 Globular vase, René Buthaud, *c*. 1925–29; the sophisticated use of crackle glaze within segmented geometric areas creates a surface effect resembling shagreen, a popular decorative finish in the Art Deco period.

104 Pieces from a tea set decorated with
Disney cartoon characters: cup and saucer and
covered sugar bowl, white earthenware with
decals featuring Mickey and Minnie Mouse,
1930s; produced under license by an unknown
maker.

105 Pair of vases, glazed earthenware, Société
des Faïenceries, Longwy; date and maker
unknown.

106 Consommé cup with saucer, porcelain, Gien (Loiret), after 1928; the "LW" monogram suggests that this ware was intended for use in a hotel or on board an ocean liner.

107 Creamer and teapot, glazed whiteware, made in Luxembourg for Robj, Paris, 1920s. Despite its functional appearance, the teapot has a major design flaw: the large lid tends to fall forward when the pot is tilted to pour the contents.

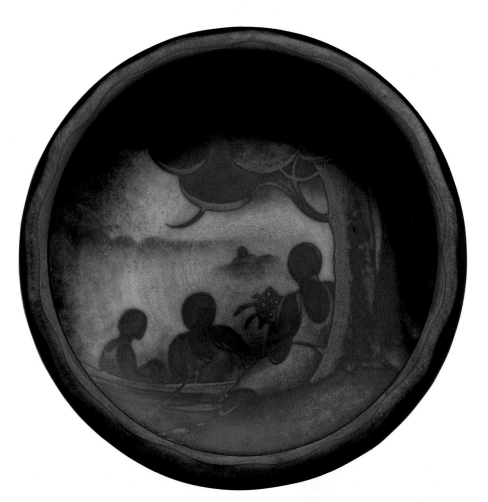

108–110 Works by Charles Catteau, one of the most prolific Art Deco masters, for Boch Frères Keramis

108 Stoneware charger, mat-glazed stoneware, 1937–39. The romanticized painted decoration, depicting a group of women in an exotic setting in the manner of Gauguin, reveals an unexpected naturalistic side of Catteau's œuvre.

109 Globular vase, stoneware with overall painted decoration depicting a stylized octopus, 1920s/1930s; a masterpiece of composition and technique.

Opposite
110 Tall vase, glazed stoneware with overall decoration of penguins, *c.* 1925–26; the artist's masterly handling of figure-ground relationships has resulted of a *tour de force* in ceramic decoration.

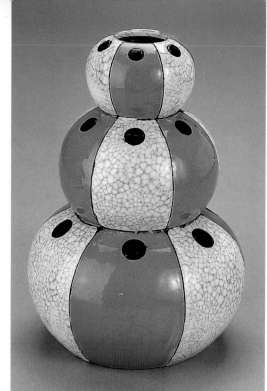

111–114 Works by Charles Catteau for Boch Frères Keramis

Above left
111 Vase, glazed earthenware, with painted decoration depicting sparrows, 1925.

Above center
112 Three-tiered vessel with alternating colored panels; date unknown.

Above right
113 Vase with overall stylized floral decoration, 1928.

Left
114 Group of vases decorated with deer; the grace and agility of deer (*biches*) led to their adoption by artists of the 1920s as a symbol of an era obsessed with movement and speed. Vases similar to these were shown in Paris at the 1925 Exposition.

115 Pitcher, glazed earthenware with abstract painted decoration, N.V. Kennemer Pottery, *c.* 1930; the style of decoration reflects the influence of De Stijl, while the streamlined handle echoes trends in engineering design.

116 Covered sugar bowl, teapot, and creamer, from "Thea" service, G.M.E. Bellefroid, De Sphinx, 1935.

117, 118 Designs by Wilhelm Kåge for the Gustavsberg "Argenta" line

Opposite
117 Urn, glazed stoneware with impressed silver details, *c.* 1928–30.

118 Chimerical figure, glazed stoneware with impressed silver details, *c.* 1939. Of the small number of animal figures made by Kåge for Argenta, this example was exhibited in the Swedish pavilion at the New York World's Fair.

119 Large urn, glazed earthenware, Herman August Kähler, Kähler Keramik, produced before 1917.

120 Centerpiece, glazed porcelain with gilding, Royal Copenhagen, 1930; this elegant piece, assembled from several separately cast sections, remains traditional in form but features an audacious use of bright orange glaze to conform with stylish Art Deco table accessories.

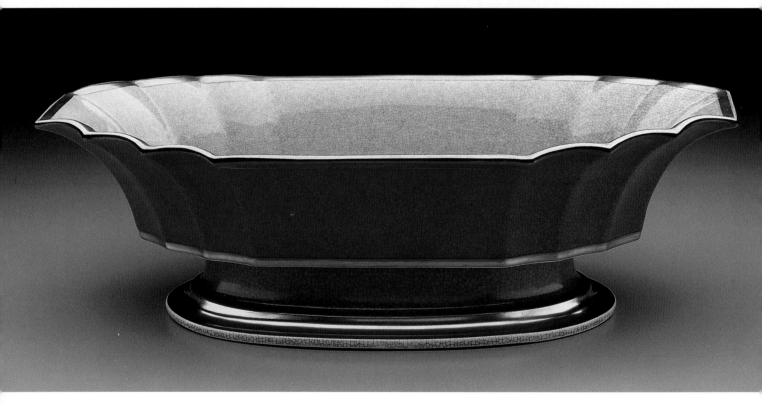

121 Male head (approx. ¾ life size) with stylized coiffure, porcelain with overall *sang-de-bœuf* glaze, Jais Nielsen, Royal Copenhagen, 1930.

122 Covered jar, glazed stoneware, Jais Nielsen, Royal Copenhagen, 1925; the expressive modelling and carved aquatic motifs are enhanced by the application of an unctuous celadon glaze.

Opposite
123 Vase, glazed earthenware, with stylized relief figures, Friedl Kjellberg, Arabia AB, 1933.

Above
124 Bowl, porcelain painted with four faces of young women on a cobalt-blue underglaze ground and trimmed with gilding, Friedl Kjellberg, Arabia AB, 1930s.

Above right
125 Covered jar with finial in the form of a baboon (probably based on a model by Karl Hansen Reistrup), glazed earthenware, Herman August Kähler, Kähler Keramik, produced before 1917.

Right
126 Covered jar with finial in the form of a fish, Greta-Lisa Jäderholm-Snellman, Arabia AB, 1930s.

127–130 Pieces designed by Gio Ponti

127 Globular vase with upturned handles and applied three-tiered neoclassical frieze, made by Ugo Zaccagnini, 1927.

Below
128, 129 Six-handled monumental urns, hand-painted maiolica, Richard-Ginori, *c.* 1923–30; the example shown on the left is entitled *La Casa degli Efebi* ("The House of the Young People").

Opposite
130 Pair of lamp-bases, hand-painted maiolica, Richard-Ginori, 1920s. The golden cords and figures of odalisques, set off against a dramatic dark-blue ground, exemplify the artist's penchant for giving neoclassical motifs a modern feeling.

Opposite
131 "Omaggio agli Snob," covered box, hand-painted porcelain, with figural group, Gio Ponti, Richard-Ginori, 1920s.

Above
132 Footed vase, glazed porcelain with painted decoration, Gio Ponti, Richard-Ginori, 1923.

Right
133 Globular vase, with painted decoration depicting aquatic motifs, Antonio Zen, Nove, 1920s; the external decoration is in strong contrast with the mottled orange glaze on the inside in imitation of Oriental lacquer.

134 Plate, maiolica, Amerigo Lunghi, U. Grazia, Deruta, 1924. The sloe-eyed female faces and the exotic headdresses are characteristic features of Art Deco stylization.

Below left
135 Vase with serpentine handles, hand-painted maiolica, Gabriele Bicchioni, Maioliche Deruta e CIMA, 1935.

Below
136 Tall vase, maiolica overpainted with luster, Ezio Cocchioni, Maioliche Deruta e CIMA, *c.* 1935.

Opposite
137 Coffee service, hand-painted terra cotta, B.M.C., *c.* 1932–34.

Opposite
140 Vase, hand-painted glazed terra cotta, form designed by Farfa, decoration by Tullio d'Albisola, *c.* 1931–32. Striking abstract decoration, incorporating stylized versions of the names Farfa and Tullio, is combined with an unusual cut-away form.

Above
138 Decanter, glazed terra cotta, designed by Nicolaj Diulgheroff, made by Torido Mazzotti, *c.* 1935–37.

Right
139 *Aerovaso*, glazed earthenware, Fillia, *c.* 1932.

Below
141 *Bullovaso* (or *Bevibullon*), glazed terra cotta, Farfa, Giuseppe Mazzotti, *c.* 1931–32.

142 Teapot, hand-painted glazed earthenware, Tullio d'Albisola, *c.* 1930.

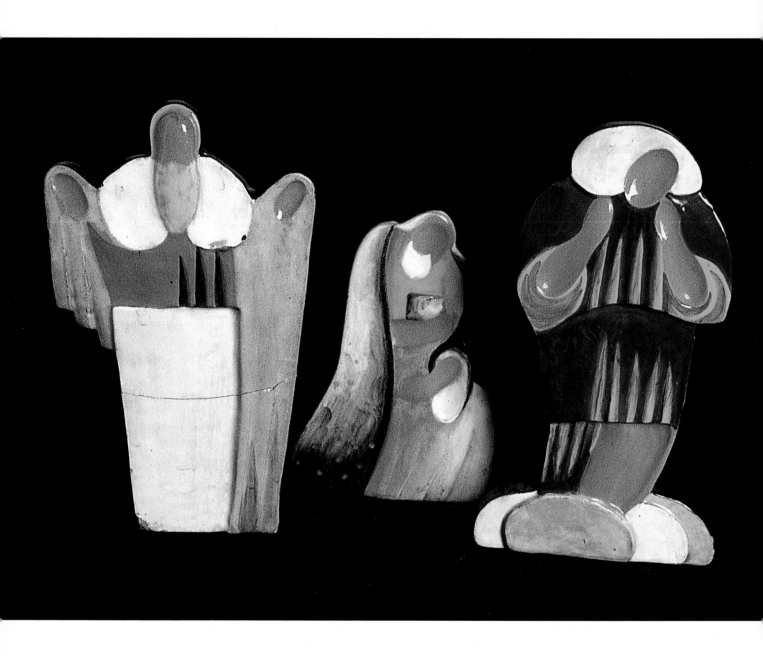

143 *The Magi*, hand-painted terra cotta figures
from a Nativity scene, Dino Gambetti and
Tullio d'Albisola, 1930.

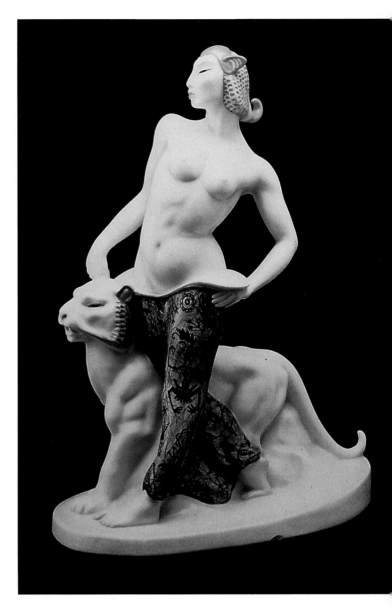

Above left
144 Vase in the form of a cyclist, hand-painted earthenware, Giuseppe Mario Anselmo, *c.* 1937–38.

Above
145 Figure with cat, hand-painted terra cotta, Sandro Vacchetti, Essevi, 1936.

Left
146 Clown, hand-painted earthenware figure, Alf Gaudenzi, 1928.

147 Pig, glazed earthenware figure
by Carl Walters, c. 1934.

Opposite, below
148 Vessel, lead-glazed earthenware by Henry Varnum Poor, 1920s; a quintessentially Art Deco shape is decorated with painted aquatic motifs.

149 Plate with still-life decoration, lead-glazed earthenware, Henry Varnum Poor, 1933.

150 Wide-mouthed footed vessel, lead-glazed earthenware with painted decoration over white slip, Henry Varnum Poor, 1920s. A still-life with pears is set against an abstract background revealing the prevailing influence of Cubism; the contrasting colored planes of the fruit produce an almost flame-like effect.

151 Three-handled urn, Fulper Pottery Company, 1920s; the overall floral decoration in relief is covered with a crystalline glaze, belying Fulper's roots as an important art pottery.

152 Vase in glazed semi-porcelain by Lorinda Epply, Rookwood Pottery, 1931; the underglaze painted decoration is typical of Art Deco, to which Rookwood (best known for its arts and crafts pottery) adapted its style.

Wares from Cowan Pottery Studio

Right
153 Hunt plate, glazed earthenware with low-relief decoration by Viktor Schreckengost, *c.* 1930–35; the serious nature of the chase, with huntsman and hounds, is relieved by the scattered birds and flowers filling the background.

Below
154, 155 Globular vase, Waylande Gregory, 1920s; this form, marketed in various decorative combinations, featured either monochrome subjects in relief (*left*) or flora and fauna forming three distinct tableaux also in relief but painted in bold underglaze colours around the body (*right*).

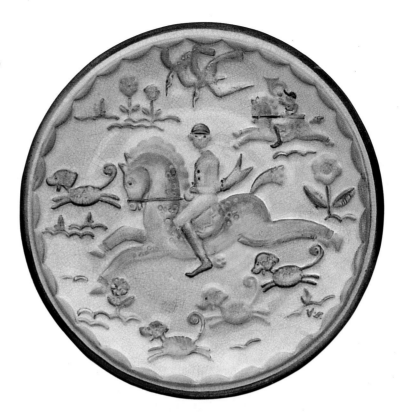

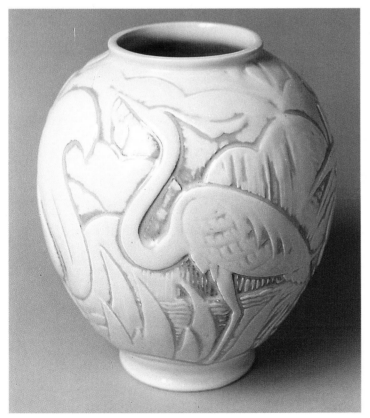

156 *Deco Delight* tea service, designed by J. Martin Stangl, *c.* 1928–29; one of several experimental Art Moderne shapes reflecting contemporary design trends produced at Fulper Pottery.

157 "Tricorne" plate and "Streamline" cup, glazed earthenware (both in "Mandarin Red"), Viktor Schreckengost, Salem China Co., 1934.

158 Pieces from the popular *American Modern* dinner service designed by Russel Wright, 1937, and produced in glazed earthenware by Steubenville Pottery from 1939.

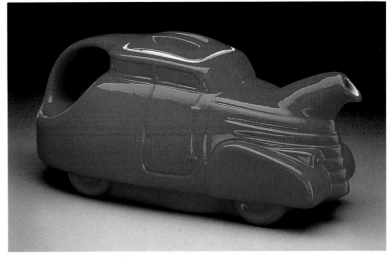

Above left
159 *Circle Vase*, porcelain, 1930s, Trenton Potteries, N.J.; a striking "machine-age" design.

Above right
160 Automobile teapot, glazed porcelain, Hall China Company, *c.* 1940.

Below
162 Slip-cast pitcher with "aerodynamic" styling designed for mass production, Hall China Company, *c.* 1932–39.

161 *Fiesta Ware* pieces in three of the original colors; glazed earthenware, designed by Frederick Hurten Rhead for Homer Laughlin Company, 1936.

163 *Cubist Cat*, glazed earthenware,
Shearwater Pottery, 1928; the faceted
modelling reflects trends in contemporary art
movements.

Opposite, above
164 *Ruffle pot*, glazed earthenware, J.A. Bauer Pottery, 1930s.

Opposite, below
165 *Futura* vase, Roseville Pottery, 1928.

Below
166 Glazed earthenware vase with contrasting luster, R. Guy Cowan, Cowan Pottery Studio, *c.* 1917.

Above
167 Ziggurat vase, factory-made glazed earthenware, 1930s; the stepped upper part of the body and neck reflects contemporary interest in archeological discoveries, especially Aztec temples.

168 Vase, glazed stoneware, by Maija Grotell, c. 1939.

169 Globular vase, lead-glazed earthenware with overall decoration of incised circles, made by Richard O. Hummel, Cowan Pottery Studio, 1930.

170 Turquoise vessel with incised decoration and mat glaze, an eloquent design by Arthur E. Baggs, 1935.

171 Footed bowl, Leon Volkmar, 1920s.

172 "Jazz Age" punch bowl, designed and decorated by Viktor Schreckengost, Cowan Pottery Studio, 1931; the sgraffito decoration exploits the contrast between the white body and the Egyptian blue glaze to maximum effect.

Left
173 *Bird and Wave*, glazed proto-porcelain figure by Alexander Blazys, Cowan Pottery Studio, *c.* 1929.

Above
174 *Mother and Child*, glazed figure group, Karoly Fülöp, 1930s.

Above
175 Plate decorated with stylized flowers and foliage, Thelma Frazier Winter, Cowan Pottery Studios, 1931.

Above, right
176 Charger, earthenware with slip and sgraffito decoration by Wilhelm Hunt Diederich, 1920s.

Right
177 Plate with scalloped rim, lead-glazed earthenware with painted decoration depicting "Jacob wrestling with the Angel," by Henry Varnum Poor, 1931.

The Myth of Leda and the Swan

178 Charger with sgraffito decoration, Viktor Schreckengost, Cowan Pottery Studio, 1931.

179 Boudoir lamp or vase, ivory bisque china, Frank Graham Holmes, Lenox China Company, *c.* 1928; the purity and translucency of the clay body is revealed when the piece is illuminated.

180 *Madonna*, crackle-glazed terra cotta, Margaret Postgate, Cowan Pottery Studio, 1929.

181 *Europa*, glazed slip-cast proto-porcelain figure, Paul Manship, Cowan Pottery Studio, *c.* 1930; the subject is similar to that of the artist's bronze sculpture of 1924.

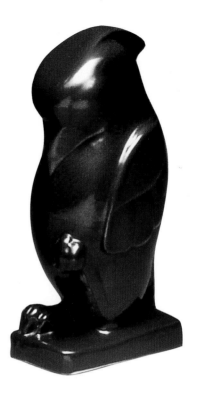

Opposite
182 *Sailing Ship*, Fulper Pottery Company, *c.* 1920–25; a romanticized treatment in which the glaze camouflages rather than reveals the subject.

Above left and right
183, 184 *Antinea* and *Introspection*, glazed proto-porcelain figurines, A. Drexel Jacobson, Cowan Pottery Studio, *c.* 1929.

Left
185 Head (on attached base), Waylande Gregory, 1928; the style reflects the strong interest in African art during this period, and in this example clay is modelled in imitation of cast bronze.

Left
186 Salt- and pepper-shakers (foreground), creamer and sugar bowl, all in the shape of birds; slip-cast porcelain with hand-painted luster decoration, maker unknown, 1920s/1930s.

Left, center
187 Creamer and sugar-bowl set, with matching tray and fixed central bird figure, all in porcelain with hand-painted decoration; maker unknown, after 1921.

Left, below
188 Small pitcher in the form of an owl, slip-cast porcelain with luster decoration; maker unknown, after 1921.

Below
189 Small pitcher in the form of a bird, after 1921. An inexpensive object of lasting charm; maker unknown.

190 Vases, porcelain with hand-painted floral decoration, 1920s/1930s; (left) Sakuraware, (right) maker unknown.

Below
191 Teapot with lid in the form of a cat's head, maker unknown, *c.* 1935; during the 1930s, Japanese manufacturers often copied the designs of English novelty teapots.

192 "Jewels" bowl, hand-painted
porcelain, Noritake, c. 1922–29.

Opposte, above
193 "Alexandra Pierret,"
porcelain figure, hand-painted and
with luster decoration, Noritake,
1920s/1930s.

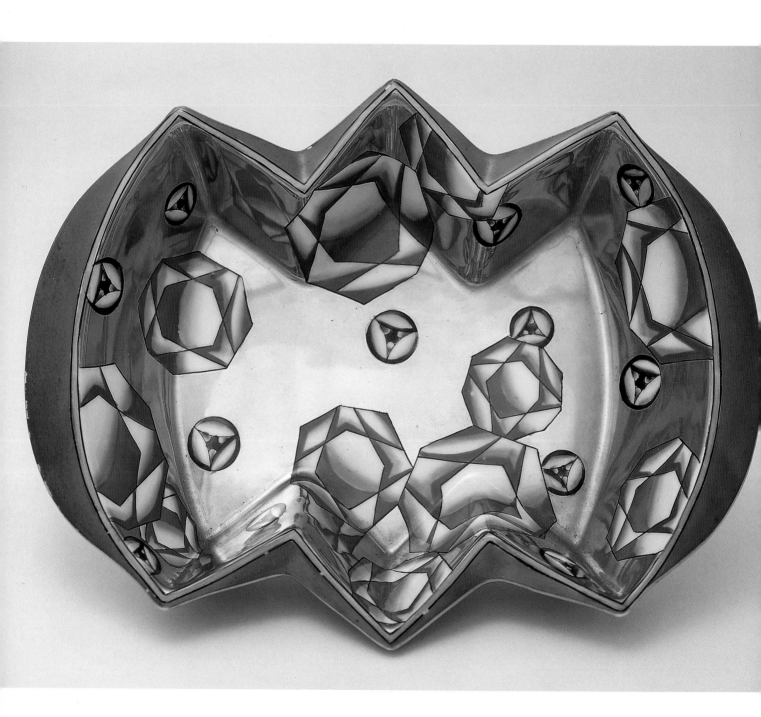

Below
194 "Arabella" covered box, hand-painted porcelain, Noritake, *c.* 1922–29.

195 Sugar basket and creamer, porcelain with hand-painted decoration depicting Chinese lanterns, Noritake, 1920s; such boldly decorated functional pieces were designed for export to the United States.

196 Tea set with conforming tray, hand-painted porcelain, 1930s; maker unknown.

197 Seven-chambered vase, after 1921; maker unknown. The design of this mass-produced model takes a thoroughly modern form, enhanced by the use of a striking yellow glaze.

198 Footed plates, 1920s/1930s; maker unknown. The traditional type of celadon-glazed plate used for serving food is enhanced by the addition of a fretwork pattern in platinum luster over a cobalt-blue glaze on parts of the upper surface.

199 Rectangular vase, glazed slip-cast earthenware, Kent Art Ware, after 1921; the design exemplifies the Modernist preference for simple geometric forms suitable for serial production.

200 Imperial Hotel china, glazed porcelain, designed by the architect Frank Lloyd Wright as part of his overall scheme for the Tokyo hotel completed in 1922. In the 1980s, this pattern was reissued by Tiffany & Co., New York.

201 "White Cap," small plate, hand-painted porcelain, Noritake, c. 1922–29.

AN A–Z OF CERAMISTS, DESIGNERS, AND FACTORIES

Cross-references to related entries are indicated by an asterisk.

Aitken, Russell Barnett. *The Futility of a Well-Ordered Life*, 1935. H. 18½ in. (47.0 cm).

Adamovich, Mikhail Mikhailovich (1884–1947). After completing his studies at the Stroganov School of Art and Industrial Design in Moscow, he received a scholarship which enabled him to study decorative painting in Italy. Two years later, in 1909, he returned to Russia, where he began painting murals in St Petersburg (known after 1914 as Petrograd) and Moscow.

After a stint in the art department of the *State Porcelain Factory, 1918–19, he served in the Red Army from 1919 to 1921. His military service proveded many important "revolutionary" subjects for his later artistic career as a porcelain decorator. He returned to the State Porcelain Factory 1921–23, and adapted various *agitprop* slogans and scenes of military life as ceramic decoration. He was active at other important Russian porcelain factories including the Volkhov Factory, 1924–27, and the *Dulevo Works, *c.* 1927–33. In 1925, he was awarded a medal at the Paris Exposition.

Adams, John (1882–1953). A British pottery designer who, with Cyril Carter and Harold Stabler, in 1921 formed *Carter, Stabler & Adams Ltd, a subsidiary of Carter & Co. Ltd (commonly known as *Poole Pottery), in which his wife Truda (later *Carter) was also a partner. He was responsible for designing many models for the firm's production and also for developing a line of glazes, both glossy and semi-mat. His *Streamline* tableware (1936) reflected the growing popular taste for modern designs during the period.

Adnet, Jacques and **Jean** (b. 1900). Twin brothers who, after World War I, worked as a team. They designed a variety of household furnishings, including carpets and furniture, for La Maîtrise, under the directorship of their mentor Maurice Dufrêne. Between 1923 and 1928 they collaborated in making figurines, animal figures, and decorative ceramic objects for *Robj. Such objects are signed "J.-J. Adnet" (a formula which has led some writers to treat the brothers as one individual, Jean-Jacques),

and were mostly made of white crackle-glazed earthenware modelled in a highly stylized manner. Some observers regard them as bordering on kitsch; although this may be true of some examples, their figures of birds in particular reveal an authentic sense of observed reality. In the mid-1920s, Jacques designed for *Boch Frères Keramis.

In 1928, the brothers went their separate ways, and Jacques, whose interior-design work followed a spare, Modernist aesthetic, became director of the *Compagnie des Arts Français. After the company closed in 1959, he was appointed director of the École Nationale Supérieure d'Art Décoratif. Jean worked as sales manager of the Galeries Lafayette department store from 1928.

Aitken, Russell Barnett (b. 1910). After studying under R. Guy *Cowan at the Cleveland School of Art, he visited Europe to complete his training with Michael *Powolny at the Kunstgewerbeschule, Vienna. When he returned to Cleveland in 1932, he established the Pottery Workshop, where he continued to investigate the modelling and glazing techniques to which he had been introduced in Austria. In 1935, he set up a studio in New York.

He was known for his caricatures of people and animals executed in a style that demonstrated the influence of his contact with the *Wiener Werkstätte. His brightly colored lead-glazed earthenware sculptures often lampooned mythical stories like Europa and the Bull, or the Virgin and the Unicorn. However, a figure entitled *The Futility of a Well-Ordered Life* earned him widespread acclaim and a $1,000 Carnegie Foundation grant when the work was first shown in 1935 in New York at a Surrealist exhibition at the Walker Gallery. This figure was a spoof on a painting by Salvador Dalí; it combined a distinctively expressive modelling style with absurd, Dalí-esque motifs.

Albisola (or Albissola). A small town situated on the Italian Riviera, Albisola was recognized as an important center of maiolica production in the 18th

Albisola, Tullio d'. *Fobia Antimitativa*, glazed terra cotta, 1929. H. 11¾ in. (29.8 cm).

Allinson, Adrian Paul. *Diana*, glazed earthenware figure, signed and dated (1922 or 1928?). H. 15½ in. (39.5 cm).

and 19th centuries. During the 1920s, it was a magnet for the Italian Futurists, whose ceramic production was centered around a pottery run by Tullio *d'Albisola and his brother Torido *Mazzotti, both of whom had been trained by their father. Although Albisola was home to other ceramics factories during this period, it was most closely identified with the work of the Mazzotti family.

Albisola, Tullio d' (Tullio Mazzotti; 1899–1971). Trained at Albisola with his father, a master-potter, and later became one of the most prolific of the Futurist ceramists (*Futurism). He showed ceramics and some sculpture at several exhibitions, but his first wide exposure came in 1929 at the Trentatre Futuristi ("Thirty-three Futurists") exhibition in Milan. His pieces were shown at virtually every important Futurist exhibition over the following years, and his work was considered the most sculptural of all the pieces shown. He also collaborated with many of the Futurists, including *Diulgheroff, *Farfa, and *Gambetti, helping them to realize their ideas in clay.

He and his brother, Torido *Mazzotti, worked both separately and jointly in their home-town of Albisola. In 1921, the Valle brothers offered them a contract to produce a number of designs, which would be sold through stores in Genoa. They accepted the challenge, but business dried up quickly. However, success came in 1925, when Mazzotti attended the Paris Exposition with samples of their wares. Business expanded rapidly, but the brothers disagreed about how production should be organized. Mazzotti was interested in industrial methods, while Tullio wanted more of a workshop atmosphere. The two used separate spaces for a time, until Nicolaj *Diulgheroff designed a new building for them in 1932; this was a combination house, laboratory, and store. Two years later, an annex was attached to provide more production space. At the beginning of World War II, when the American and French governments placed restrictions on Italian imports, profitable markets were lost.

Allinson, Adrian Paul (1890–1959). An artist and sculptor who studied at the Slade School of Art, London. Though known primarily as a painter, he applied his decorative style to diverse projects such as stage sets, poster designs, and ceramic sculpture. In *Diana*, which depicts a leaping deer behind a supine female, he evokes some of the recurring themes of the Art Deco style: the mythic, idealized female is featured with an animal known for its agility and speed. This work was shown in 1928 at the Arts and Crafts Exhibition Society, Royal Academy, London. He created other stylized sculptural works using exotic animal subjects, such as toucans.

Altman, Natan Isaevich (1889–1970). After attending art school in Odessa, he studied painting from 1910 to 1912 at Marie Vasilieva's Free Russian Academy in Paris. Around this time, his work was shown in avant-garde exhibitions, including the "Knave of Diamonds" and "0.10" (the show, held in Petrograd in 1915, at which *Malevich introduced Suprematism to the public). He taught in various schools shortly before and throughout the 1920s. Altman sketched many portraits of Lenin (one of these was used by *Adamovich to adorn a porcelain plate), and in 1918 he decorated Palace Square in Petrograd for the first anniversary of the October Revolution. A banner designed for this project ("The Land is for the Working People" or "The Land is for the Workers") was later adapted in red and green for use on a porcelain plate. Ceramic wares decorated with political slogans were a common means of disseminating so-called "agitational propaganda" (*agitprop*) during the early years of Communism, notably on porcelain blanks from the *State Porcelain Factory.

American art pottery. The wares so described were produced by dozens of potteries in the United States between about 1875 and 1940 (*art pottery).

Anselmo, Giuseppe Mario (b. 1913). Italian ceramist who began his career working with Tullio *d'Albisola. At first he worked as a ceramic painter, but in 1928 he took up modelling. Following the Futurist predilection for depicting motion, repetition, and speed, he often used airplanes and bicycles as subjects.

He continued to work with Tullio in the new studio designed by Nicolaj *Diulgheroff, and participated fully in the Futurist movement both in facilitating the execution of designs by others and in the creation of his own bas-relief designs. He was also associated with Alf *Gaudenzi in Genoa. In 1930, he won the gold medal at the Futurist "Arti e Mestieri" (Arts and Crafts) contest in Rome. As a member of the Genoa group, he participated in many Futurist art exhibitions, including the Mostra Futurista di pittura, scultura e arte decorativa, 1931. During the Italian campaign in East Africa he ceased his artistic pursuits, but resumed his work in 1937, when he returned to Albisola.

Arabia AB. The leading Finnish manufacturer of ceramics, this company was originally founded in 1874 in Helsinki by the Swedish company *Rörstrand, with the aim of marketing domestic wares in the vast contiguous Russian market. The company first produced European-style tableware and decorative objects using as decoration transfer prints supplied by Rörstrand. In 1916, Arabia became independent and began to develop its own

Archipenko, Alexander. *Walking Woman*, painted terra cotta, 1937. H. 25½ in. (64.8 cm).

styles that reflected modern design trends. In 1922, the factory was modernized, and the company's range of products expanded to include not only domestic wares, but sanitary and industrial items. These years also saw the beginning of a continuing tradition of working with individual artists. In the late 1920s, Greta-Lisa Jäderholm-Snellman's stylish designs added to Arabia's increased standing in the marketplace. Its modern image was also enhanced during the 1930s by the work of Friedl Kjellberg (1905–89), though she was better known later for her "rice porcelains," first produced in the 1940s.

With the arrival of Kurt Ekholm as artistic director in 1932, the company opened its doors to artists, making Arabia the center in Finland for both mass-produced and studio ceramics. The following year, the designer Toini Muona (1904–87), who had joined the firm in 1931, won a gold medal at the first Milan Triennale. Arabia's design philosophy, firmly based in functionalism, evolved throughout the 1930s and 1940s. By the 1960s it had become the style now referred to as "Scandinavian modern." This style is deeply rooted in both the Modernist functionalist ethos and the Social Democratic political system which prevails in Scandinavia.

Archipenko, Alexander (Aleksandr; 1887–1964). Russian-born sculptor who studied in Paris at the Ecole des Beaux-Arts. In 1923, he emigrated to the USA, where he remained for the rest of his life. During the recession of the 1920s, he was hired by several New York department stores (including Lord & Taylor, Macy's, and Saks Fifth Avenue) to design window displays. However, he was primarily known for his sculpture, creating stylized figurative forms that show the influence of Cubism and of his formative years in Paris. He sometimes used clay as an inexpensive substitute for bronze, but at other times he made ceramic sculptures that exploited the material for its inherent qualities. Throughout his career, his work was shown extensively in museums and galleries; in 1987, the Hirshhorn Museum and Sculpture Garden, Washington, D.C., mounted a major retrospective exhibition.

Art Deco (*c.* 1910–1930). Following on the heels of *Art Nouveau, true Art Deco developed in France, and was quickly adopted in one form or another by architects and designers in other European countries. Originally, when the style was revealed to the public at large at the Exposition Internationale des Arts Décoratifs et Industriels Modernes of 1925 (the Exposition had originally been planned for 1914, but World War I intervened), it was referred to as *art moderne* or *style moderne* (referring to French Art Deco). Beginning with "Les Années '25: Art Déco/Bauhaus/Stijl/Esprit Nouveau," an exhibition held in 1966 at the Musée des Arts Décoratifs in

Paris to commemorate the 1925 show, the phrase "Art Deco" was adopted generally. In America, the name was popularized following two important exhibitions, both entitled "Art Deco": in New York at Finch College Museum (1970), and at the Minneapolis Institute of Art (1971).

The style, which encompassed all the applied arts, attracted the best practitioners in each field. Among the titans of Art Deco design who immediately come to mind are Jacques-Emile *Ruhlmann, René Lalique, Jean Dunand, Edgar Brandt, René *Buthaud, Maurice Dufrêne, Paul Follot, Louis Süe, André Mare, Paul Iribe, Paul Poiret, and André Groult. Their work represented a cross-section encompassing glass, ceramics, furniture, metal, fashion, and bookbinding. Stylistically, true Art Deco, like the complex times that engendered it, can best be characterized by a series of contradictions: purist vs. ornamental, tectonic vs. fluid, ziggurat vs. streamline, symmetrical vs. irregular, to name but a few. The iconography chosen by Art Deco artists to express the period is also laden with contradictions. Fair maidens in 18th-century dress seem to coexist with chic sophisticated ladies and recumbent nudes, and flashes of lightning illuminate stylized rosebuds. Imagery drawn from newly excavated archaeological sites such as Tutankhamen's tomb was also popular. The style encompasses so many diverse aspects that it is not easy to sum up, except to say that one knows it definitively when one sees it.

Artěl Cooperative. A conglomerate of craft workshops in Prague, modelled on the *Wiener Werkstätte, which produced ceramic, metal, and wood artefacts from Czech Cubist designs. Ceramic designs featured a distinctive style characterized by boldly faceted, fluted, or ribbed geometric shapes, which were loosely based on crystalline forms. Ceramics in this style were manufactured by the firm of Rydl and Thon in Svijany-Podolí, and were often highlighted by the addition of linear decoration, usually in black, red, or gold. The wares often bear an "Artěl" mark.

Although the primary focus of *Czech Cubism was on architecture, the artists applied the same fervor to ceramics as they did to buildings: the production of artefacts offered them a special way of realizing their unique conception of form, matter, and energy.

Artigas, José Llorenz (Joseph-Llorenz; 1892–1971). Spanish painter and studio potter who was active in Barcelona before moving to Paris where, from *c.* 1923 to 1941, he collaborated with artists, most notably Raoul *Dufy (1922–30 and 1937–39) and Albert Marquet (1933). During this period his work included modelled ceramic planters painted by Dufy and by Nicolas Rubio Tuduri. An important collaboration was his work with Joan Miró on large ceramic murals for the UNESCO Building, Paris, in 1958.

art moderne or **art décoratif**. The name first given to the innovative modern designs of *Art Deco. In America, confusion reigns because the term *art moderne* or its anglicized version "art modern" was adopted to cover a range of modern styles including Art Deco and others associated with the Machine Age. American modernity was so eclectic that labels such as "Jazz Moderne" and "Zig-Zag Moderne" were also adopted.

Art Nouveau. The name of this style was derived from that of the Paris shop, La Maison de l'Art Nouveau, opened by Siegfried Bing in 1896. In Germany and Austria the style was called *Jugendstil* and, in Italy, *Stile Liberty*. Art Nouveau, which reached its peak in the last decade of the 19th century and continued into the early years of the 20th, is readily identifiable from its distinctive whiplash curves and flowing lines derived from nature and the human figure. Characteristically, components are presented in an asymmetrical format. The style was reflected in designs for every part of the man-made environment—from architecture to tableware, furniture to household fixtures—and as such it paved the way for *Art Deco. The malleability of clay made it easy for studio potters and designers alike to produce curvaceous forms typical of this style.

art pottery. Art pottery first developed in England as a reaction to the industrialization of the ceramics industry, which had occurred almost completely by the mid-1850s. The Great Exhibition of 1851 showed up the shortcomings of total industrialization in design and, spurred on by the critic John Ruskin, a reassessment of the means of production ensued. Ruskin's idea was that the roles of artist/designer and craftsman should be united in the production of aesthetically pleasing goods, abandoning the presumed hierarchical separation of roles.

Art pottery was made both by individual potters and in specially created studios set up by leading manufacturers. Working not necessarily from the *Arts and Crafts ideal, but as a means of attracting an increased share of the market, large, established potteries were quick to adopt some form of "handcraft." Doulton created its Lambeth Studio in London for this purpose, and *Mintons opened its Art Pottery Studio in 1871, while *Wedgwood had a studio directed by Alfred and Louise *Powell in which they revived the art of freehand painting. Many well-known artists, designers, and architects supplied ideas. At Wedgwood, complex patterns with their roots in the Arts and Crafts tradition were applied to wares by skilled paintresses. Smaller potteries were already engaged in limited serial production of decorated accessories and ornamental wares and, by comparison with larger operations, could more easily bridge the gap between design and production. Interest in art pottery waned by around the 1930s, as modern styles started to dominate the scene and the work of studio potters gained an audience. In a very general sense, one can think of art pottery as the work produced by art potters (as opposed to the artist-potters who followed) by means of limited serial production in either large factories or smaller potteries. That definition, however, does not take into account the compelling aesthetic component of art pottery, which has a very distinctive style, albeit a gloriously varied one.

Across the Atlantic, literally dozens of art potteries sprang up in America—among them *Rookwood, Grueby, van Briggle, *Teco, *Fulper, *Robineau, *Weller, Newcomb, Overbeck, and Marblehead. Although each pottery developed its own distinctive style, they all resonated with an "arts and crafts" aesthetic. Decoration based on natural forms and the use of popular glazes, such as mat green and turquoise, were characteristics shared in common by the products of many of the potteries. Most of the art potteries were still producing at the dawn of the modern era when *Art Deco and *Bauhaus-inspired styles began to dominate, and some actually produced Art Deco pieces. After the Arts and Crafts movement petered out, the values that it had established were carried on in a different way by artist-potters who sought to make ceramics that expressed the individual, using tradition-based means of production.

Arts and Crafts Movement. The 19th-century social and artistic reform movement which profoundly affected attitudes toward hand-craft in England, Continental Europe, and the USA. The theoretical basis for the movement, which came as a reaction to rampant industrialization in England, was formulated by the critic John Ruskin (1819–1900) and the designer William Morris (1834–96), whose idea it was to establish craft workshops based on the medieval guilds system. Morris's firm—Morris, Marshall, Faulkner & Co.—was founded in 1861 for the production of sturdy, unornamented furniture. His wallpaper and fabric designs, in particular, are some of the defining visual manifestations of Arts and Crafts style. Many members of the Pre-Raphaelite circle, including Ford Madox Brown, Dante Gabriel Rossetti, and Sir Edward Burne-Jones, worked for the firm. The company's commitment to designs which exhibited "fitness of purpose" paved the way for the "form follows function" ideal striven for, decades later, by many Modernists.

Ashtead Potters Ltd. *The Wembley Lion*, modelled by Percy Metcalfe, produced as the official souvenir of the British Empire Exhibition held in 1924; the angular modelling reflects the influence of Cubism. H. 14 in. (35.6 cm).

A.E. Baggs

In the field of ceramics, the response to the Arts and Crafts Movement was enormously rewarding, and came in the form of so-called *art pottery. The ideals of the movement were followed by the Art Workers' Guild (1884) and the Arts and Crafts Exhibition Society (1886) in England, and were promulgated by them. In the United States, a group that shared the Arts and Crafts philosophy, the American Art Workers' Guild, was formed in New England (1885).

Arzberg. Bavarian porcelain-manufacturing center which began to establish an importance comparable to that of *Limoges during the 19th century. In 1931, the Carl Schumann factory produced the *Arzberg 1382* service designed by Dr Hermann *Gretsch. This is thought to be the first time that a German manufacturer used a simple, Modernist design for tableware. Featuring a combination of uncluttered geometric shapes devoid of ornament, *Arzberg 1382* aptly reflects the modern era, but its soft, round forms also hark back to some traditional ceramic designs. Perhaps this combination of seeming opposites, historicism and traditionalism, explains the long-lasting appeal of the service. Today, many of the Arzberg factories are consolidated under the name Hutschenreuther AG.

Ashby Potters' Guild. In 1909, Pascoe Tunnicliffe, who hailed from a family of potters, started the Ashby Potters' Guild in Woodville, Derbyshire, a studio pottery that produced hand-thrown decorative and utilitarian wares in glazed earthenware. The pottery was known particularly for its crystalline glazes, known as *rouge flambé*, and for ruby and blue lusters. In 1913, the Copenhagen Museum acquired one of Ashby's crystalline glazed pieces, and in 1920, the Guild's wares were shown at the British Industrial Arts Exhibition. After a partnership was formed with William Ault's pottery in 1922 the combined business was called Ault and Tunnicliffe.

Ashtead Potters Ltd. Pottery at Ashtead, Surrey, founded in 1923 by Sir Lawrence Weaver to provide work for disabled ex-servicemen. Aided by experienced potters from the Victoria Works in Ashtead, they initially manufactured earthenware specialty items and tableware with simple decoration (landscapes; bold, monochrome colors; or transfer-printed designs). By the mid-1920s the factory was producing nursery ware decorated with E.H. Shepard's illustrations for *Winnie the Pooh*.

Ashtead's best-known piece was Percy Metcalfe's design for *The Wembley Lion*, which was the official souvenir of the British Empire Exhibition held at Wembley in west London in 1924. During the 1930s, the firm produced modelled figurines, some designed by Phoebe *Stabler. From 1926 to 1936,

Ashtead Potters' production was stamped with a mark depicting a tree on a hill and "Ashtead Potters, Made in England."

Attwell, Mabel Lucie (1879–1964). Known primarily as a children's book illustrator, she began designing nursery wares for *Shelley Potteries in 1926. She illustrated works by Lewis Carroll, the brothers Grimm, and Hans Christian Andersen, but it was her own designs—especially those in three dimensions depicting chubby-cheeked children—for nursery ware that amused several generations of British children. The whimsicality and wit of her designs were welcome during the Depression, and that characteristic quality continues to contribute to the popularity of these wares as collectibles.

Augarten, Wiener Porzellan-Manufaktur. Manufacturer of fine porcelain established in 1922 at Schloss Augarten, Vienna, continuing the earlier production of the Vienna State Porcelain works. Augarten made a wide range of tablewares and fine decorative objects, including models of the famous Lipizzaner horses of the Spanish Riding School. Tableware was sometimes decorated in a lively manner using an unusual combination of polychrome floral motifs within detailed geometric patterns. In 1928, a dinner service by Josef *Hoffmann was produced by Augarten, and designs by other members of the *Wiener Werkstätte, including Michael *Powolny and Vally *Wieselthier, were executed around the same time. Production of fine porcelain continues today, including several tea sets originally designed by Hoffmann.

B

Baggs, Arthur Eugene (1886–1947). A talented student of Charles F. *Binns, he helped to initiate the idea of the studio potter in the United States, and was also instrumental in establishing serious criteria for the teaching of ceramics at university level there; he believed that firm technical foundation in ceramics engendered the production of art. He taught pottery at the Ethical Culture School and the School of Design and Liberal Arts in New York, 1913–20, and thereafter at the Cleveland School of Art. In 1928, he became a professor of ceramic arts at Ohio State University, where he remained until his death. Baggs also fulfilled professional commitments with R. Guy *Cowan (from 1925 to 1928) and with Marblehead Pottery in Massachusetts (from 1904 until it closed in 1936). He became owner of the latter pottery in 1915.

Although much of Marblehead's production embodies the aesthetic concerns of *art pottery, Baggs's own work sometimes demonstrates the influence of Modernism in his use of abstract, incised

Bauhaus. Coffee pot designed by Otto Lindig, Bauhaus Keramik, c.1923–24. H. 7¼ in. (18.6 cm).

decoration on simple hand-formed pots. He was also known for carving outlines of flowers, fruits, animals, or sometimes marine subjects, before glazing in a single color. Simplicity in form and decoration was the *leitmotiv* of Marblehead's production of primarily hand-thrown wares designed by Baggs.

Balla, Giacomo (1871–1958). A participant in the Futurist movement, which was founded on principles propounded in one of several manifestos of which he was co-author. One tenet of *Futurism was the idea that artists should move freely among creative disciplines, although Balla himself was known primarily as a painter. By 1918, he was widely respected for his precise, systematic style which, ironically, was perceived to be emotionally charged.

The Casa d'Arte Bragaglia produced his "modern ceramics" in 1918, and he also independently designed vases and plates. That same year, he co-authored with Marinetti the *Color Manifesto*. In 1925, he exhibited work at the Paris Exposition. Throughout the 1920s, he designed vibrantly colored plates and floor tiles, and sometimes worked for Roma Rocchi. He also collaborated with Riccardo Gatti in creating a coffee service that was shown at the Esposizione Internazionale di Barcellona in 1929. By the early 1930s he slowly distanced himself from the Futurists, and by 1937 a complete ideological separation had taken place.

Ballets Russes. The startling stage presence of the Ballets Russes under the direction of Serge Diaghilev was first seen in Paris in 1909. Ballets were designed not only by Léon Bakst, but also by Jean Cocteau, whom Diaghilev once directed to "Astonish me!". This charge was taken to heart by Cocteau, as well as by his collaborators, Pablo Picasso, Erik Satie, and Léonide Massine, whose combined efforts produced *Parade*. Both Picasso's Cubism and the Orientalism seen in Bakst's stage sets and costumes directly influenced French Art Deco designs in all media; one of his costume designs also provided the basis for decoration on a Russian porcelain dish. The work of Josef *Hoffmann, Otto Wagner, and Adolf Loos in Austria, and of Clarice *Cliff in England reflected the international influence of the Ballets Russes. Presented on stage in a spectrum of vibrant colors, they first appeared in London in 1911, immediately transforming interior color-schemes and profoundly affecting decorative styles of the period.

Barbier, Georges (1882–1932). French artist and designer. Although not known directly for ceramic work, he produced noteworthy graphic and theater designs, which were influenced by the *Ballets Russes and 18th-century fashions; these had a direct influence on some contemporary painted ceramic decoration. Some of his depictions of elegantly

attired women were reproduced on powder boxes, plates, and vases. (Particularly, the Japanese firm *Noritake borrowed freely from his work.) During the late 1920s, he had a brief stint in Hollywood, as a result of which his style became known to the American public.

Baudisch-Wittke, Gudrun (1907–82). A leading figure in the *Wiener Werkstätte's ceramic design department from 1926 to 1930, she made tall, fluted vases, and dishes, and designed lamps for production. Her modelled heads and freestanding figures were made of painted terra cotta, and although by the late 1920s she was smoothing out their surfaces, her work remained audacious and highly expressive.

Having gained a reputation for ceramics, textile design, and bookbinding, she established her own studio in Vienna in 1930. She subsequently worked in Berlin (1936–42), and by 1943 established a second studio in Hallstatt. She signed her work variously GUDRUN BAUDISCH, GB/W, GBW, or with a cipher in the form of an H within a circle.

Bauer Pottery, J.A. Originally a family business established in Kentucky in 1883 to produce earthenware and stoneware for domestic use. After a brief closure, John A. Bauer brought many of his employees to California, where he opened a new pottery in Los Angeles in 1905. Due to its abundance of raw materials, California was ideally suited for potteries, and Bauer became (along with Gladding McBean & Co., Pacific Clay Products, Vernon Kilns, and Metlox Poppy Trail Manufacturing Company) one of the "Big Five" American dinnerware producers located there.

From the time of its arrival, the company produced utilitarian wares and a line of molded art pottery, and also cornered the market in flower pots. "Beer crocks" made for home brewing were popular during the Prohibition years. However, the firm became best known for its brightly colored dinnerware, in a range of "mix-and-match" colors, introduced in 1930. Such wares proved immensely popular during the Depression, and Bauer's line antedated *Homer Laughlin's *Fiesta Ware* by six years.

Bauhaus (Das Staatliche Bauhaus Weimar). The Bauhaus was a school with a uniquely integrated program for instruction in design and architecture with architects and artists as teachers. Although the school was short-lived (1919 to 1925 at Weimar; 1925 to 1933 at Dessau), the ideas it espoused have had a lasting effect on modern architecture and design, most notably as seen in architecture in the International Style and in the birth of industrial design as a professional field of endeavor. The ideals upon which the Bauhaus was based were foreshadowed by William Morris, whose ideas

Bayes, Gilbert. *Mermaid*, garden figure in Polychrome Stoneware, Royal Doulton, 1937.

Bernardaud, L., & Cie. Small vase decorated in black, red, and beige, promoting a Parisian furrier, 1923; inscribed on the base "Edité pour la maison à la Reine d'Angleterre Fourrures. L. Bernardaud & Cie." H. 6 in. (15.0 cm).

inspired the *Arts and Crafts Movement in England, and the Deutscher Werkbund (1907–33) in Germany. Dozens of studies have been made of the Bauhaus, and many of its leading practitioners, some of whom emigrated to the USA (including Josef Albers, Marcel Breuer, and Walter Gropius), have achieved legendary status.

The demands of pottery-making made it necessary to set up the Bauhaus pottery in the stables of a Rococo castle at Dornburg, 15½ (25 km) miles from Weimar. Here, from 1920 to 1925 (when the main school was moved to Dessau), the pottery came very close to achieving one of its original goals, that of making well-designed functional ceramics at a profit. (The Bauhaus was first established with the idea that the workshops would, in time, make a profit to support its educational activities, though for the most part this did not happen.) Gerhard *Marcks, the Master of Form, approached functional ceramics using the formal considerations of sculpture as his criteria, and Max Krehan, the Workshop Master, supervised the technical aspects of pottery-making. Other ceramists who made significant contributions were Theodor *Bogler, Otto *Lindig, Marguerite *Friedländer-Wildenhain, Margarete *Heymann-Marks, and Lucia Moholy.

Typically, Bauhaus pottery featured unadorned, clean shapes designed for maximum functional efficiency. Sometimes they show the heritage of German folk pottery, while also exhibiting the reductionist tendencies of Modernism. When displayed on a shelf in a typical, spare Bauhaus living environment, such pieces with rounded forms act as a kind of human "punctuation" mark within the strict horizontal and vertical axial approach characteristic of the International Bauhaus style.

Bayes, Gilbert (1872–1953). During his long association with *Royal Doulton (1923–39), this distinguished academic sculptor revolutionized the production of modelled garden and architectural ornaments and fountains. His work came to international attention in 1925 at the Paris Exposition, where he was awarded a gold medal and a diploma of honor for a fountain made of Polychrome Stoneware (a highly durable material developed and trademarked by Doulton). Although he created many works for buildings and gardens using this material, his most ambitious project, completed in 1939, was a frieze 50 ft (15 m) in length for the facade of Doulton House illustrating "Pottery through the Ages."

Bell, Vanessa (1879–1961). English painter and designer. She made household objects at the Omega Workshops (1913–19), which were associated with the renowned literary circle known as the Bloomsbury Group, of which her sister Virginia Woolf was a member. Her ideas for surface decoration showed

the influence of French Post-Impressionism and were painted with freely flowing floral designs and abstract patterns. They were perfectly suited to the cluttered domestic interiors of the time, notably at Charleston, the house in Sussex to which she moved in 1916 with Duncan *Grant, her long-time friend and collaborator.

In 1934, Clarice *Cliff commissioned her to decorate tableware for A.J. *Wilkinson Ltd. Later, some of her designs for the Omega Workshops were adapted for production using simplified motifs and a limited palette. One such pattern, *Vanessa*, was a floral design, and a dinner service designed in 1934 for Newport Pottery, Burslen, shows one of her designs "tamed" for mass-production.

Bellefroid, Guillaume Marie Edmond (1893–1971). Dutch artist who became design director at *De Sphinx in 1929. Under his tutelage the firm produced dinner services, domestic ware, and decorative pieces using distinctively modern design idioms, including those mimicking sleek machines. The example he set served not only to enhance the public's perception of the Dutch pottery industry, but also raised the esteem in which the industrial designer was held.

His approach to design was rooted in the *Bauhaus ethos, as well as in his belief that good aesthetic values could be achieved even within the constraints of industrial production. This philosophy is borne out by several services designed by him before World War II, including the stylish, streamlined *Thea*. The *Maas* service of 1932 included a sugar bowl without handles, a radical design feature which was economical in terms of production. He remained at De Sphinx until 1946 (except for a wartime break, 1942–45), and subsequently worked as aesthetic advisor for the porcelain works N.V. Mosa, Maastricht, 1950–67.

Bernardaud, L., & Cie. A French porcelain factory established in *Limoges at the end of the 19th century for the manufacture of decorated tableware and ornamental ceramics. Some of the latter were shown at the 1925 Paris Exposition. The firm also made promotional pieces for individual clients. The firm introduced the first fully functional tunnel kiln in Limoges in 1949. It continues to produce fine porcelain today, with members of the Bernardaud family directing the operation, as they have done continuously since *c.* 1895.

Besnard, Jean (1889–1958). Son of the French painter Albert Besnard (1849–1934), Jean was an artist-potter known for making vases with incised or impressed surface decoration that often resembled lace, and for his painted decoration inspired by the pointillism of Impressionist painting. He was also recognized for producing luxurious pieces decorated with gold and platinum lusters. Although his work is said to have been inspired by Mediterranean, tribal, and Savoie pottery, he transformed these historical models into highly individual statements, often in the forms of figurative or animal-shaped pots.

He exhibited regularly in Paris at the Salon des Artistes Décorateurs, the Salon d'Automne, and the Salon des Tuileries throughout the 1920s and 1930s. He won a silver medal at the 1925 Paris Exposition. His noteworthy technical innovation was a white enamel glaze with a bad "fit"—which contracted during firing to create the impression of shagreen or sharkskin, a popular decorative finish during the period. His simple forms provided an appropriate background for complex, detailed surface treatments. Some works with impressed surface marks are related in kind to African pottery that mimics basketry.

Beswick, John (d. 1936). After training at Tunstall Pottery, in 1920 he started to work at his father's firm J.W. Beswick Ltd, Gold Street Works, Longton, Staffordshire. His ideas furthered the kitsch side of Art Deco through the production of an extensive line of novelty wares that showed the English penchant for exploiting the *trompe l'œil* aspect of clay modelling by "disguising" one thing as another. Under his direction the company produced a great number of functional wares in shapes including butterflies and pansies, and even introduced an embossed lettuce pattern that was similar to a *Carlton Ware design. In 1934, his *Cottage Ware*, with pieces shaped like an English country cottage (the idea was not new, having originated in the 19th century), was introduced in functional forms ranging from biscuit boxes to teapots. The popular taste for kitsch, and later for nostalgia, is confirmed by the fact that *Cottage Ware* remained in production until 1971.

In 1937, *Sundial Ware*, which incorporated elements such as an Aztec-inspired ziggurat shape made into a handle, was introduced posthumously, and soon rivaled *Cottage Ware* in popularity, remaining in production into the 1950s. At the same time, Beswick was making animals and witty figurines which were produced in Longton by Shaw and Copestake under the trade name "Sylvac." Single-color, mat glazes in green, blue, and oatmeal enlivened his designs for *Moderne* and *Shadows* which were in keeping with the Art Deco styles of the era.

Beyer, Henri-Paul-Auguste (1873–1945). Before becoming a ceramist *c.* 1905, he had followed the family tradition of making stained glass. Around 1914, he settled in Lyons and learned the technique of making salt-glazed stoneware after spending some time in Vallauris (Alpes-Maritimes), later made famous by Picasso's ceramics.

He created figural groups of saints, as well as whimsical birds and animals, from thrown, coiled, and pinched clay; he also made pitchers and vases. In its time his impressionistic style was too advanced for the public—in fact, it resembles a certain genre of 1950s stoneware. In his early work he explored the use of high-fired glazes on forms derived from Oriental models, and in 1932 he began working in a studio attached to the *Sèvres factory. He left for La Borne (Cher) in 1942, and there with a number of other potters including E. Joulia, J. Leart, and V. Ivanoff, re-introduced stoneware, thus effecting a revival of the medium in France.

Bimini Werkstätten (Bimini Werkstatt für Kunstgewerbe Gesellschaft m.b.H.). Incorporated in 1923 in Vienna, the company manufactured and sold furniture, toys, and decorative ceramics. (Bernhardine) Dina Kuhn (b. 1891), who was also associated with the *Wiener Werkstätte, was the ceramics designer for Bimini from 1926 to 1931. She created tiles, figures, plaques, candlesticks, vases, and jars—a range which represented the main output of the factory. Although the palette employed at Bimini is more saturated than that typically used at the Wiener Werkstätte, many of the figurative pieces produced by the two workshops have a witty expressiveness in common. After several corporate reorganizations, the company closed in 1940.

Bing & Grøndahl Porcelaensfabrik. Factory founded in Copenhagen in 1853 by the brothers Jacob Herman Bing and Meyer Herman Bing (both Danish art dealers) and Frederik Vilhelm Grøndahl (a sculptor and designer), for the production of porcelain figures and reliefs. Toward the end of the 19th century the firm's art director Pietro Krohn (1840–1905) created the renowned *Heron* service, which exhibited many of the charactistics associated with the *Art Nouveau style.

At the Paris Exposition of 1925 the company presented expressively modelled works by Jean Gauguin (d. 1961). During the 1920s and 1930s the firm produced decorative and sculptural forms in a distinctively modern idiom, sometimes reflecting the influence of Cubism. Knud Kyhn and Alex Salto (1889–1924) were among the leading designers of the period. As one of the two major Danish ceramics factories, Bing & Grøndahl showed its wares at all the important international design exhibitions, often winning prizes for its outstanding products.

The firm's continuing prosperity has resulted, in part, from its willingness to engage fine artists as designers. Some of these, such as Nielsen and Gauguin, achieved international success; in 1939, their work was exhibited at the New York World's Fair. After World War II, the company opened a new factory to produce dinnerware, devoting the

Bing & Grøndahl. Globular vase by Marie Smith, glazed porcelain with airbrushed decoration in gray and beige depicting an owl, 1920s. H. 10⅞ in. (25.5 cm).

Boch Frères Keramis. Five-part vase, glazed earthenware with abstract painted decoration; underglaze mark "Keramis Made in Belgium." H. 8 ⅝ in. (22.0 cm).

Boch Frères

Blazys, Alexander. Russian folk dancer with musicians, glazed porcelain figures, Cowan Pottery Studio, 1927. H. of dancer 10 in. (25.5 cm).

older workshop to the creation of art wares; the factory continues to produce dinnerware and ornamental objects. Its line of commemorative Christmas plates, a series started in 1895, remains in production.

Marks include a cipher depicting three towers, and often feature the abbreviation "B&G" and the name "Kjøbenhavn" or "Copenhagen" and/or "Danish China Works."

Binns, Charles Fergus (1857–1934). A leading teacher who influenced a generation of noted ceramists, including Arthur *Baggs, R. Guy *Cowan, and Charles *Harder. At the age of 14 he became an apprentice at the Royal Worcester Porcelain Works, where his father, Richard William Binns, was a director. He wrote articles describing his interest in ceramic techniques; they appeared in *Ceramic Technology*, *Pottery Gazette*, and *The Craftsman*. His book *The Potter's Craft* (1922) inspired a generation of ceramists.

He moved to the United States in 1898 and was appointed principal of the Technical School of Sciences and Art in Trenton, New Jersey. In 1900, he became first director of the New York State School of Clayworking and Ceramics (from 1932 the New York State College of Ceramics at Alfred University). His own work in glazed stoneware was commemorated in a posthumous exhibition (1935) at the Metropolitan Museum of Art, New York. He was a charter member of the American Ceramic Society, founded in 1899, and was associated with the English Ceramics Society, the Boston Society of Arts and Crafts, as well as other arts organizations.

Blazys, Alexander (1894–1963). Born in Lithuania, he had by the fall of 1925 emigrated to the United States and was living in Cleveland, Ohio. He is best known for the ceramic figures he modelled for R. Guy *Cowan, he was instrumental in shifting the emphasis of the Cowan Pottery Studio's production toward decorative sculptural works. In 1926, he received first prize at the Cleveland Museum's annual "May Show" (an exhibition of works by local artists) for two small bronzes entitled *Russian Dancers*;

the following year, his *Russian Dancers* were shown in ceramic versions produced by Cowan. However, in that same year he ended his association with Cowan, but continued to produce ceramics at the Cleveland School of Art, where he taught until 1938.

B.M.C. Italian firm founded during the 1930s in Sesto Fiorentino (Tuscany) by Barraud, Messeri, and other partners. Production included everything from figurines of the Madonna and Child to more modern designs for tea sets.

Boch Frères Keramis. Belgian manufacturer. The Boch family first began producing pottery in 1767 in Luxembourg. In 1839, after the borders of Luxembourg and Belgium were changed, the Boch family settled in Belgium, opening the Keramis factory at La Louvière (Saint Vaast) in 1841. The factory's output imitated the distinctive, well-known Delft and Rouen faiences until just after the turn of the century.

It was not until Charles *Catteau became artistic director in 1907 that the company began to produce sophisticated modern ceramics. By the 1920s, it was thriving under the leadership of Catteau, who used simple forms as a background for very complex painted designs on stoneware. Boch Frères and the French company *Longwy were both outstanding in their use of distinctive glazing techniques which were meant to produce a finish resembling *cloisonné* enamel. With this technique, multiple colored glazes are applied separately to a crackled or plain ivory ground. Catteau's technical expertise, coupled with his boundless visual imagination and intelligent exploitation of relationships between decorative subjects and their grounds, fueled the dynamic designs typical of his work for the company. Its ware were often marked with an impressed outline or a printed line drawing of a wolf and the words "KERAMIS / MADE IN BELGIUM." The trade names "Keramis" or "Grès Keramis" were also used, as was a shield flanked by the initials "BF."

Böck, Josef, Wiener Porzellan-Manufaktur. The factory, founded in Vienna in 1828, which initially produced earthenware, later became renowned for its porcelain, due in part to its association with the *Wiener Werkstätte and the Kunstgewerbeschule. These two institutions were centers of creative activity after the turn of the century, and the firm worked with some of the most prolific designers and artists of the era, including Josef *Hoffmann, Dagobert *Peche, Michael *Powolny, and Vally *Wieselthier.

The factory was begun by Josef Böck, whose son of the same name controlled the company during the period under discussion. The Böck family oversaw

Bollhagen, Hedwig. Lidded boxes, glazed earthenware. H. 3½ in. (9.0 cm) and 6¼ in. (15.7 cm).

the management of the business until 1960, when it was acquired by Haas & Cjzjek.

Bo Fajans. Swedish manufacturer; see Dahlskog.

Bogler, Theodor (1896–1968). After studying architecture and art history in Munich in 1919, he entered the *Bauhaus in 1920. Shortly thereafter, he began training in the Bauhaus ceramics workshop at Dornburg. In 1923, he was given his own design studio; in 1924, he became business manager of the Bauhaus workshop, where he worked with Gerhard *Marcks, Max Krehan, and Otto *Lindig. Bogler's collaborations with Lindig were particularly productive. Together they explored the use of high-fired earthenware bodies which would not require glazing. Their goal was the creation of prototypes that took into consideration the needs of serial production. They designed components which could be assembled into a number of different functional forms. By 1925, Bogler had departed from the Bauhaus and was appointed art director at *Velten-Vordamm. During this time he sometimes used stripes of contrasting colors and widths as decoration on earthenware and stoneware.

At the age of 49, Bogler converted to Catholicism and entered a Benedictine monastery, of which he had become abbot by 1939; in 1948–49, he directed the monastery's artistic workshop, and again from 1951.

Bollhagen, Hedwig (b. 1907). After receiving technical training in ceramics at Höhr-Grenzhausen, the German center of stoneware production well known for its progressive designs, she worked from 1927 to 1930 at *Velten-Vordamm; there, she was able to perfect her skills under the direction of Hermann Harkort, who encouraged her to produce designs suitable for adaptation to serial production. During this formative period, she also came into contact with leading *Bauhaus pottery designers such as Gerhard *Marcks, Theodor *Bogler, and Werner *Burri.

She put many of their ideas about producing cost-efficient but well-designed tableware into effect when she established her own workshop in 1934 in the pottery that had formerly been *Haël-Werkstätten. To her own pottery, which she called "HB," she brought along a number of the women painters who had worked at Velten-Vordamm. Initially, they reproduced some of her old patterns, although she soon began creating new designs. She was one of the few women ceramists in Germany to become an independent entrepreneur. Like Bogler and Burri, who sometimes worked for her, she developed a lively linear, banded decorative treatment, which she first worked out on unique pieces. Charles Crodel, a painter, joined her pottery

and helped in the development of technical aspects. Thereafter, they were able to produce architectural ceramics and garden ornaments on a much larger scale than everyday domestic wares. Although the workshop ceased operating during World War II, it reopened and still continues in production.

Bonfils, Robert (1886–1971). One of three artists chosen to design posters for the 1925 Paris Exposition, he was very versatile, creating ceramics and textiles in addition to working on canvas and paper. He designed for *Haviland & Cie of Limoges in the late 1920s and also produced designs for *Sèvres.

Bonifas, Paul-Ami (1893–1967). Swiss ceramist. He received a traditional education in Switzerland as well as some technical art training, especially in jewelry engraving in his father's studio. In 1913 the Swiss School of Ceramics opened in Cavannes-Remens with Bonifas in attendance, but it closed following the outbreak of World War I, prompting him to set up a studio in France at Versoix. In 1919 the studio burned down and Bonifas moved to Paris. There he met Amédée Ozenfant (1886–1966) and Le Corbusier (1887–1965) and was immediately swept up, literally and figuratively, by *L'Esprit Nouveau*, "the illustrated review of contemporary activity." He became general secretary of the magazine 1921–22. He established close ties with Ozenfant and Le Corbusier, although by 1925 his relations with the latter had faltered as a consequence of theoretical disagreements about ornament. The enduring influence of the two men is, however, apparent in Bonifas's work, especially in the black forms of the 1930s, which, in the opinion of Ozenfant, achieve the required level of *purisme*. In these the question of ornamentation is moot—the forms with black gaze make a singular, coherent statement that altogether sidesteps the notion of ornamentation. A little later, he created a group of *faïences blanches* to complement the black wares.

In 1925, he was invited to judge the ceramics section of the Paris Exposition. Subsequently, he returned to Ferney-Voltaire and reopened a small studio, where he produced earthenware and some stoneware. He made a number of black pieces which were exhibited in Paris at the Salon d'Automne in 1927. Despite critical success, Bonifas was bankrupt by 1934. He briefly worked in Ferney-Voltaire again but, following the German occupation of France, he returned to Switzerland in 1940 and then emigrated to the United States. Following his retirement from the Department of Fine Arts at the University of Washington, Seattle, in 1959, he again devoted himself to ceramics.

Following the path of several other Modernists, Bonifas was interested in making single pieces and in producing small series (usually 12) by modified industrial means. He had little interest in creating a totally new formal vocabulary, as he believed that the 7 or 8 "perfect" ceramic forms had been created many centuries before and these could be called into service at will. His later forms seem to contradict this notion, for they are uniquely his own.

Brain, E., & Co. Ltd (Foley China). Many talented artists and designers of the modern era were associated with the Staffordshire porcelain manufacturer E. Brain & Co. In 1903, William Henry Brain, his father E. Brain (d. 1910), and, G. Hawder directed Robinson & Son at Foley China Works, Fenton, founded in the 19th century, and noted for its utilitarian tableware. William Brain was instrumental in introducing decorative wares into the factory's production prior to World War I. Despite this expansion, by the late 1920s the company faced economic hardship due to the General Strike of 1926.

From 1930 to 1946, Brain worked closely with Freda Beardmore (b. 1910), who had been employed as company designer. Her *Savoy* shape and various patterns with abstract or floral decoration helped to revitalize the factory's products and increase business. In 1932, Thomas Acland Fennemore was appointed Managing Director of E. Brain & Co.with the goal of further improving commercial pottery standards, and thereby, sales. He expanded the range of products and launched new designs aimed at mass distribution. Additionally, he formed an experimental association with A.J. *Wilkinson Ltd, with both companies engaging well-known artists to design tableware (originally twelve were invited, but the list grew to 26); they included Vanessa *Bell, Frank *Brangwyn, Gordon *Forsyth, Barbara Hepworth, Dame Laura *Knight, Graham Sutherland, Clarice *Cliff and Billy Walters. Each artist's work was produced in bone china and earthenware, with Clarice Cliff adapting the designs for industrial production; in 1934, the work was shown in London at Harrod's department store in an "Exhibition of Modern Art for the Table," which was a critical success—it even received accolades from Nikolaus Pevsner—but a commercial flop.

During the 1920s, Foley China, as the company was known, produced a *Cube Teapot* in a variety of patterns, some of which were alien to its strict Modernist shape. In 1930, the company launched a pattern called *Pallas*, an audaciously curved shape decorated with a number of Art Deco designs, and in 1933 its *Langham* pattern competed directly with Shelley's *Regent* design. While maintaining a "modern" appearance, Foley China remained committed to a policy of restraint in design and combined with efficient function.

E. Brain & Co. acquired Coalport China Ltd in 1958, and became part of the *Wedgwood Group

in 1967. During the Art Deco era, the company prevented Wileman & Co. (*Shelley Potteries) from marketing their lines in America under the Foley name, already registered as a trademark.

Brangwyn, Sir Frank (1867–1956). A well-known painter who designed ceramic decorations for *Royal Doulton, among other firms, and also became internationally known for his textiles, carpets, and furniture. He worked as an artist for E. *Brain & Co. and was also associated with A.J. *Wilkinson Ltd, where one of his designs for a charger was painted by Clarice *Cliff. His improvised decoration for ceramics captures the spirit embodied by the *Arts and Crafts Movement. He was a protégé of Arthur Heygate Mackmurdo (1851–1942), one of the originators of *Art Nouveau in England. From 1882 to 1884 he worked with William Morris, but eventually his principal interest was the growing field of industrial design, in which he concentrated on making affordable furniture. In 1941, he was knighted for his contributions to art and design. Viewed with hindsight, his career can be seen to have embraced all the design movements of his time, with Brangwyn ending up a Modernist devoted to fulfilling consumer needs.

Brush-McCoy Pottery. The history of Brush-McCoy is tied to that of the J.W. McCoy Pottery (founded in 1899 in Roseville, Ohio, by J.W. McCoy) and the Nelson McCoy Sanitary and Stoneware Company (founded in 1910 by J.W.'s son). The first wares produced at J.W. McCoy Pottery were primarily utilitarian, but soon a line of artware was introduced. The company formulated a mat green glaze which proved popular. The second artware line, *Loy-Nel-Art* (1908), named after McCoy's two sons, was decorated by hand with embossed and incised patterns, and then glazed in mat brown or green. It was similar to superior *Rookwood ware.

In 1908, George S. Brush had joined the J.W. McCoy Pottery as manager, and after a reorganization in 1911 became its owner. From that time the company traded as Brush-McCoy Pottery, and in 1925 it became Brush Pottery Company, with G.S. Brush as president from 1931.

The Nelson McCoy Sanitary and Stoneware Company, also in Roseville, Ohio, became a leader in making mass-produced kitchen utensils, and in 1926 began a successful artware line. From 1933, the company traded under the same Nelson McCoy Pottery. In 1934, an English designer, Sidney Cope, joined the company, and his style imparted a quirky angularity to even the most modest of McCoy's flower pots and vases. McCoy wares produced in the 1930s and early 1940s were among the cheapest American-made pottery, yet Cope gave the line a unique personality.

Buthaud, René. Amphora-shaped vase with decoration in the ancient Greek manner depicting an athlete; signed "RB." H. 14¼ in. (36.2 cm).

René Buthaud

His designs were strongly modelled, featuring stylized leaves and flat disks on larger vases and elongated Cubist animal forms. Most of these were glazed in a simple palette of flat white, yellow, pink, and a distinctive aqua. Cope-designed cookie jars for McCoy often exhibit the same jaunty stylization as the vases and planters, featuring triangular eye-sockets and crisp uncluttered lines, as in the classic "Mammy" jar, produced from 1940 until 1957. His later work for McCoy gradually moved away from the Art Deco style.

Bucher, Hertha (1898–1960). After studying at the Vienna Kunstgewerbeschule under Michael *Powolny, as well as under Cizek, Boehm, and Strnad, she was associated with the *Wiener Werkstätte. Along with other workshop members, she showed her work in the 1920 Kunstschau; in Munich at the Deutsche Gewerbeschau two years later; and in 1925 at the Paris Exposition. Her style of modelling the female head and figure, along with that of her peers such as Susi *Singer and Vally *Wieselthier, contributed to the recognition achieved by Wiener Werkstätte ceramics. Her modelling, lumpy in her early work, became smoother over time, but remained distinctively "Viennese." In fact, some of her ceramics share an aesthetic commonality in surface treatment with the sexually charged watercolors of Egon Schiele (1890–1918). Her output was diverse, and included chimneys and grates for the Bauer apartment designed by Josef *Hoffmann.

By 1920 she had established her own ceramics workshop in Vienna, producing a wide range of wares, including figures, garden ornaments, decorative accessories, and tableware. She worked as a freelance porcelain modeller for the Wiener Porzellan-Manufaktur *Augarten, creating a line of signed figures and accessories. Later in her career, she was a member of the Austrian Werkbund and the Wiener Frauenkunst.

Bunzlau region. Now in Poland, the area around Bunzlau (Boleslawiec) was a thriving center of ceramic production from the Middle Ages to World War II. The region first became known for its folk patterns, featuring indigenous animals and flowers as well as heraldic symbols, on a slip-coated red-clay body. After the area fell to Prussia in the nineteenth century, its wares were spread through German imperial markets, and the "Bunzlau coffee pot" became a common household item. In 1897, the Königliche Keramische Fachschule (Royal School of Ceramics) was founded, and a subsequent revival of interest in folk ceramics helped to confirm the popularity of the region's wares.

C. 1929, Bunzlau decorators opened a new chapter in the history of painting ceramic wares by applying their designs with an airbrush. Shapes inspired by Bunzlau's traditional repertoire were stencilled and sprayed with geometric iconography reflecting the influence of some contemporary avant-garde art movements, including *Futurism, Suprematism, and *De Stijl. Individual firms within the region tended to follow the most popular local designs, hence ceramics with similar styles would frequently emerge from different workshops.

Burri, Werner (1898–1972). Trained at the *Bauhaus ceramics workshop, he took over the design direction at the pottery in *Velten-Vordamm in 1926, replacing Theodor *Bogler. The Bauhaus ideal of merging art and technique would be the cornerstone of Burri's style. His designs were often similar to Bogler's, combining sober, simple shapes with linear decorations which show the influence of Mondrian, and, more importantly, were easy to mass-produce. Unlike Bogler, however, he did not give his works sharp, "metallic" corners that emphasized their design, but used rounder, softer edges, thus lending his vessels a more overtly ceramic quality. In the 1930s, he sometimes worked at the workshop of Hedwig *Bollhagen, creating unique pieces that demonstrated his commitment to an aesthetic of formal harmony. From 1941 to 1963, he taught ceramics at the Keramische Fachschule (School of Ceramics) in Berne.

Buthaud, René (1886–1987). Trained as a painter at the École des Beaux-Arts in Bordeaux. His studies there influenced his work in clay, which became his primary medium in 1918. He exhibited examples of his work at the 1925 Paris Exposition before returning to Bordeaux, where he established a studio and taught painting and decorative arts at the École des Beaux-Arts.

He used crackle glazes to decorate the simple stoneware forms he designed and which were made for him by local potters. When creating vessels with abstract decoration, he sometimes worked with lusters or turned *craquelure* into what he called *peau de serpent* (snakeskin)—an effect which showed the influence of tribal art, especially that of Africa. Some of his best-known pieces are painted with supine female nudes, thus exploiting the particular shape of a ceramic vessel as a "canvas." After 1940, he concentrated mainly on images of women: stylized odalisques, idealized female figures, and mythological goddesses including Venus. Although his pieces painted with nudes fetch high prices at auction, it is still possible to find his exquisite abstract pieces at reasonable cost. He was under contract to Galerie Rouard, Paris, where he exhibited regularly from 1928 to 1965. During this long period, he habitually signed other works that he produced "J. Doris."

Carlton Ware. Pitcher with raised enamel decoration of fairyland figures and flowers, c.1930. H. 7 in. (17.8 cm).

Carlton Ware
MADE IN ENGLAND
"TRADE MARK"

Carlton Ware

B. F. K.

Ch. Catteau.
D. 1056

Charles Catteau

Carter, Stabler & Adams. Cylindrical vase with abstract geometrical decoration, c.1925. H. 11 in. (28.0 cm).

C

Calm-Wierink, Lotte (b. 1897). A ceramic modeller trained at the Vienna Kunstgewerbeschule, she was a member of the *Wiener Werkstätte, 1918–25, where she was responsible for some of the workshop's first successful ceramic output. She hand-modelled figures and figural groups in the distinctive expressive style now associated with several of the workshop's artists. In 1927, she married and left Vienna to travel to the Far East and India with her husband.

Carlton Ware. Trade name used by Wiltshaw & Robinson for decorative and novelty art wares made of earthenware and porcelain at the Carlton Works, Stoke-on-Trent, established in 1890. In 1920, the firm exhibited at the British Industrial Arts Fair, where its luster decoration and wide range of original colors, including mother-of-pearl, various shades of turquoise, orange, black, and a deep red were well received. The company also introduced *Cloisonné Ware*, with a richly colored surface treatment featuring yellow and black on a crazed gold background. Some of its raised enamel decoration is similar to *Wedgwood's *Fairyland Lustre*. Carlton Ware's abstract and floral designs exemplify the era, as do their sunbursts, lightning bolts, and motifs derived from Tutankhamen's tomb (discovered in 1922).

The wares in general seem to step into the modern era of ceramic decoration, while remaining rooted in history, a situation due, in part, to the use of Chinese-type body shapes. However, not all pieces are historically based, as is indicated by the "Machine Age" toast rack (pl. 63). In 1932, due to economic difficulties, the company was acquired by Birks, Rawlins & Company. In 1958, it was renamed Carlton Ware Ltd. The factory closed in 1989.

Carstens, C. & E. Business begun c. 1900 at Reichenbach, Thuringia, for manufacturing porcelain, by two brothers, Christian and Ernst Carstens. Their activities expanded to include factories in Rheinsberg, Hirschau, Georgenthal, Uffrecht, Sorau, Neuhaldsleben, and Gräfenroda. Several of these factories produced ceramics with distinctive decoration made with an atomizer.

Carter, Truda (Gertrude) **Adams** (*née* Sharp; 1890–1958). While studying at the Royal College of Art in London, she met John *Adams whom she subsequently married. Beginning in 1921, their combined talents created much of the ornamental ware produced by *Poole Pottery, where they were partners. *C.* 1931, she married Cyril Carter (Chairman of the company and grandson of one of its founders), though she continued to collaborate with her former husband, including work on surface decoration for his *Streamline* shape.

Working with floral designs derived from faded Jacobean embroideries and from common peasant patterns, she evolved a subtle polychrome palette for her ceramics. These were often freely interpreted in hand-painting by two senior paintresses, Margaret Holder and Ruth Pavely; their distinctiveness set her decorative designs apart from those used by many rival potteries, especially in Stoke-on-Trent. In 1925, she won several awards at the Paris Exposition. Some of her patterns were still produced after her retirement in 1950.

Carter, Stabler & Adams Ltd. A subsidiary of Carter & Co. Ltd, established in 1921. The original firm, founded by Jesse Carter in 1873, remained a family-run business until 1913, when Harold *Stabler was invited to join as a partner, and his wife Phoebe became a figure modeller. Carter, Stabler & Adams was formed when John *Adams and his wife Truda joined the firm. They greatly influenced the direction its designers would take, with John designing many of the shapes and Truda creating patterns with floral decorations that would become a hall-mark of *Poole Pottery wares during the 1920s and 1930s. The new company also employed a number of other designers working outside the factory, including Minnie McLeish, D.M. Batty, and the artist Edward Bawden. At the 1925 Paris Exposition the firm earned two gold medals, and in 1936 achieved popular success with John Adams's *Streamline* shape for tableware.

Catteau, Charles (1880–1966). As a young man, he studied at *Sèvres and worked at the Nymphenburg porcelain factory in Bavaria. For the better part of his career, however, he worked in Belgium at *Boch Frères Keramis, which he joined in 1906, becoming artistic director only a year later and remaining with the company until 1945. He introduced hand-thrown ceramics into its production, creating both their forms and decorative motifs. His first works of note were vases which, though painted with simple floral patterns, achieved unusual textures through imaginative layerings of glaze, sometimes imitating *cloisonné* enamel. Later works, with stylized patterns of flora and fauna, earned him a reputation for creating sophisticated and commercially successful ceramics. His brilliant turquoise glaze on a crackled ivory ground recalled the early individualized palette of the French sculptor and ceramist Edmond *Lachenal, while other works reflected the influence of Japonisme, African tribal art, and the Modernist avant-garde.

He earned international acclaim when a series of his vases won the Grand Prix at the 1925 International Exposition in Paris. His growing prominence earned him a teaching position at the Ecole Supérieure Industrielle de La Louvière, which he used to recruit students, decorating the factory's vases with their designs. In 1945, he retired to Nice, where he lived until his death.

Cazaux, Edouard (1889–1974). Born into a family of potters from the Landes region of France, he studied design at Mont-de-Marsan. He produced a wide range of earthenware and stoneware plates and vases. Although he learned many technical aspects of ceramics from his father, with respect to clay and glaze technology he was known to be an innovator throughout his career. After moving to Paris in 1907, he worked in the studio of Georges Garing, formerly of the Manufacture Nationale de *Sèvres, who helped him increase his knowledge of a variety of materials and glazes. Into the 1920s, Cazaux, who became known as a sculptor, also experimented with glass and bronze. During this time he was a respected teacher, and he also exhibited at important shows of the day, including the annual Salon d'Automne and the Salon of the Société des Artistes Décorateurs (1922–33 and 1942). He was on the selection committee for the 1925 Paris Exposition, and in 1933 was appointed a Chevalier of the Légion d'Honneur.

For his own work he drew on diverse subjects: religious and mythological themes, including Adam and Eve, the Muses, Prometheus, and nymphs. He combined thick glazes providing a luxurious polychrome finish with forms that are noteworthy for their freshness. From 1920 to 1930, he worked with white earthenware, making stylized figurative, animal, and botanical forms, often engraved or in high relief and glazed in copper red. Many of these designs were inspired by birds and African and Asian art. His vases and bowls sometimes display a gilt or white crackled finish.

Ceramiche Rometti. Factory established by Settimio and Aspromonte Rometti at Umbertide (Umbria) in 1927. Its products are of very high quality with a distinctively Art Deco stylistic touch. The factory quickly developed its industrial side, thanks to the direction of Dante Baldelli, a close relative of the Romettis. Corrado Cagli, who began working there in 1928, was known as something of an eccentric and an individualist who resisted both the avant-garde Futurist movement and the prevailing trend of Fascist politics in Italy. In their collaborative efforts Baldelli had the business expertise and practical knowledge, while Cagli, who had no formal training, developed a complex, narrative style that had a lasting effect on the firm's production. After Cagli left in 1930, many pieces made by the firm still reflected his personal style, even though he was not directly involved in their production.

In either 1933 or 1936, the company became known as S.A.C.R.U. (Società Anonima Ceramiche Rometti, Umbertide) with Baldelli as its technical

director. The factory eventually began phasing out Cagli's designs and concentrating on more traditional pieces.

Ceramiche Zen. North Italian factory founded *c.* 1870 in Nove, near Venice. In the 19th century, this region began to develop as one of the main areas for the production of porcelain and maiolica in Italy. While the Baroque style was important in the company's early years, Antonio Zen (son of the founder) was responsible for many designs in the present century in the Art Deco style. Historically, the factory was noted for its openwork and overall hand-painted decoration. Consistently fine-quality designs combined with skilled craftsmanship enhanced its reputation. The factory continues production today under the grandson of Antonio Zen, who shares the same name.

Chekhonin, Sergei Vasilievich (1878–1936). While still a student at the Baron A. Stieglitz Central School of Technical Design, he began working part-time at the Imperial Porcelain Factory, St Petersburg. From 1897 to 1900, he also studied painting under Ilya Repin at Princess Mariia Tenisheva's School. Later, he studied at the Free Studio of St Petersburg, as well as at Savva Manontov's Abramtsevo Ceramic Workshop in Moscow. In 1907, he began working at Petr Vaulin's ceramics factory near St Petersburg, where he produced majolica panels to decorate the Hotel Metropole in Moscow. From 1910 to 1924, he was a member of *Mir iskusstva* and exhibited with them. He was, from 1918 to 1923, art director of the renamed *State Porcelain Factory in Petrograd, in which capacity he made a commitment to artistic innovation and also tried to recruit artists for the factory. The power of the Revolution inspired him not only in his own creations, but in his ability to motivate others. His own graphic talent led him to create many innovative slogans, emblems, inscriptions, and monograms. He combined avant-garde imagery with traditional Russian religious ikons which were thought to make the unseen world tangible, and his work also borrowed from folk art. One of his slogans was "The kingdom of the workers and peasants shall have no end." Although he designed postage stamps and paper and silver money, his involvement with ceramics continued as director of the Volkhoy Ceramics Factory near Novgorod, and from 1925 to 1927 following his return as director of the State (now Lomonosov) Porcelain Factory. In 1928, he emigrated to Paris.

Cliff, Clarice (1899–1972). One of the few English women of her day who, after becoming a paintress, was eventually employed as a designer in the ceramics industry, despite the fact that she did not have a middle-class background. At the age of thirteen she

FANTASQUES
HAND PAINTED
Bizarre by
Clarice Cliff
NEWPORT POTTERY
ENGLAND.

Clarice Cliff

Compagnie des Arts Français. *Automne*, glazed earthenware panel with a stylized representation in relief showing an allegory of Autumn, Paul Véra, *c.*1920.

Susie Cooper

was working as an enameler, and by 1916 she had begun her lifelong association with A.J. *Wilkinson Ltd, initially working as a lithographer. After taking evening classes in 1924–25 at the Burslem College of Art and attending the Royal College of Art in London in 1927, she worked full-time at Wilkinsons. In 1929, the firm introduced her *Bizarre* wares, which became an immensely popular line and established her as one of the leading designers of the era. Her wares have since remained extremely popular with collectors.

It was her own idea to call her early designs *Bizarre*, but it was A.C.A. Shorter (the head of Wilkinson and her future husband) who decided to adopt the name for an entire line. Early *Bizarre* ceramics encompassed novel, colorful designs hand-painted by her on stock earthenware forms. However, her innovative decorations called for new forms, and eventually *Bizarre* came to include many shapes produced by combining circles, squares, triangles, and cones. Perhaps the most extreme of these new designs, but which did not utilize geometric forms, was *Le Bon Dieu*, teaware in knobby, twisted irregular shapes, painted with green and brown tones recalling trees and moss. After the *Bizarre* line, she produced a succession of original and imaginative works. The *Age of Jazz* figures of 1930 were to be used as a centerpiece "when listening to a dance band on the wireless." However, as the decade progressed, the taste for such baroque pieces as her *Queer* figures, a series of grotesques, waned. After the *Bizarre* line ceased production in 1941, she became increasingly involved with administration.

Compagnie des Arts Français, La. In the years following World War I, artists working in different media often joined forces to produce decorative arts that aimed at ensemble or "total design." One of the most successful collaborations was the Compagnie des Arts Français, formed in 1919 by Louis Süe (1875–1968), an architect and designer, and André Mare (1887–1932), a painter, furniture designer, and bookbinder. They designed interiors and all the objects necessary to furnish them—ceramics, clocks, lamps, fabrics, wallpapers, carpets, silverware, etc. Their style drew on the elegance of the Louis Philippe period, manifesting itself in furniture by abundant curvilinear outlines, lacquer finishes, and carved wood details.

For the 1925 Paris Exposition, Süe and Mare created a pavilion called "Un Musée d'Art Contemporain." Rivaling *Ruhlmann's "Pavillon d'un Collectionneur" in acclaim, their presentation immediately brought them international attention. A large ceramic dinner service exhibited in their pavilion featured scalloped shapes and stylized floral finials. They also exhibited a series of ceramic bas reliefs of reclining nudes executed by Paul Véra (1882–1971) and José Martin.

Cooper, Susie (Susan Vera; b. 1902). One of the most influential industrial ceramic designers to emerge in 20th-century Britain. Born in Burslem, Staffordshire, she attended night classes at the local art school with the aim of becoming a fashion designer; however, she soon became interested in ceramics and in 1922, with the encouragement of Gordon *Forsyth, obtained work with A.E. *Gray & Co. Her talent was quickly recognized by Edward Gray, who had the prescience to create "designer labels," promoting her work with the back-stamp "Designed by Susie Cooper." (This was also done with the work of other designers during the 1920s, including Charlotte *Rhead and Clarice *Cliff.)

She established her own decorating atelier in the fall of 1929. Despite the difficulties caused by the worldwide economic depression of the 1930s, it was from this platform that she launched a revolution in

Cowan Pottery Studio. Allegorical figure of *Radio* by Waylande Gregory, glazed porcelain; a photograph of this figure was reproduced on the cover of *Design*, April 1935. H. (approx.) 21 in. (53.3 cm).

COWAN

R. Guy Cowan

tableware by designing stylish, functional, yet cost-conscious earthenwares. Her factory produced breakfast sets, tea and coffee sets, jugs, cruets, and dinnerware were made for a middle-class market. In 1932, her first stand at the British Industries Fair caused a sensation, as crowds admired her well-known banded patterns and the Royal Family acquired several items, including a triangular lamp base decorated with a clown. At this Fair she also introduced two innovative shapes, *Curlew* and *Kestrel*, which remained popular until the late 1950s.

It was in the heyday of production during the 1930s that the classic Susie Cooper style—elegance combined with utility—developed. In spite of various setbacks (including the effects of World War II and several disastrous fires), her business mostly thrived throughout the 1940s and 1950s. Early in the 1950s, she seized an opportunity to become not just a decorator but a manufacturer of bone china and merged with R.H. & S.L. Plant. In 1966, the entire company was subsumed by the *Wedgwood Group, for whom she occasionally continues to produce designs.

Cowan, R. (Reginald) Guy (1884–1957). Born into a family of Ohio potters, he studied under Charles F. *Binns at the New York State School of Clayworking and Ceramics, Syracuse, New York, in 1911, then moved to Cleveland, where he taught pottery at a local high school. In 1913, he opened his first studio, the Cleveland Pottery & Tile Company. The workshop produced functional pottery and lead-glazed buff clay and terra cotta tiles until Cowan suspended production to join the US Army during World War I. After the pottery closed in 1917, it was awarded first prize at the International Show of the Chicago Art Institute.

After returning from military service in 1920, he opened the Cowan Pottery Studio, and began producing well-designed, commercially viable red-clay slip-cast pieces using gas-fired kilns. After studying at the John Huntington Polytechnic Institute in Cleveland, he went into full-scale commercial production in 1921, setting up a network of retail stores nationwide and selling his wares through department stores such as Wanamaker of Philadelphia, Halle Brothers of Cleveland, and Marshall Field of Chicago. At this time the studio switched to high-fired porcelain wares decorated with brightly colored glazes. By 1925 the pottery, using the most modern equipment, employed 40 people and made a vast range of products including vases, figurines, doorknobs, fountains, flower holders, and wall-plaques. *Lakeware*, a mass-produced line begun in 1928, was notable for its flower-containers. Perhaps the studio's most successful series of commercial products sprang from Cowan's innovative figurine-shaped flower frog combined with a bowl of complementary design.

Their popularity allowed the pottery to expand its distributorships.

Cowan dedicated his studio to the production of wares of high artistic quality, and consequently became a forum for some of the most-talented ceramists of the day. He employed or commissioned many artists, including Alexander *Blazys, Edris *Eckhardt, Waylande *Gregory, Margaret Postgate, Viktor *Schreckengost, Richard O. *Hummel, and Thelma Frazier *Winter. Often produced in limited editions of 50 to 100, figures designed by these artists were especially popular and won awards at the Cleveland Museum of Art's annual "May Shows." However, in spite of increasing creative successes, the Depression quickly sank the studio into bankruptcy and it closed in 1931. In 1933, Cowan moved to Syracuse, New York, where he worked for the Onondaga Pottery Company until his death.

Czech Cubism (1910–25). In Czechoslovakia, a group of Bohemian architects including Josef Gocár, Vlastislav *Hofman, Pavel *Janák, Josef Chochol, and Jirí Kroha began designing in a style that reflected the "simultaneous" abstraction of French Cubist painting filtered through their own deeply felt ideology. However, the Bohemian vision went well beyond the canvas: its most original and startling manifestations were in architecture and the applied arts, where the structure of functional objects was rendered in abstract form, so as to "liberate" the inherent energy thought to be contained within form and material. In addition to Cubism, Bohemia was exposed to the influence of northern European art in 1905, when paintings by Edvard Munch were exhibited in Prague. The extreme expressiveness and emotional content of his art seemed also to be absorbed into the Czech Cubists' style.

During the time this style was developing, various interdisciplinary groups producing furniture, textiles, metalwork, glass, and ceramics were established in Europe. The *Wiener Werkstätte (1903–32) and the Deutscher Werkbund (1907–33) were two such organizations, whose attitudes exerted a profound influence on the production of crafted objects and furniture. Czech Cubist objects were produced by the *Artěl Cooperative, founded in 1908. Those who designed ceramics were Bedrich Feuerstein, Jozef Havlicek, Vlastislav Hofman, Jaroslav Horejc, Pavel Janák, Jirí Kroha, Antonin Prochazka, and Rudolf Stocker; their designs were manufactured by the firm of Rydl and Thon.

Interestingly, the Czech Cubist aesthetic imbued small-scale domestic objects with a monumentality normally associated with architecture or sculpture: in effect, the object activates space like a piece of sculpture, and this quality is unique among functional ceramics.

D

Dahlskog, Ewald (1894–1950). An accomplished painter, he also designed for the ceramics and glass industries in Sweden. In Stockholm, he studied first at Centraltryckeriet from 1905 to 1908, and later attended the Royal Institute of Technology and the Royal Swedish Academy Art School. Beginning in the 1920s, he traveled to France, Italy, and Tunisia, where he continued his art education. From 1924 to 1926 he worked in Paris as a freelance illustrator and journalist, while simultaneously pursuing his career as a painter.

Returning to Sweden, he joined Kosta in 1926, leaving there in 1929 for Bo Fajans, where he stayed for the rest of his life. In 1930, some of his work for Bo Fajans, which was characterized by a solid, architectonic presence, was shown in "Stockholmsutställningen," the main exhibition of Swedish art and industry. Later, the work found its way to London, where it was included in an exhibition at Dorland House, Regent Street.

By 1930, according to *Pottery Gazette and Glass Trades Review*, Dahlskog's work—which was part of the "functionalist" tradition that dominated Scandinavian design—was beginning to lose its neoclassical and neo-baroque underpinnings in favor of a reductive Modernism which reflected the influence of the *Bauhaus.

Danko, Elena Y. (1898–1942). Recruited by Sergei *Chekhonin, art director of the *State Porcelain Factory in Petrograd, she worked there as a painter after studying fine arts at Alexander Murashko's school in Kiev (1915), and in Moscow at the studios of Ilya Mashkov and Fedor Refberg (1915–18). Between 1918 and 1941, she worked on and off at the factory, primarily decorating the work of her elder sister, Natalya. In addition to writing plays for puppet theatre and children's books, she studied the history of ceramics, and wrote a history of the State (from 1925 Lomonosov) Porcelain Factory.

Decœur, Emile (1876–1953). One of the most accomplished potters working in France between 1910 and the 1930s, he was apprenticed to Edmond *Lachenal in 1890, and established his own atelier in Fontenay-aux-Roses (Seine) in 1907. He made stoneware and porcelain vases decorated with incised or painted motifs such as spirals, roses, and geometric patterns. Working in Paris after World War I, he rejected the exuberance associated with Art Nouveau and Oriental-type designs, preferring simple forms with uncluttered lines enhanced by monochromatic glazes. This slight shift in purpose paralleled his experimentation with satin and mat glazes. In the mid-1920s, he created many of his finest vases, cups, and bowls, sometimes interpreting Chinese shapes. These featured a range of colored glazes, including green, yellow, pink, white, violet, or blue, which created sublimely subtle effects. From 1939 to 1942, he worked at *Sèvres, and was a consultant there until 1948.

Delaherche, Auguste (1857–1940). Although he had trained in stained glass and precious metalwork, Delaherche produced art pottery of such quality that his contemporaries called him the "poet of stoneware." In the early 1880s he began experimenting with functional wares that resembled the pottery of his native Beauvais. Many examples were slip-coated and featured either thumb-prints or fluting as decoration. In 1887, he befriended Ernest Chaplet (1835–1909), who pioneered the rebirth of studio pottery in France, and bought the latter's Paris studio in Rue Blomet, Vaugirard. In Chaplet's former studio, over the next ten years, he produced Japanese-inspired work featuring the use of thick glazes. His experiments were rewarded when he received a gold medal at the 1889 Exposition Universelle in Paris.

He established a studio in Armentières, near Beauvais, in 1894, and continued to experiment with glazes, though he no longer used decoration in relief. In 1904, after a brief Art Nouveau phase, he worked increasingly with porcelain, generally making small, unique pieces carefully coated with aventurine or honey-colored drip-glazes. In 1910, he began producing porcelains decorated in the manner of Chinese Fukien ware, in which perforations in leather-hard clay fill with glaze during firing, creating diaphanous, translucent patterns. By the 1920s, he had abandoned floral patterns, relying for embellishment solely on superimposed layers of his unique glazes.

Deruta e CIMA (Maioliche). In 1920, Biagio Biagiotti, with partners, founded the Società Maioliche di Deruta (Deruta Maiolica Company). Biagiotti's ambitious plans included the creation of a national consortium of major ceramic factories, but on realizing the difficulties inherent in such a project, he abandoned it, and instead formed a union of ceramic factories in central Italy. Under the direction of Biagiotti and vice-president Giuseppe Baduel, the Società Maioliche di Deruta and the Consorzio Italiano Maioliche Artistiche (Italian Consortium for Artistic Maiolica), known as CIMA, created a strong domestic market, and eventually they became well-known throughout Europe and the Americas, exporting large quantities of wares. During this period, Biagiotti established "La Salamandra," a new venture (housed in a former convent in Perugia); it concentrated almost completely on the North American market, specializing in "collage" pieces either decorated with colors that

Emile Decœur

Auguste Delaherche

Diederich, Wilhelm Hunt. Plate with decoration depicting a cowboy mounting his horse, 1926. D. 15 in. (38.1 cm)

merged together, or painted with varying tones of the same color.

In 1927, the two factories in Deruta and Perugia, which employed a total of 400 people, were modernized, including the installation of electric kilns, along with other new equipment. Even after modernization, production consisted for the most part of traditional wares influenced by Italy's long ceramic history, though occasionally designs did reflect contemporary aesthetic trends.

De Sphinx. Along with Société Céramique, this company (called Petrus Regout & Co. before 1899, having been originally established as a glassworks in 1834), was one of the giants of Dutch pottery production. It produced ornamental and domestic pottery, in addition to hotel ware (beginning in 1933), tiles, fireproof earthenware, and sanitary products. Designs for domestic and ornamental wares were mostly based on 19th-century models, but with the weakening of the market for these historical styles and the development of new technologies and materials, this situation began to change. The transformation was aided by new educational opportunities: in 1917, the Quellinus School in Amsterdam, specializing in industrial arts and crafts, set up a ceramics department, and from 1922 a State School for Pottery existed in Gouda.

After Edmond *Bellefroid became design director in 1929, De Sphinx was a forceful presence in the modern design movement. His designs brought the company success, while his design philosophy influenced the entire Dutch ceramics industry. Société Céramique merged with De Sphinx in 1958, forming N.V. Sphinx-Céramique. The company produces tiles and sanitary products, and made domestic pottery and hotel ware until 1969.

De Stijl. A loose confederation of Dutch artists, architects, and a poet who shared deeply felt beliefs about art and society. The group's name was derived from the magazine *De Stijl* ("The Style"), begun in 1917 by the painter Theo van Doesburg (1883–1931). He had help from a reluctant mentor/collaborator, Piet Mondrian (1872–1944), recently returned to the Netherlands from Paris, where he had discovered Cubism. Through the magazine, the group's ideas found a wider audience, especially in France and Germany. In 1918, the group issued their first manifesto, which laid out the foundation for art, architecture, and design rooted in the harmonious relationship of squares and rectangles in a horizontal/vertical relationship, using a palette of primary colors. The group's practitioners believed that by restricting the means of art, individual expression could be eliminated, and through the resulting universality they hoped to solve the problems of the world. Even though The Netherlands was not

directly involved in World War I, it is more than likely that this search for Utopia was a direct result of the social upheaval caused by the war. In De Stijl there also exists a corrective undercurrent that has its origins in Holland's Calvinist history and prevalent puritan theology.

Although De Stijl artists and architects were not known for ceramics, the visual manifestation of their style—pure, geometric forms and primary colors—helped to define the Modernist aesthetic. De Stijl's transformation of Cubism into pure abstraction was absorbed by the *Bauhaus, and later became part of the International Style. An emphasis on both geometric form and decoration became *leitmotivs* of the Modern movement, which encompassed all expressive forms, including ceramics.

Diederich, (Wilhelm) Hunt (1884–1953). Although Diederich had a Hungarian father and was born in Hungary, his mother came from an American family distinguished in the arts: his grandfather was the painter William Morris Hunt, and his great-uncle the architect Richard Morris Hunt. After studying sculpture in Paris and Rome, at the age of 20 he attended the Pennsylvania Academy of Fine Arts, Philadelphia. A peripatetic artist, he simultaneously maintained homes in America, France, and Germany.

He is known for very accomplished, highly individual work in several media, including wrought iron, using animal imagery in fire screens, chandeliers, and weathervanes. Though trained as a sculptor, he felt strongly that his work should be both functional and accessible to a wide audience. His interest in ceramics began in 1923 during a trip to Morocco; his early pieces were often painted with stylized animal figures. He sometimes used imagery depicting cowboys with their horses, which he drew directly from his own fond memories of having worked as a cowboy in Arizona, New Mexico, and Wyoming. Throughout his career, he used animal themes; greyhounds and ibexes were favorite subjects (the latter having been a source of inspiration for many artists of the era). In addition, he borrowed freely from ancient Egyptian, Greek, and Mesopotamian sources.

In 1927, he was awarded a gold medal for his pottery by the Architectural League of New York. His production in earthenware consisted both of individual pieces and of designs for mass-production. In 1928, his work was included in the International Exhibition of Ceramic Art at the Metropolitan Museum of Art, New York, but by the end of the decade he was no longer working in clay.

Dimitrov Factory. After the October Revolution of 1917, social issues dominated the outlook of this Russian factory in the Moscow area. Topics such as industrialization, the collectivization of agriculture, foreign policy, and the cultural revolution were reflected in designs for mass-produced wares. Often the designs of T. Podryabinnikov were combined with ornamentation based on industrial motifs, depicting workers and women tractor operators.

Disney cartoon characters. The earliest incarnation of Mickey Mouse, "Mortimer Mouse," appeared in 1927, and the first *bona fide* Mickey Mouse film was *Steamboat Willie*, copyrighted in 1928. In 1930, the Staffordshire firm Paragon China announced that it had signed a deal with Walt Disney for exclusive world rights to use cartoon characters as decoration on their bone china. A series of twelve portrayals reproduced on decals was expanded, but by the mid-1930s Paragon's rights either expired or were infringed, for several other companies began featuring the characters. In England, for example, Wade, Heath & Co. (Burslem) created a line of nursery ware featuring Mickey, Minnie, and Pluto (each character purportedly drawn by Walt Disney himself). Mickey Mouse is also featured on a French platinum-banded earthenware tea set; the mark on these pieces indicates that a licensing agreement was in effect, even though the specific factory is not mentioned.

Diulgheroff, Nicolaj (1901–82). Born in Bulgaria, the son of a typographer, he arrived in Italy in 1926. He completed his studies in Turin at the Architecture School of the Accademia Albertina di Belle Arti in 1932. There, he first came into contact with *Futurism. At this time he dedicated himself to painting, while also designing furniture, lamps, crystal, and ceramics. In 1928, he participated in the Futurists' display at the XVI Venice Biennale, and that same year he was represented in the Futurist Pavilion at the Esposizione Internazionale in Turin. From 1931 to 1932 he worked at the Casa Mazzotti in *Albisola; there, he incorporated decorative elements into his work, which was dedicated to finding solutions to the problems of function usually associated with ceramics, while working in an innovative, modern style.

Dufy, Jean (1888–1964). A painter and water-colorist from Le Havre, he was the brother of the painter Raoul *Dufy. He decorated porcelains commissioned by William Haviland, of *Haviland & Cie, Limoges, from 1915 to 1925. He also created relief borders named *Serpent*, *Syringa*, and *Feuille de Chêne*, as well as painting foliage and floral patterns for Haviland. His energetic style forthrightly reflected the influence of the Fauve painters. He exhibited examples of his work produced by Haviland at the 1925 Paris Exposition, and subsequently worked for the *Compagnie des Arts Français.

From 1934 to 1936, he worked at the Manufacture Nationale de *Sèvres.

Dufy, Raoul (1877–1953). Though known primarily for his Post-Impressionist paintings and woodcuts, particularly his illustrations for Guillaume Apollinaire's *Le Bestiaire*, he also worked extensively in the applied arts. He is equally well known for his colorful textile designs, some of which were created for the influential Parisian couturier Paul Poiret (1879–1944). His tapestry designs, some of them executed by leading manufacturers such as Gobelins, and his fabric designs for the firm of Bianchini-Férier are considered by some commentators to be the best of the period.

Like his brother Jean, he also became interested in ceramics. From *c*. 1922 to 1930 he worked in clay, and in the mid-1920s began designing for *Sèvres. Periodically during the 1920s and 1930s, he worked with the Spanish-born potter *Artigas, creating vases, fountains, and indoor planters painted with Dufy's signature motifs: dancers, flowers, nymphs, and fish. In 1927, they began to collaborate with the Parisian architect Nicolas Marubio. This highly productive team created decorative ceramics with architectural lines and miniature landscapes including live plants that alluded to the Japanese *bonsai* tradition.

Dulevo Works. Formerly known as the Kuznetsov Works, this Russian company produced Suprematist designs on porcelain cups, saucers, and plates. Unlike the representational, moralizing style of *agitprop* ceramics, Suprematist decoration sought to "represent" such ideas as weightlessness or infinity using simple geometric shapes painted on white porcelain. While social realism predominated at other factories, Suprematism (*Malevich) held sway at Dulevo during the 1920s and 1930s. One of the company's best-known designers was the avant-garde painter Vassily *Kandinsky.

Duxer Porzellan-Manufaktur. A Bohemian factory which, from the 1860s to the mid-20th century, produced an extensive range of figurines and ornamental wares under the trade name Royal Dux. The history of the factory was tied via its owner, E. Eichler, to the Blankenhain porcelain factory in the Thuringian region of Germany. In 1918, the merged factories were acquired by C.&E. *Carstens.

The Royal Dux line was characterized by the production of exotic figurines that tended to have soft silhouettes accentuated by gilt decoration. Subjects include snake charmers, Spanish dancers, belly dancers, and all forms of stylized showgirls and animals. Although the figurines sometimes border on kitsch, they have found an enthusiastic audience in the collectibles market.

Eckhardt, Edris. *Alice and the White Rabbit*, figural group awarded 1st Prize at the May Show, Cleveland Museum of Art, 1936.

Lorinda Epply (see pl. 152)

E

Eckhardt, Edris (b. 1907). In 1932, she graduated from the Cleveland School of Art where, during her final year, she had been part of a collaborative ceramics program between the Cowan Pottery, Cleveland School of Art, and Cleveland Museum of Art. After her studies she set up her own studio and experimented with glaze chemistry. She became part of a pilot program for the Public Works of Art Project in 1933–34. For this she produced a series of small-scale sculptures for libraries based on themes from children's literature, including *Alice in Wonderland* and *Green Mansions*. The figures attracted much attention and in 1939 Eleanor Roosevelt commissioned one inspired by *Huckleberry Finn*.

Eckhardt was made local director of the ceramic sculpture division of the Welfare Art Program (WAP). She continued in this office until it closed in 1941. Thereafter she taught at the Cleveland Institute of Art, and exhibited in the May Shows held at the Cleveland Museum.

Epply, Lorinda (1874–1951). After attending the Cincinnati Art Academy, she studied ceramics at Columbia University, New York. She is best known for her work at the *Rookwood Pottery, where she spent her entire creative career, from 1904 to 1948. At Rookwood she was given a great amount of artistic freedom, consequently her work, outstanding for its experimental glazes is among the most individualistic produced there. Along with work by William Hentschel, examples of her pottery were chosen to represent the firm in New York at the Metropolitan Museum of Art's 10th Annual Exhibition of Industrial Art in 1926–27.

F

Fabbri, Giuseppe (b.1902?). A dedicated Italian journalist and author, he began organizing sales of Futurist ceramics in Faenza in 1928. He requested designs from *Balla, Dal Monte, Rizzo, Benedetta, Dottori, and others, and had them produced by Ricardo Gatti, Orgolani, and Bucci. These ceramics were shown at the Mostra Futurista (Futurist Show) in Faenza. In April 1929, the Turin publication *La Città Futurista* (The Futurist City) announced: "In Faenza, Filippo Tommaso Marinetti has inaugurated the first Futurist ceramics show, organized by Giuseppe Fabbri, with an acclaimed polemical speech." Fabbri urged the ceramists to "commercialize" their work and had a particularly strong influence on Gatti. During the 1930s, Fabbri's influence diminished in Italy, after he moved to Africa.

Farfa (Vittorio Osvaldo Tommasini; 1881–1964). In 1919, he was introduced to F.T. Marinetti, thereby beginning his exposure to *Futurism. By way of this connection he supplied, in 1930 and 1931, a series of dynamic ceramic models which were executed by Tullio *d'Albisola. In 1930, the first group was shown in the Futurist exhibition at the Galleria Pesaro in Milan, and in 1931 others were included in the Mostra Futurista: Pittura, Scultura, Aeropittura, Arti Decorative, Architettura (Futurist Show: Painting, Sculpture, Aeropainting, Decorative Arts, Architecture), held in Chiavari, in addition to other shows at the Galleria Pesaro. In 1932, his ceramics were included in the Mostra Fotografica Futurista (ceramiche) (Futurist Photography Show [Ceramics]), and also in Nuove Ceramiche Italiane (New Italian Ceramics) at the Hôtel Montparnasse, Paris. He also showed ceramics in the Mostra d'Arte Futurista, Pittura, Scultura, Arte Decorative, (Futurist Art Show, Painting, Sculpture, Decorative Art) at the Galleria d'Arte in Savona.

In 1932, the year in which Marinetti crowned Farfa in Genoa with an aluminum helmet and proclaimed him the "national poet of record," Tullio deemed his work "mechanical ceramics," but, although his forms may seem derived from mechanical parts, in fact they show enormous formal invention. Their "mechanical" nature also imbues them with a sense of irony generally not seen in ceramics. After this initial spurt of prodigious activity in ceramics, however, Farfa produced only the occasional plate.

Fau & Gaillard. French company established *c.* 1920 to produce figural ceramics designed by Léon Leyritz and Do Canto. The proprietors collaborated with artists such as Le Jan, Delabassé, Willy-Georges Wuilleumier, and Maurice Guiraud-Rivière. Some of their commissions were exhibited at the 1925 Exposition in Paris. The company remained active until the 1930s.

Fillia (Luigi Colombia; 1904–36). Italian ceramist who used his mother's maiden name. He often collaborated with Tullio *d'Albisola. From 1929 to 1930, he designed a series of decorative plates with patterns based on a combination of geometric shapes. In 1932, he made a series of *aerovasi* (literally, "air vases"), evidence of the Futurist fascination, even in ceramic form, with the appearance of mechanization. *Aerovasi*—miniature non-representational sculptures—double as functional objects. He also worked as a painter and writer, and was a proponent of rationalist architecture. Except for occasional trips to Paris, all his work was done in Turin.

Flögl, Mathilde (1893–1950). A porcelain modeller who was associated with the *Wiener Werkstätte from 1916. She was known for her lively style, which was evident in ceramic figures and simple, stylized

Farfa. Stepped columnar form in glazed terra cotta (made in collaboration with Tullio d'Albisola), 1932. H. 8⅝ in. (22.0 cm).

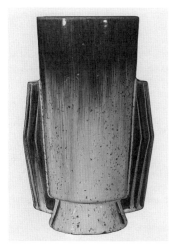

Fulper Pottery Co. Vase, buff-colored stoneware with blue *flambé* and crystalline glaze, c.1930. H. 8¾ in. (22.3 cm).

forms. She also undertook engraving on glass, as well as freehand and stencilled wall decorations, and was the author of a history of the Wiener Werkstätte (1928). By 1931 she had opened her own studio in Vienna, where she worked and taught.

Foley Potteries. Founded in the late 1820s by John Smith at Fenton, Staffordshire, this pottery was acquired in 1872 by James F. Wileman and Joseph Shelley. In 1896, the latter's son, Percy, took over control of the business, with the idea of using the talents of well-known artists to enhance the status of the factory. One such artist, Rowland Morris, created a teaware line called *Dainty White* which became so popular that it remained in production until 1966. Frederick H. *Rhead, as art director 1896–1905, helped to develop new lines issued with Italianate names, e.g. *Intarsio* and *Urbato*.

In 1898, the works expanded to encompass earthenware production, and pieces such as busts of military leaders were also made to commemorate British and foreign events. A mother-of-pearl glaze was introduced in 1920, and Walter Slater expanded decorative schemes to maximize colors with Oriental-style patterns. In 1925, *Shelley Potteries was established, and the company enjoyed tremendous success under this name.

Forsyth, Gordon Mitchell (1879–1952). A ceramic designer and painter, and an influential educator. His best-known student was Susie *Cooper, whom he persuaded to switch from fashion to ceramics, but he also influenced other students such as Jessie Van Hallen and Freda Beardmore. His two books, *The Art and Craft of the Potter* and *20th Century Ceramics*, were important to modern ceramists and other educators. In his teaching and writing he followed Modernist design principoles that originated in the *Bauhaus, and believed that art had a place in industry.

After training in Aberdeen and attending the Royal College of Art, he studied in Italy on a fellowship. In 1900 he worked at the Royal Lancastrian Pottery. He became art director of Minton, Hollins, & Co., 1903–05. In 1920 he became Superintendent of Art, coordinating the programs of schools throughout Stoke-on-Trent. He also worked as an advisor to the British Pottery manufacturers' Association.

Friedländer-Wildenhain, Marguerite (1896–1985). Born in Lyons to an English mother and a German father, she attended schools in France, England, and Germany, and eventually studied sculpture at the Hochschule für angewandte Kunst in Berlin in 1914. In 1916–17 she worked as a designer at a porcelain factory in Rudolstadt. In 1919, she entered the *Bauhaus, where she studied ceramics under

Gerhard *Marcks, experimenting with functional forms such as molded mugs with monochromatic glazes. When Marcks left the Bauhaus in 1924, she followed him in 1925 to the ceramic workshop of the Kunstgewerbeschule Burg-Giebichenstein in Halle, and taught there.

In 1929, she began designing for the *Staatliche Porzellan-Manufaktur, Berlin (KPM). In 1930, she designed the well-known *Halle* service, a complete porcelain table service that showed the influence of the Bauhaus in its rational design concept. Here, functional pieces were made of a combination of simplified shapes derived from geometry that fit mass-production standards, while retaining a strong aesthetic appeal. The service was sometimes celadon-glazed, and in 1931 concentric gilt bands by Trude *Petri-Raben were added as decoration. In 1930, Friedländer also designed the *Burg-Giebichenstein* dinner service, which featured a modelled surface with grooved rings. This service reflects her attempt to incorporate craft-like design elements in wares intended for mass production.

With the advent of the Third Reich, KPM was accused of employing a "non-Aryan" artist, i.e. Friedländer-Wildenhain, (her name was deleted from the 1938 catalogue celebrating the 175th anniversary of KPM); in 1933, she had married Frans Wildenhain and moved to Holland. There, in 1937, she designed faience for *De Sphinx. In 1940, she emigrated to the United States, where she taught at the California College of Arts and Crafts in Oakland. Her long career as a studio potter and teacher influenced a generation of American ceramists.

Fülöp, Karoly (1893–1963). The medieval art of Hungary and a monastic education contributed greatly to Fülöp's artistic vision. He originally studied art in Budapest, Munich, and Paris, and had moved to New York by 1921. He exhibited his work there throughout the 1920s and 1930s, but moved to Los Angeles in 1931, where he opened a school of decorative arts. Although the subject matter of his works was often spiritual, stylistically they showed the influence of French Cubism. How he came to work in clay is not known, but he sometimes liked to create ensembles comprising a fully three-dimensional ceramic sculpture that was combined with a carved wood relief.

Fulper Pottery Company. Operating from 1805 in New Jersey, the Fulper Pottery was known primarily for domestic products such as cooking utensils and crockery made of high-fired stoneware. In 1909, when the art-pottery line *Vasekraft* was initiated, the factory's output had grown to include all kinds of household and decorative wares, and it was this line that put the pottery on the map. Wares were decorated using multiple color glazes that had

Goldscheider. *Bat Girl*, glazed figurine, Friedrich Goldscheider, 1930s. H. 19⅝ in. (49.0 cm).

captivating names such as "café au lait" and "elephant's breath." Some, such as *"famille rose"* and "Ashes of Roses," imitated historical glazes and were said to cost ten times more than "ordinary" colors.

Under J. Martin Stangl's technical direction from 1911 to 1915, the company produced a number of important mat, crystalline, and mirror glazes which were awarded prizes in the Panama-Pacific Exposition of 1915. Despite his success, Stangl left the firm and worked from 1915 to 1920 with the Haeger Potteries, where he developed a line of artware that was marketed in 1917. In 1930, Stangl acquired the pottery, continuing to make artware on a limited scale until 1935. Thereafter he shifted the emphasis to dinnerware. Although the Fulper name is identified mostly with art pottery, some of Stangl's own designs were decidedly modern. In 1955, the name of the firm was changed to Stangl Pottery Company, and it operated as such until the death of its owner in 1972.

Futurism. The Italian Futurist movement was founded in 1909 by the poet and editor of *Poesia*, Filippo Tommaso Marinetti (1876–1944). It was at first a literary movement, but quickly attracted painters such as Giacomo *Balla, who evolved an exciting approach to arts of all kinds. By 1911, paintings clearly identified as "Futurist" were being produced and shown. From the outset the movement was widely discussed all over Europe and America, and, in fact, the first Futurist manifesto appeared in France on the front page of *Le Figaro* (20 February 1909). With cries of "Drain the canals of Venice!," "Burn the museums!," and "Let's kill the moonlight!," traditional ideas were unceremoniously banished, and attempts were made to translate rhythms of the machine and the anxiety about advancing technologies into tangible forms. The Futurists were entirely interdisciplinary: besides ceramics, they created paintings and sculptures, wrote articles, poetry, and plays, and even published a cookbook. They often participated in more than one of these activities simultaneously, and took themselves very seriously, issuing "manifestos" which outlined in detail how to approach each art form. One such manifesto, *Ceramica e Aeroceramica*, set out the necessary steps for making ceramics in the Futurist style.

Through their work in every medium, the Futurists hoped to infiltrate middle-class homes with appropriate symbols that would transform their owners' way of life. Although much of their work served a functional purpose, they were not immune to pure flights of fancy. For example, besides making vases and tea sets, they created tiles, and Tullio *d'Albisola even planned a ceramic road that would lead, like all roads in Italy, to Rome. Curiously, several Futurists created ceramic crèches (Nativity scenes); while the abstracted figures were stylistically unusual for their time, such religious imagery, in general, seems at odds with their goal of modernizing Italy through avant-garde art.

G

Galvani. Italian company founded by Giuseppe Galvani in 1811 in Pordenone for the production of ceramics of a traditional type. However, in 1929 the factory collaborated with the Futurist painter Giacomo *Balla, making a dinner service with individual plates decorated in single colors. This "revolutionary" idea firmly planted the factory in the modern era.

Gambetti, Dino (b. 1907). An architect by training, he took part in 1929 in the Mostra dei Presepi per Famiglia (Family Nativity Show), where he showed ceramic work made in collaboration with Tullio *d'Albisola. In 1931, he showed both paintings and ceramics at the Mostra Futurista di Pittura, Scultura e Arte Decorativa (Futurist Show of painting, sculpture and decorative art) in Chiavari.

Gaudenzi, Alf (1908–?). In 1932, examples of his work were included in the Nuove Ceramiche Italiane (New Italian Ceramics) exhibition in Paris, the Mostra Futurista di Pittura, Scultura e Arte Decorativa (Futurist Show of Painting, Sculpture and Decorative Art), and the Mostra Fotografica Futurista (ceramiche) (Futurist Photography Show [Ceramics]) in Trieste. Although he made some memorable modelled works in clay, he was better known for his work as a painter and scenographer (maker of stage sets).

Gensoli, Maurice (1892–1972). He began working as a decorator at *Sèvres in 1921 and became head of the porcelain studio in 1924. At the 1925 Paris Exposition he exhibited decorative porcelain panels. In 1928, he became head of the design studio at Sèvres, where he remained until 1959. Under his direction the iconographic repertoire of Sèvres expanded to include stylized waves, sea shells, exotic animals, and human figures sculpted in a cubistic style. While he decorated classical forms created by other artists such as Henri *Rapin and Frédéric *Kiefer (after 1936), Gensoli himself was an imaginative designer with a deep understanding of the technical aspects of ceramics. His taste for exploiting contrasts—the texture of clay and the sheen of glaze—led him to "sculpt" directly on the surface of porcelain.

Goldscheider. In 1885, Friedrich Goldscheider (1845–97), an Austrian entrepreneur, established a ceramics business in Vienna, producing earthenware

Grant, Duncan. Footed vase, c.1930.

A.E. Gray & Co. Ltd

and porcelain. The company developed its refined techniques making reproductions of classical and Renaissance sculptures for the Österreichisches Museum für Kunst und Industrie, Vienna, using marble, alabaster, and artificial stone. The firm was also known for producing terra cotta figures, animals, and decorative objects. It held a patent for a process whereby objects modelled in clay, as well as in cement, could be bronze-plated. A bronze foundry was opened in Paris in 1892, followed by enterprises in Leipzig and Berlin, creating an international manufacturing and retail business on a scale unparalleled at the time.

After Friedrich's death, his widow Regina (who remarried in 1901), brother Alois, and son Walter ran the Vienna business, which was converted to a public company in 1910. When Walter left in 1916, Regina Goldscheider-Lewit was in sole charge until her death in 1918. The Paris-based subsidiary, lost in 1914, continued trading under the name of Arthur Goldscheider; it had its own display at the 1925 Exposition, showing works by artists such as Max Blondat, Pierre le Faguays, Pierre Lenoire, and the *Martel brothers.

During the 1920s, the Vienna firm again became a public company, under the management of Walter and Marcell Goldscheider. Business expanded rapidly, with sculptures in bronze and ivory by such artists as Josef Lorenzl and Bruno Zach being reproduced in polychrome cast plaster and ceramic bodies. Walter Goldscheider opened a branch of the company in Trenton, New Jersey, in 1938. He returned to Vienna in 1950. The business was eventually liquidated in 1954, at which time the rights to some of the company's wide range of models and the use of the Goldscheider name. When it was wound up in 1954, the rights to the use of the Goldscheider name.

Goupy, Marcel (1886–?). Known primarily as a designer of glass and ceramics, he had studied architecture, sculpture, and interior decoration at the École des Arts Décoratifs in Paris. He worked as a silversmith and jeweler before joining the Paris retailer Georges Rouard in 1909; until 1954, he designed ceramics, silver, and enameled decorative and utilitarian glass, and became known as the "soul of the house." He also selected designs proposed by other artists for production. His ceramic designs were sometimes decorated with animal, flower, and butterfly patterns.

He also designed porcelain table services for Théodore *Haviland of Limoges, e.g. *Antibes*, in rose, black, and gold, and *Marquises*, with stylized flowers and birds. Examples of his designs were included in the 1923 Exhibition of Contemporary Decorative Arts. Others, including those manufactured by *Boch Frères Keramis, were exhibited in 1925 at the Paris Exposition (where he was the vice-president of

the jury for glass), and in 1966 at the Musée des Arts Décoratifs. In the late 1920s and early 1930s, Goupy and Jean *Luce both designed elegant tableware for *Sèvres. In the 1920s, he and Paul Follot were also designers for *Wedgwood on a freelance basis under the art director, John Goodwin.

Grant, Duncan (1885–1978). Though known primarily as a painter associated with the Bloomsbury Group, he became involved in decorating ceramics. From 1913 to 1919 he was co-director, with Vanessa *Bell, of the Omega Workshops, where he worked on plates, bowls, and vases. He rarely participated in the production of the pieces themselves but, although the majority of his work was not intended for mass production, E. *Brain & Co. did produce some of his patterns for tableware. His style was, in part, influenced by Roger Fry (1866–1934), founder of the Omega Workshops, who had studied ancient and Oriental ceramics, though his own loose line and calligraphic markings were distinctive in their own right. Although interesting as a painter and proficient as a ceramic decorator, Grant's greatest contribution to the visual side of the Bloomsbury Group was his collaboration with Vanessa Bell at Charleston, Sussex. Although not specifically Art Deco, conceptually the house presented a "total" design, like many modern interiors of the period.

Gray, A.E., & Co. Ltd (Gray's Pottery). Albert Edward Gray (1871–1959) was a glass and pottery salesman who grew dissatisfied with the wares that were available to his customers. He envisioned modern tableware that was well designed, artistically appealing, yet moderately priced, and in 1907 sought to realize his dream by establishing his own firm. Though he apparently never produced any design of his own, he was a businessman with an ability to recognize artistic talent, and so greatly influenced the development of functional, modern ceramics in England. The company specialized in creating decorations that would often be either finished or executed wholly by hand. To this end, it commonly recruited young talent to paint undecorated wares bought from other manufacturers, and in this way was also able to keep abreast of current trends. Perhaps the best known of its young designers was Susie *Cooper, who was given free rein to create her own designs (1922–29).

Gray once remarked that "Colour is courage," and in the 1920s his firm became known for its freehand floral motifs, polychrome lusters, and transfer-printed designs. In the 1930s, the firm was able to make significant use of "push-banding," whereby shaded bands could be hand-painted in bright, clear colors using a brush and turntable. (Susie Cooper developed many patterns using this technique.) This method yielded dramatic results,

Gregory, Waylande. *Europa and the Bull*,
earthenware group, 1938. H. 23¼ in.
(59.0 cm).

W
GREGORY
Waylande Gregory

Grimwades Ltd

Grotell, Maija. *The City*, glazed
stoneware, 1935. H. 10⅝ in. (27.0 cm).

but was not overly labor-intensive, and thus helped
Gray to achieve his vision of high-quality objects
which could be sold at relatively low prices. Though
A.E. Gray produced a number of animal models and
masks, it did not generally produce many figures,
concentrating instead on tablewares.

Gregory, Waylande de Santis (1905–71). A
noted modeller, he first studied at the Kansas State
Teachers' College and later at the Kansas City Art
Institute. While still a student he worked at the
Midland Terra Cotta Company in Cicero, Kansas,
which provided his first introduction to clay. He was
invited by Lorado Taft to serve a residency at the
Chicago Art Institute, and in 1928 accompanied
Taft to Italy and studied in Florence.

That same year, he became a modeller for R. Guy
*Cowan. One of his limited edition works, *Diana
and Two Fawns*, was awarded first prize at Cleveland
Museum's May Show, 1929. Besides stylized figurative pieces such as *Burlesque Dancer* (1929–30), he
designed vases decorated in low relief.

He left the Cowan Pottery Studio in 1932
and became an artist in residence at Cranbrook
Academy of Art, Bloomfield Hills, Michigan. Later
he taught at Cooper Union before setting up a studio
in New Jersey. He received a commission for *The
Fountain of Atoms*, 1939–40, a work weighing more
than a ton which was exhibited at the World's Fair.
This won him a commission to design a mural
80 ft (25 m) wide for the Municipal Arts Center in
Washington, D.C. Thereafter, Gregory's reputation
declined, and in order to support himself he was
forced to manufacture limited-edition figurines.

Gretsch, Dr Hermann (1895–1950). A leading
designer for the German tableware industry, he also
worked as an interior designer. He studied at the
Technische Hochsule in Stuttgart with Bonatz
and Schmitthenner, 1922–23, and took courses
in ceramics and graphics at the Stuttgart Kunstgewerbeschule. In 1932, he began working as an
industrial designer for *Villeroy & Boch, where he
redesigned their dinnerware lines; *Freia* was one of
his best-known patterns of this period. In 1931, he
designed the sensuous *Arzberg 1382* service for the
Carl Schumann factory in *Arzberg: geometrifi-
cation of form signals the intended purpose of each
piece. Popular appreciation of the Modernist virtues
of this service, which was awarded a gold medal at
the Milan Triennale of 1936, resulted in it remaining
in production into the 1960s.

An important member of the Deutscher Werkbund, he became head of the Werkbund division of
the Reichskammer der Bildenden Künste (State
Chamber of the Visual Arts). Following the demise
of the Werkbund, Gretsch and a Stuttgart colleague
tried to revive it on an informal basis. In 1940, his

ideas were published in a book entitled *Gestaltendes
Handwerk* (Creative Handicrafts).

Grimwades Ltd. The Staffordshire pottery known
as Grimwades Ltd from 1900 was first established
in 1886 as Grimwade Brothers at Winton Pottery
in Hanley and Elgin Potteries in Stoke-on-Trent.
Around 1913, it acquired two other potteries:
Rubian Art Pottery Ltd in Fenton and Atlas China
Company Ltd. All combined to produce decorative
tableware and accessories during the 1920s and
1930s. Although best known for its floral patterns
including *Delhi Ware* and *Chintz*, Grimwades Ltd
also produced pieces that relied solely on form for
their visual interest. The company trademark
"Royal Winton Grimwades, England" is usually
back-stamped. Occasionally, the hand-painted
name of the pattern is also found.

Grotell, Maija (1899–1973). Trained as a painter,
designer, and sculptor in Finland, she also did post-
graduate work with the artist/potter Alfred William
Finch, a native of Brussels who taught in Finland. In
1927, she emigrated to the United States, where she
studied under Charles Fergus Binns at Alfred University. She subsequently began a long teaching
career, first at the Henry Street Settlement in New
York and later at the School of Ceramic Engineering, Rutgers University, New Jersey. In 1938, Eliel
Saarinen invited her to become a member of the
teaching staff of Cranbrook Academy of Art in
Michigan, where she was head of the ceramics
department until 1966.

As a teacher, she hesitated to interfere in her
students' creative endeavors, for she was interested
in individual differences and in the process of creative discovery. Her own pieces were notable for
their strength and simplicity and were of two basic
types—globular and cylindrical. She also developed
a range of colors to suit her style. Later, she became
known for her unique glazes. She won twenty-five
major awards and educated several leading artists,
among them Richard DeVore, Toshiko Takaezu,
and Suzanne Stephenson

Guillemard, Marcel (1886–1932). First known for
his furniture designs for the manufacturer Kriéger
in the Faubourg Saint-Antoine, Paris, he was often
associated professionally with Louis Sognot (1892–
1970). Following World War I, he succeeded Sognot
as the top designer/decorator at Atelier *Primavera
(part of the department store Au Printemps). The
works created by Atelier Primavera were sold in a
salon set up within the store to display furniture and
home furnishings. (At the time, all the major Paris
department stores had similar salons.) He played a
central role in designing Atelier Primavera's display
at the 1925 Paris Exposition.

Gulbrandsen, Nora. Tea set, porcelain decorated with sprayed and painted bands of color graduated from black through gray to yellow, highlighted with orange, Porsgrund, c.1929–31.

Gustavsberg. *Argenta* vase, glazed stoneware with impressed silver decoration, Wilhelm Kåge, 1930s. H. (approx.) 10⅛ in. (25.5 cm).

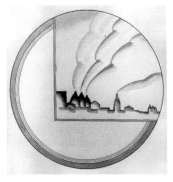

Haggar, Reginald. Design for a plate in Art Deco style, 1932, prepared for Mintons Ltd; the decoration depicts bottle ovens (traditional coal- or wood-fired kilns formerly used in the production of ceramic wares).

Stylistically, his work in all media, including ceramics, showed the influence of some of his associates, most importantly Sognot. He absorbed the prevailing painting style, Cubism, and utilized the Modernist vocabulary, which was deeply rooted in geometry, to create forms made by a combination of simple geometric shapes.

Gulbrandsen, Nora (1894–1978). After training at the National College of Art and Design in Oslo, she worked in ceramics, enamel, glass, metal, and graphic media. As art director of the Porsgrund porcelain factory, south of Oslo, where she worked from 1928 to 1945, she established a style for decorative and table wares based on modern shapes, thus replacing the forms of her predecessor, Hans Flygenring. She appreciated the forms and patterns of the modern movement for their own sake, without attaching political significance to them. Her work was allied visually more with *Art Deco and Jazz Moderne than with the romantic idealization of folk-art traditions practiced by some designers in Norway, and demonstrated an awareness of the work of Russian Constructivists and of the *Bauhaus. However, her goal was also to create designs suited to modern industrial manufacturing processes.

Gustavsberg. Swedish factory. From 1929 until 1952 it produced a line of decorative objects and table accessories called *Argenta*, designed by Wilhelm *Kåge and featuring a glazed white earthenware body with applied silver decoration. Typically, the forms are thick-bodied and are glazed either blue-green or blood-red, the latter quite rare. The silver decoration falls into several thematic categories: mythical and realistic female nudes; male warriors; sea creatures, and flowers. In addition, pieces sometimes have diaper-patterned floral borders or abstract patterning. Each piece is marked either with silver (indicating an early date) or printed in black or gold with "Gustavsberg" and "Made in Sweden" in addition to a model number and annual date letter (starting with "A" in 1929), and the anchor logo of Gustavsberg. Hand-thrown pieces are marked "hand drejad." *Argenta* ware is noteworthy for its fine quality: simple, neoclassical forms with exotic decoration mostly of marine subjects that reflect Sweden's close association with the sea. Pieces are either hand-thrown or mold-made, and although both types are the same in general appearance, the hand-formed pieces are heavier.

H

Haël-Werkstätten. German company whose factory at Marwitz achieved artistic acclaim during the 1920s, even though much of its pottery resembled that of *Velten-Vordamm. It produced forms in stoneware and faience that were hand-painted with banded decoration in an abstract and Cubist style meant to enhance their simple shapes. Much of this decoration was successful due to the painters' skillful use of a broad brush to apply concentric bands of color, sometimes in soft, graduated tones. Some of the pottery's production was rooted in local peasant pottery traditions, using red clay with mat glazes. In 1934, the company closed and Hedwig *Bollhagen took over the premises.

Haggar, Reginald George (1905–88). After he completed his studies at the Royal College of Art, London, he was appointed art director at *Mintons in 1929. Besides working as a designer, he was also a painter, writer, and lecturer. He was especially receptive to the Art Deco style, and among his first designs for Mintons were *Les Vases Modernes*, which employed geometric styling and moved the firm's production into the modern era. (When first produced, these designs did not find a receptive audience within the company.) Notably, in 1931 Haggar designed a cube-shaped tea set (similar ones were produced by other manufacturers) for the Cunard Steamship Company. The square, flat-bottomed pieces, while practical on board ship, were sometimes inappropriately decorated, for example with the printed pattern *Indian Tree* (a *chinoiserie* subject), which underscored Mintons' reluctance to embrace fully modern design idioms. He also designed several dinnerware patterns, including *Modern Art*, which features figures of women (inspired by Jean Dupas) against rocky landscapes; *Noah's Ark* (1930), featuring stylized houses, animals, and people, all in bright primary colors; and *Mexican* (1932), a pattern prefiguring the popular dinnerware lines of *Homer Laughlin and other American factories made in the late 1930s.

Haggar prepared Mintons' exhibits for the 1935 Royal Academy Exhibition and the 1934 "English Pottery Old and New" at the Victoria and Albert Museum. In 1935, he was replaced as art director by John *Wadsworth. He became a consultant designer to the Campbell Tile Company, and was Master-in-Charge of Stoke School of Art 1935–41.

Hald, Edward (1883–1980). Swedish designer, whose international educational background also included commercial training in England and Germany, 1903–04. In Dresden he studied architecture and painting at the technical Academy, and in 1907 he moved to Copenhagen to study at the Artists' Studio School with Johan Rohde. Between 1908 and 1912, he traveled and studied in Germany, England, Italy, France, and Denmark. His varied education left him with an unprejudiced approach to design, allowing a fruitful interchange between fine art and design concepts in his work. In fact, his

Harder, Charles. Vase, glazed stoneware. H. 9½ in. (24.1 cm).

Hall China Company

Theodore Haviland
Limoges
FRANCE
COPYRIGHT

Haviland & Cie

Grete Heymann-Marks (see pl. 9)

studies in Paris with the painter Henri Matisse influenced the decorative subjects he chose for glass, which reflected Parisian café society. Although not formally trained as a glass blower, he designed glass for Orrefors from 1917 to 1944, and became managing director in 1933. At the same time until 1927, he was also a freelance designer for *Rörstrand, where he created a popular ironstone (earthenware) pattern with transfer-printed decoration called *Halda*. This pattern, which easily fell within the style that the British critic Morton Shand had dubbed "Swedish Grace," had a modern flair while still evoking tradition. Hald's fellow countryman Gregor Paulsson included an illustration of *Halda* in his book *Vackrare Vardagsvara* (1919), which argued for good design in everyday products. From 1923 to 1944 Hald designed for Karlstrona, where he was also art director.

Hall China Company. Founded by Robert Hall in East Liverpool, Ohio, in 1903, the company has since 1911 been principally concerned with the production of heavy-duty institutional pottery and kitchenwares. Since most of its clientele preferred traditional forms, often liberally decorated with decals or trimmed with fired-on gilding, Hall's forays into dramatic modern styling have been relatively few, the most notable instances being novelty teapots and kitchen jugs introduced in the late 1930s, which are particularly striking in the company's famous "Chinese-red" glaze. Several designs seem to have been directly influenced by the forms of *Homer Laughlin's popular *Fiesta Ware*. Notable examples included: the *Banded* and *Safe-Handle* kitchenware lines, the *Streamline* jug and the *Basketball* teapot (1938). Several teapots displayed original features: *Streamline* (1937), with an interlocking notched lid and ring finial; *Surfside* (1937), formed like a stylized conch shell; *Rhythm* (1939), an ovoid shape; and, most remarkable of all, *Football*, with a ribbed body topped by a flaring handle, and the notched lid discreetly tucked on the side of the pot (now quite rare, this design was produced only from 1938 to 1941). A more conservative Art Deco novelty teapot was made in 1939 for the New York World's Fair: this features the symbols of the fair (trylon and perisphere) embossed in gold on a cobalt-blue glazed body.

The company, which continues to produce hotel ware today, has reissued several of its more popular Art Deco shapes, notably the 1938 *Doughnut* pitcher and the *Streamline* jug.

Harder, Charles M. (1889–1969). American studio potter. He studied at Texas A & M University and in the US Army training corps, and completed his training at the Art Institute of Chicago in 1924. While teaching at the New York State College of Ceramics, Alfred University, he continued his own studies with Charles Fergus *Binns. He became a full professor at Alfred in 1931, but left in 1935 to do research in Chicago. When he returned to Alfred in 1936, he reorganized the ceramics program so as to comply with New York State educational standards.

In 1937, he was awarded a gold medal at the International Exposition, Paris—an award which reflected the growing sophistication of American studio pottery. He won the Binns Medal of the American Ceramic Society the following year, and became a fellow of the society in 1947. In his work he tended to use impressed marks enhanced by glaze as the only decorative elements.

Haviland & Cie. Company founded in 1864 by David Haviland and his two sons, Charles and Théodore, to manufacture porcelain in the *Limoges area. For more than half a century Haviland enjoyed the reputation of creating fine porcelains with traditional floral designs. When Théodore died in 1919, his son William inherited the business and decided to develop a new kind of tableware using modern design idioms. At the 1925 Paris Exposition the company made a stunning showing with a collection of witty animal ceramics designed by Edouard-Marcel *Sandoz, featuring rabbit salt- and pepper-shakers, duck pots, etc. Equally impressive were Jean *Dufy's sgraffito renderings on vases; his *Châteaux de France* series won Haviland an "Ex-Competition, Member of the Jury" award.

These successes led the company to experiment with shapes and designs that increasingly acknowledged achievements in modern painting. Some of these new shapes were decorated by Suzanne *Lalique, who worked for Haviland until 1931. She painted clean, brightly colored floral and sometimes geometric motifs on the various wares. In the following years, decoration was kept to a minimum in favor of colored pastes or typeface initials in red, gold, or platinum. Such simple decorations, which enhanced the natural beauty of the porcelain, were extremely popular. Although the firm suffered severe setbacks during the Depression and World War II, it managed to survive, and still produces fine porcelain wares today.

Heymann-Marks, Grete (Margarete; b. 1899). After studying art in Cologne and Berlin, she entered the *Bauhaus in 1919 and trained with the Swiss painter Johannes Itten. At the end of 1921, she left the Bauhaus to teach pottery to children in Cologne, and in 1922 she began working at *Velten-Vordamm. By 1923 she was designing for the Artistic Ceramics Co. Ltd of *Haël-Werkstätten. The significance of this body of work is that she created utilitarian wares reflecting a thorough commitment to modern design in form and pattern, abandoning the tradition of folk

Hoffmann, Josef. Tulip coffee pot with creamer and covered sugar bowl designed by Hoffmann, Wiener Porzellan-Manufaktur Augarten, c.1935.

pottery sometimes evident in the work of Bauhaus colleagues. In 1934, she emigrated to England, where, through an introduction to Gordon *Forsyth, she secured employment as a designer at *Mintons in Stoke-on-Trent. Also, during this period she taught briefly at the Burslem School of Art. Just before World War II, she designed *Grete Pottery at Mintons*, for which she had her own back-stamp. In 1938, she left due to differences with the art director, John *Wadsworth.

She also did freelance design work for two Stoke-on-Trent potteries: at Ridgway she had her own backstamp, "Grete Pottery at Ridgway, Shelton," and at E. *Brain & Co. (Foley China) she and Freda Beardmore collaborated on white porcelain dinnerware, as well as children's ware. She also created designs for Johnson Brothers.

In 1938, with the aid of her husband Harold Marks, she founded Grete Pottery in Stoke-on-Trent. Using ceramic blanks acquired from Gosse and *Wedgwood, she created Modernist surface patterns, some of which were stylized flowers and polka dots, using mat glazes with strong colors. The wares were marketed through a number of leading stores, including Heals. During World War II, the pottery was forced to close, and in 1946 she moved to London, where she began making and exhibiting studio pottery.

Hoffmann, Josef (1870–1956). Best known as an architect, he was also a prolific designer of furniture, glass, metal, and ceramics. In 1897, he co-founded the Vienna Secession with the architect Joseph Olbrich, the designer Koloman *Moser, the painter Gustav Klimt, and several others. Their purpose was to break down the barriers that existed not only between life and art, but also between the fine and applied arts. During this period, he sought to create not just architectural plans, but *Gesamtkunstwerk* (or

total art work), in which everything down to ladies' fashions would fit coherently into a design scheme. His masterpiece, the Palais Stoclet (1905–11), Brussels, variously described by its owners as "the most perfect house in the world" and "a house for angels," had a complete interior design by the architect, even including porcelain and teaspoons. Although considered by some to be the last great *Jugendstil* work, the design of the building relies not on typical curves but almost entirely on right angles and checkerboard motifs, except for the dining-room murals by Gustav Klimt.

Influenced by the ideas of the Glaswegian Charles Rennie Mackintosh and the English *Arts and Crafts Movement, Hoffmann grew increasingly interested in the integrity of materials, the precepts of functionalism, and the union of artist and craftsman. With this in mind, he and Moser, together with a financier named Fritz Waerndorfer (1867–1939), founded the *Wiener Werkstätte in 1903, with the aim of creating everything for the home, including ceramics. With his partner Moser, he made designs for the porcelain manufacturer Josef Böck, and some of the products were decorated by Dagobert *Peche. He designed the Austrian Pavilion at the 1925 Paris Exposition, and also exhibited a number of ceramics. In the early 1930s, the porcelain manufacturer *Augarten produced his *Tulip* coffee set; its scalloped form contrasts sharply with Hoffmann's earlier purely geometric work.

Hofman, Vlastislav (1884–1964) An architect and artist who studied at the Czech Technical University from 1902 to 1907, and thereafter worked in the buildings department of the City of Prague. Together with fellow-architects Josef Gocár (1880–1945), Josef Chochol (1880–1964), and Pavel *Janák, Hofman was associated with the inauguration of *Czech Cubist architecture and design in Prague.

Janák, Pavel. Group of vases in different decorative styles made in 1911; the pieces are seen against a complementary fabric background. H. of tallest vase 13 in. (32.5 cm).

Fiesta

Homer Laughlin Company

His writings contributed to the theoretical basis of the movement and, among the work of members of the group, his ceramic designs were most consistent with its stated ideology. He is remembered for his wide-ranging production, which also included painting, the applied arts, and, after 1919, stage design. Although his work was created in the Czech Cubist spirit, he sought to introduce both psychological and kinetic elements with the intention of exploring the "inner capacity of matter." Later, this goal was more easily accomplished in his work as a scenographer. Hofman was a member of *Artĕl Cooperative and the Mánes Association of Plastic Artists. He won a gold medal at the Paris Exposition of 1925 and the Grand Prix at the Milan Triennale in 1937.

Homer Laughlin Company. This American commercial pottery began by making well designed white cups and saucers decorated by E. Lycett. Vanity sets decorated with raised designs in gold and dark colors were shown in the late 1890s, and by 1905 the company owned three factories producing hotel ware and dinner services. The arrival of Frederick H. *Rhead as art director in 1927 launched the company into the consumer market. His *Fiesta*, designed specifically for mass production, was of high quality and reasonable price; it was available in five contrasting colors, which were intended to be "mixed and matched" by the purchaser, allowing a certain level of self-expression on the part of the homemaker. *Fiesta Ware* was not the first pattern made to mix and match, although it is the best-known example, and it caused a veritable design revolution. In 1986, the firm began to re-issue *Genuine Fiesta* (using original molds), while examples of the vintage wares remain popular collectibles.

Hummel, Richard O. (*c.* 1899–*c.* 1976). After training as a potter, he began working at Cowan Pottery Studio (*Cowan) *c.* 1912, and modelled many of the workshop's art pottery vases; he also experimented with glaze formulas, developing the Oriental red for which Cowan became well known. In 1928, he became advisor to the company on matters of ceramic technology. At about this time, he began to produce unique, hand-thrown vessels signed with his initials and marked with the Cowan cipher. In 1929, one of these pieces received an honorable mention at the Cleveland Museum of Art's annual May Show, and the following year, one of Hummel's pieces received second prize in the pottery section.

I

Imperial Porcelain Factory, St Petersburg. See State Porcelain Factory, Leningrad.

J

Jacobson, A. Drexel (Albert Drexler Jacobson; 1895–1973). After studying sculpture at the Beaux Arts Institute of Design, New York, under Solomon Borglum, followed by military service, he attended the American Academy in Rome in 1920, and in 1925 studied at the British Academy there. Following studies at the École de la Grande Chaumière, Paris, he returned to New York, where he taught pottery and ceramic sculpture at the Greenwich House Pottery. During the early 1930s, while working on various WPA projects, he taught at New York University, the Brooklyn Museum Art School, and the Silvermine Guild of Artists in Norwalk, Connecticut.

Throughout his career he made both functional objects and ceramic sculpture, using mostly porcelain and stoneware for the former and earthenware for the latter. Although he was not a resident designer working for R. Guy *Cowan, he produced a number of porcelain pieces for the Cowan Pottery Studio on a freelance basis *c.* 1928, including *Introspection* [bird], *Giulia* [woman's head], *La Rêveuse* [female head with hand], *Antinea* [mythological head], and a set of pelican bookends. These were highly stylized works whose conception and execution reflected Art Deco sensibility. He later made abstract sculpture and figurative garden ornaments in line with changing styles. His work was included in several of the Ceramic National Exhibitions, Syracuse, N.Y., between 1936 and 1958. He was also president of the New York Society of Ceramic Arts during this period.

Janák, Pavel (1882–1956). Primarily known as an architect and urbanist, he was one of the leading theorists of *Czech Cubism in addition to being a founding member of *Artĕl Cooperative. From 1906 to 1908, he studied in the master's course under Otto Wagner at the Vienna Academy of Fine Arts, and later, with Josef Gocár, Josef Chochol, and Vlastislav *Hofman, was an early protagonist in the practice of Cubist architecture and design in Prague. He was a professor of architecture at the School of Decorative Arts, Prague, from 1921 to 1942. He set forth many of his ideas in an essay ("Od moderní architektury k architekture" [From Modern Architecture to Architecture]) published in *Styl*, vol. 2., a monthly journal of architecture, crafts, and urban aesthetics edited by Zdenek Wirth. Beyond the impact of Janák's writings, his work in architecture, furniture, and ceramics consistently reflected the ideas that he expounded.

In 1911 and 1912, a time of intense productivity, he created ceramics that were, for the most part, concavely or convexly polygonal, outlined in black and gold. This choice of palette directly reflected the

Jourdain, Francis. Bottle and large shallow dish, both wheel-thrown, earthenware with artist's initials "FJ" in blue slip, c.1919–25. H. of bottle 10½ in. (26.0 cm); d. of dish 12½ in. (31.5 cm).

influence of the *Wiener Werkstätte, while also—especially when black-and-white zigzags were applied—giving objects a dynamic presence in accordance with Czech Cubist ideas. One of his best-known ceramics, a covered box in crystalline form, exhibited the Czech Cubists' predilection for using the structure of an inorganic crystal as a model. In ceramic form, in particular, his work, along with that of the other Czech Cubists who made designs that conformed to their ideology, reflected the constraints of traditional means of production.

Jesser-Schmidt, Hilda (b.1894). With Susi *Singer, she studied at the Kunstschule für Frauen and Mädchen, a private art school for girls founded by the Secessionist painter Adolf Böhm. Then, from 1912 to 1917, she attended the Vienna Kunstgewerbeschule (School of Arts and Crafts), and studied with Josef *Hoffmann. He chose her as an artist for the Künstlerwerkstätte (artists' workshops) of the *Wiener Werkstätte, where she maintained a studio from 1916 to 1921. There, she designed, among other things, postcards, textiles, toys, glass, wooden boxes, ceramics, and embroidery. Her glass, leatherwork, and painted boxes were featured among the thirty-five artists—all members of the Wiener Werkstätte—who exhibited together at the important Kunstschau Wien in 1920. Also noteworthy were her engraved and enameled glass wares made in Bohemia. Her ceramics, designed for the Wiener Werkstätte, helped distinguish its production which had begun in 1916–17. She also designed porcelain wares made at the *Wiener Porzellan-Manufaktur Augarten. She taught at the Kunstgewerbeschule 1922–67, and was also a member of the Austrian Werkbund and the Wiener Frauenkunst (Vienna Women Artists).

Jourdain, Francis (1876–1958). Son of the Belgian-born architect Frantz Jourdain (1847–1935), he was a painter, engraver, and designer. In his paintings he often depicted luminous floral gardens. In 1911, he was awarded a Grand Prix at the International Exhibition in Turin. That year, he began to design ceramics, carpets, textiles, wallpaper, and furniture. In 1912, he founded the Ateliers Modernes, beginning with a single artisan responsible for carrying out his Modernist concepts for furniture, which tended to be very spare. By the end of World War I, Ateliers Modernes had developed into a factory producing simple, affordable items, including dinner services, which were sold through his Paris shop, Chez Francis Jourdain, from 1919. His decorative schemes for interiors ranged from offices to apartments, and he often won over prospective clients by inviting them into his own home.

He was closely affiliated with Pierre Chareau, Robert Mallet-Stevens, Eileen Grey, and René

Herbst, all of whom were members of the Société des Artistes Décorateurs. In 1928, he co-founded the Union des Artistes Modernes. For the 1925 Paris Exposition, he designed the French Embassy's gymnasium and smoking room, as well as a smoking carriage which had been commissioned by the Paris–Orleans Railway.

Joyce, Richard (1873–1931). An English potter, noted for his modelling and painting, mostly in luster, of a variety of animals, including leopards, lions, cattle, fowl, and fish. Before he joined *Pilkington's Tile and Pottery Co. in 1905, he worked at the Bretby Art Pottery as a painter and designer, as well as for Moore Brothers. He executed his own original designs, as well as objects designed by other artists.

K

Kåge, Wilhelm (1889–1950). Early training at the the Valand Art School in Gothenburg, and with the painter Carl Wilhelmsson in Stockholm, influenced his work as art director of *Gustavsberg (1917–49). He came to international attention when his wall decorations won a Grand Prix at the 1925 Paris Exposition. His successful fusion of fine arts criteria with craft and manufacturing methods produced objects that reflected Edward *Hald's views as expressed in *Vackrare Vardagsvara*, which became a touchstone for many designers of his generation. His stacking dinnerware, *Pratika*, well illustrates this, but he is best known for his *Argenta* line, with its distinctive impressed silver decoration.

The search for a Scandinavian style based on functionalism and compatible with democratic social codes was accompanied by the simultaneous development of another, more decorative style. In some of Kåge's work, one observes not only Swedish classicism, but also a kind of stylization more typical of the languid side of Art Deco.

Kähler Keramik. Danish factory established in 1839 by Joachim Christian Herman Kähler to produce earthenware, particularly stoves; it has passed from father to son ever since. When Herman August Kähler inherited it in 1872, he introduced several new glazes, including a red metallic finish, exhibited in the 1880s, which received a silver medal at the 1900 International Exposition in Paris. He later concentrated on decorative wares, particularly vases, notable for their simple forms and floral decorations painted in luster. In the 1920s, Herman J. Kähler and his brother Nils continued to produce luster-wares. Many of these pieces were modelled by Jens Thirslund, chief designer at the factory, 1917–41. Thirslund introduced the use of painted lusters in 1919, and it was his work (and that of the painter

T11

Frédéric Kiefer

and sculptor Karl Frederick Hansen-Reistrup) that the company exhibited at the New York World's Fair in 1939.

Kandinsky, Vassily (1866–1944). Russian painter; though educated as a lawyer, he decided in 1896 to devote himself to art. From *c.* 1910 his early abstract works and a tract "On the Spiritual in Art" (1912) made him one of the leading Modernists of the day. Like the *Bauhaus artists with whom he would work during the 1920s, he advocated the concept of the *Gesamtkunstwerk*. Though known mostly as a painter, in 1921 he began to decorate porcelain, and from there it was a natural step for him to create several designs for the *State Porcelain Factory, Leningrad. The abstract decoration which he applied to porcelain cups were consonant with the vanguard style of his paintings.

Kennemer Pottery. Dutch manufacturer. Konrad Mertens (1889–1953) and Eelke Snel (1889–1939) designed ceramics for the Utrecht company De Vier Paddenstoelen until 1920, when they left to found the Kennemer Pottery at Velsen. After a year of partnership, Mertens left and—as sole proprietor— Snel subsequently merged Kennemer with the workshop of the potter Anton Cornelius van Ee (1908– 55). This partnership ended in 1939, when Van Ee decided to go his own way, and Snel died only a month later.

Kiefer, Frédéric (1894–1977). Thanks to his family background (his father and grandfather were both potters), no part of the ceramic-making process was unknown to Kiefer. Consequently, his technical expertise as a modeller and glaze technician earned him the respect of many leading French ceramists of his day. In 1936, he was named "Meilleur Ouvrier de France" (Best Worker of France) and began to design at *Sèvres, where he remained until 1947. While working there, he collaborated with leading ceramists such as *Decœur, Dalpayrat, *Soudbinine, and *Gensoli. Though Kiefer learned his technical skills from his Alsatian forebears, his work was highly influenced by the aesthetic traditions of the Far East, especially China, Korea, and Japan. His work with glazes was also significant, and he employed a porcellaneous stoneware body, which was described as *porcelainique*. A single firing at high temperature vitrified both clay and glaze, resulting in rich surface nuances.

Knight, Dame Laura (1877–1970). An accomplished painter and printmaker working in linocut, lithography, woodcut, and etching, even before her dinner service, *Circus*, of 1934 established her reputation as a ceramic decorator. At E. *Brain & Co., the art director Thomas Acland Fennemore was among

the first in the field to invite artists to submit designs for ceramic production; between 1932 and 1934, Knight was invited to design tableware. Aside from the practical restriction of having to use existing ceramic shapes, she had complete artistic freedom, with the goal of improving the company's commercial appeal. Her original design resulted in *Circus*, which was marketed as a copyrighted edition in earthenware by A.J. *Wilkinson. The sauceboat, specially modelled for the project, is decorated with painted swags and zigzags in colors and gilt, with a handle shaped like a female acrobat. The dinner plate features a transfer-printed pattern based on a circus scene, painted in red, green, yellow, and brown. The choice of a painted subject such as the circus for a dinner service typified the spirit of modern ceramic decoration.

Königliche Porzellan-Manufaktur, Berlin (KPM). See Staatliche Porzellan-Manufaktur.

Kyhn, Knud (1880–1969). After studying painting and sculpture in Copenhagen, he worked first as a designer for *Bing & Grøndahl (from 1913) and at *Royal Copenhagen (1905–23). In 1925, he opened his own workshop, but later continued to design for Bing & Grøndahl (1933–35). That year, his work received critical acclaim at the Paris Exposition, along with that of several other Danish designers including Jais *Nielsen. Primarily known as a sculptor, he specialized in modelled stoneware and porcelain animals. Many of the pieces he designed for the Royal Copenhagen factory were celadonglazed, reflecting the contemporary Danish interest in Chinese and Japanese ceramics.

L

Lachenal, Edmond (1855–*c.* 1930). A Parisian ceramist and sculptor who worked with Auguste Rodin and served as chief designer in the workshop of the noted 19th-century ceramist Théodore Deck. He founded his first atelier at Malakoff, near Paris, and later moved to Châtillon-sous-Bagneux (Seine). He designed earthenware and porcelain painted with birds and flowers either in the new Japonisme style, or decorated in relief with landscapes and flowers in Persian style. His Japanese-inspired designs were often sculpted in naturalistic floral relief and suffused with richly colored glazes. By 1890, he was able to achieve a consistent quality with glazes having a velvety finish, resulting from the use of hydrofluoric acid. His vases were sometimes decorated with stylized, plant-inspired motifs. He also designed enameled glass at the Daum Frères factory in Nancy, and displayed examples of his stoneware furniture at the 1900 Paris Exposition Universelle. He was the father of Raoul *Lachenal.

Lachenal, Raoul (1885–1956). The son of Edmond *Lachenal, he took over his father's studio at the turn-of-the-century. There, he produced high-fired stoneware and porcelain, examples of which were first exhibited in 1904. In 1911, he established his own studio at Boulogne-sur-Seine, near Paris, where he produced vases, bowls, and plates in simple, symmetrical shapes that recalled Oriental wares. Often these pieces were decorated with geometric patterns, sometimes in high relief, against a velvety black or salmon-pink background. He favored mat and *flambé* glazes and the use of enamels in bold combinations of green, orange, red, gold, black, and white. Some of his pieces have a white crackled finish, while others are decorated in a complex style imitating *cloisonné* enamel, sections of the design being outlined with glazes of different colors. He also produced wares decorated with a distinctive Egyptian blue glaze, a line that was marketed in New York through Carol Stupell.

Lalique, Suzanne (b. 1899). Daughter of the noted glass artist René Lalique, she was a painter and designer of textiles, wallpaper, and ceramics. During the Art Deco period, she designed ceramics for *Sèvres and *Haviland & Cie, where she worked from 1925 to 1931 (she married Paul Haviland in 1928). At this time her plate designs featured grapes and grapevines in black, silver, and green, and bore her signature in blue.

Lallemant, Robert T. (1902–54). A ceramist and designer, he attended the École des Beaux-Arts in Dijon before becoming an unpaid apprentice in a Parisian ceramist's atelier and subsequently opened his own ceramic workshop. He specialized in ivory-glazed vessels in a unique combination of cubic, spherical, cylindrical, and flat shapes. His bold abstract painted decorations showed the influence of Cubism. He also rendered the seasons, sports, travel, marine subjects, signs of the zodiac, flowers, animals, and other subjects in a graphic, representational style. Although he explored a wide range of subject matter for use as painted decoration, even including a world map on a spherical pot, he regarded decoration as being secondary to form. He experimented until he found the ideal shape, then made a mold to permit reproduction in large numbers. Though most of his forms were composed of multiple geometric shapes, some were inspired by the machine aesthetic or the stepped contours of a Mayan pyramid. He did not believe in designing a "*pièce unique*," and his work, produced in quantity, was sold inexpensively at Paris department stores; one such was Le Printemps, for which he created a special line.

With Jean Luce, he was a founding member of the Union des Artistes Modernes (U.A.M.), whose goal was to spread *l'esprit moderne*. Between 1925 and

1929 he exhibited regularly at the Salon des Artistes Décorateurs, but despite great success in the field, he stopped designing in 1939 to become a full-time businessman.

Lapshin, Nikolai Feodorovich (1889–1942). A Russian graphic artist and painter, he studied at the drawing school of the Society for the Encouragement of the Arts in Petrograd (St Petersburg) and at the studios of Yan Tsionglinsky and Mikhail Bernstein. From 1920 to 1923 he worked for the *State Porcelain Factory, where he employed the Suprematist vocabulary of circles, squares, and triangles for decorative patterns on a variety of plates, teacups, etc. A white porcelain service he painted in 1921–23 in pink and black earned him a gold medal at the 1925 Paris Exposition.

Lenci. An Italian factory founded in Turin by Enrico Scavini and Elena König Scavini in 1919 for the production of dolls, wooden furniture, and carpets. Lenci ceramics, first made in 1928, elicited a positive critical response, quickly finding an appreciative audience. In October 1929, a British magazine, *The Studio*, gave Lenci's production a favorable review, so boosting the firm's sales potential outside Italy. Between 1929 and 1937, the year in which Elena König Scavini gave up control of the company, many well-known artists then working in Turin lent their creative skills, providing original designs for Lenci; they included Gigi Chessa, Mario Sturani, and Sandro *Vacchetti (who eventually became director of the company).

Lenoble, Emile (1876–1939). A French artist and potter who designed commercial earthenware before joining the pioneering 19th-century ceramist Ernest Chaplet in Choisy-le-Roi (near Paris) in 1904. There, he made light-bodied stoneware decorated with arabesques and flowers, often incised and painted in enamel, or modelled in low relief and well adapted to his pure, free-flowing forms. He later became known for his carved and modelled geometric designs. Inspired by Chinese Song Dynasty and Korean ceramics, he painted the surface of many of his bowls and cylindrical vases in beige, black, and white. After 1913, he used dark-blue and turquoise glazes, some with a crackled effect. Many Art Deco designers, such as Jacques-Emile *Ruhlmann and Pierre-Paul Montagnac, commissioned pottery from him and applied their own decoration.

Lenox China Company. The predecessor of Lenox, the Ceramic Art Company, was established in 1889 by Walter Scott Lenox (1859–1920) and Jonathan Coxon in Trenton, New Jersey. Lenox, who had a very particular view of the kind of ceramics he wished to make, worked first at Ott and Brewer from

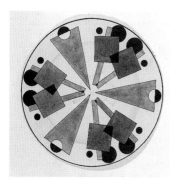

Lapshin, Nikolai. Design for a plate, watercolor, 1920s. D. of plate 8½ in. (21.6 cm).

Lessore, Thérèse. Plate, Josiah Wedgwood & Sons Ltd, 1922.

1881 to 1884 as apprentice and then art director, and then at the Willets Manufacturing Co., where a Belleek-type hard porcelain named Art Porcelaine (1887) was made. By 1906, Walter Lenox had the controlling interest in the Ceramic Art Company, which was renamed the Lenox China Company. A very translucent, ivory-colored clay body—less shiny than Irish Belleek, but equally translucent—was developed, and with it the variety of wares. Initially, the Ceramic Art Company had been known for elaborate ornamental wares embodying the artistic values of the Aesthetic Movement, but between 1906 and 1918 the focus of the firm's production shifted to dinnerware.

Lenox wanted to model the company's dinnerware lines on those made for European royalty and the aristocracy, hence he strove to achieve perfection in form and decoration. His concepts were executed by the designer Frank Graham Holmes. In 1934, a set was made for the State Dining Room at the White House. During the 1930s, such plates with elaborate gold decoration sold for $800 each, putting them outside the reach of most consumers. Holmes made his mark not only in the area of design, but as a spokesman for the firm. In 1925, Herbert Hoover, United States Secretary of Commerce, invited him to participate in a four-person commission attending the 1925 Exposition in Paris. Two years later, at a trade meeting, he urged American manufacturers to steer clear of European designs and create their own patterns. However, despite his own admonition, he invited the Russian *émigré* artist Simon Lissim, whom he had met in Paris, to work as a consultant designer for Lenox.

With the arrival of John M. Tassie in the late 1930s, Lenox entered a new era. Through increased efficiency in production, costs came down and it was possible for the company to cater to the middle-class market, which had thus far been dominated by European producers, e.g. those based in Staffordshire. During the decalomania craze, in 1917, Lenox began using lithographic transfers for decorating; under Tassie, this became a favored means of cost-cutting. To maintain a high standard, Lenox enhanced these essentially flat designs by the addition of raised enamels, which allowed dinnerware to be decorated by a combination of hand and printed means.

Lessore, Elaine Thérèse (1883–1944). A member of a distinguished family of French artists and ceramists. Her grandfather, Émile, had worked in England at *Wedgwood and her father, Jules, was a member of the Royal Institute of Painters in Watercolours, while her sister, Louise Lessore *Powell, had her own career at Wedgwood and also worked independently.

Thérèse attended the Slade School of Art, where she studied painting, and, with her sister, was also associated with May Morris through the Royal School of Needlework. Her entry into the world of ceramic decoration at Wedgwood came through her sister. From 1920 to 1924, she designed a series of dishes and plates, one of which reflected contemporary café society, as well as dealing with more traditional art subjects such as the nude, but portraying them in a neo-Impressionist manner. This style reflected her earlier connection with Vanessa *Bell and Duncan *Grant, both of whom she had met through the London Group which she had co-founded with her first husband, Bernard Adeney, in 1913. Through Lessore, Bell and Grant were able to design for Wedgwood. In 1926, Thérèse married the painter Walter Sickert.

Limoges (Haute-Vienne), France. Ever since kaolin, one of the essential ingredients of porcelain, was discovered in nearby Saint-Yrieix in 1769, Limoges has been a center of French soft-paste porcelain production. The region has many ceramic factories (including *Haviland & Cie, Raynaud & Cie, and L. *Bernardaud & Cie), and its name is associated throughout the world with well-designed, quality tableware. By the end of the 19th century, technological advances in manufacturing, together with the use of designs created by artists, assured the continuing success of the region's ceramic factories. In the period between the two World Wars, high-style designs made Limoges porcelains even more popular with the public. Many consumers, especially brides choosing dinnerware patterns, have come to regard "Limoges" as synonymous with fine French porcelain in general.

Limoges. Porcelain tea and coffee service, 1930s; individual pieces are decorated with stylized figures engaged in various leisure activities. H. of coffee pot 9¼ in. (23.5 cm).

Lindig, Otto (1881–1966). After training as an artist and modeller, he studied sculpture at the Staatliche Kunstgewerbeschule, Berlin, under Henry van de Velde (1863–1957). In 1920, he went to study ceramics at the *Bauhaus with Gerhard *Marcks,

Longwy. Large vase decorated with blue and turquoise enamel on a cream-colored crackle glaze, Société des Faïenceries, Longwy, c.1925. H. 22 in. (56.0 cm).

Longwy (see pl. 92)

Luce, Jean. Plate, glazed porcelain, Théodore Haviland & Cie, Limoges, 1925. D. 9¾ in. (25.0 cm).

whose pottery studio he headed in 1922. His ideas about beauty and the formal qualities of clay itself were crucial to the development of the Bauhaus ceramic aesthetic. He believed that functional wares like teapots and pitchers should be well designed, simply shaped, and unornamented. His work consistently stressed the sculptural elements of a piece over more strict ceramic qualities. This was apparent in the oft-imitated sharp, convex rims that he developed by high-firing earthenware until it warped. Form and material predominated in his works, and his use of a hard, fine clay obviated the need for glazing.

Löffler, Berthold (1874–1960). A painter, designer, and graphic artist who worked in Vienna for the better part of his career. In 1905, he began teaching at the Kunstgewerbeschule and the following year, in collaboration with Michael *Powolny, founded the Wiener Keramik, where he was responsible for decorating many of the studio's figurines. Wiener Keramik specialized in creating glazed-earthenware figures in a profusely ornamental style featuring curlicues, curves, putti, and flowers that had little in common with the *Wiener Werkstätte's early purist style. After 1907, Wiener Keramik products were distributed by the Wiener Werkstätte.

Some of Löffler's figurines also portray traditional East and Central European elves in a style that uses angled cubistic perspective combined with a sensuous curvaceousness typical of Art Nouveau. He also made vases and jars with geometric patterns featuring the black-and-white checkerboard motif that characterized Wiener Werkstätte design. He executed various Wiener Werkstätte commissions, including tiles for *Hoffmann's Palais Stoclet, Brussels, and the Cabaret Fledermaus.

Lomonosov Porcelain Factory, Leningrad. See State Porcelain Factory.

Longwy (Meurthe-et-Moselle). A factory located in the French town of the same name, the Société des Faïenceries Longwy evolved from a pottery business begun in a Carmelite convent at the end of the 18th century by the Huart de Nothomb family. Émaux de Longwy, a subsidiary established in 1875, specialized in the production of brightly colored ceramics decorated with Oriental and Middle Eastern motifs. The factory also produced tiles and decorative pieces such as *L'Enfant aux pigeons*, which was decorated by Eugène Carrière.

Following World War I, Longwy began producing Art Deco ceramics with naturalistic and geometric motifs in crackle and *cloisonné*-type enamels. Pilgrim bottles, round or triangular boxes, and octagonal flasks were decorated in typical Art Deco style with female nudes and stylized flowers. Longwy also

executed pottery designs for the Paris department stores Au Bon Marché and Le Printemps, producing many of Claude Lévy's designs for Atelier *Primavera during the 1920s. The factory still makes fine earthenware and enamels, many in Art Deco style.

Luce, Jean (1895–1964). The son of a French dealer in porcelain and glass tablewares, he became interested in glass while working in his father's shop. In 1923, he left to begin learning glassmaking. Though he taught at the Collège des Arts Appliqués and was a technical adviser at *Sèvres, he was principally a designer, creating ceramic and glass models which were executed by others. After establishing his own studio in 1931, he designed complementary sets of glasses and porcelain dinnerware; one such set was made for the liner *Normandie*.

Stylistically, he was always interested in the relationship of ornament and form. His glass was sandblasted or engraved with abstract, geometric motifs, and he sometimes used stylized, floral hand-painted or stenciled decorations on ceramics, which were Art Deco in spirit, while his designs for glass were more truly avant garde. During the 1920s, he designed porcelain for *Haviland & Cie, Limoges, which was decorated with elegant combinations of finely drawn lines embellished with gold and platinum to create patterns that occasionally depict stylized clouds, angular solar rays, and zigzags.

M

Makeig-Jones, Daisy (Susannah Margaretta; 1881–1945). A designer for *Wedgwood, she was best known for her series of wares which often broke with the company's traditional choice of shape, pattern, and color. She developed a pattern called *Fairyland Lustre* which featured butterflies and exotic fruits, as well as dragons, goblins and fairies in a style that emphasized their grotesque aspects. Her subjects were printed with a gold outline of vividly colored luster grounds applied to bone china. Although her shapes recalled those of 18th-century porcelain, she treated her subject matter in a manner which followed that of book illustrators such as Edmund Dulac, using stippled colors under luster to create dream-like landscapes and figures. Her early work focused on nursery ware and toy tea sets, dessert plates, and bowls patterned with soldiers, animals, or illustrations from the tales of Hans Christian Andersen. She also decorated tableware, including tea and coffee sets, and created subject matter for the firm's range of luster wares.

Malevich, Kasimir Severinovich (1878–1935). Russian artist. Suprematism, introduced by Malevich, provided a visual analogue to the contemporaneous Constructivist movement in

Russia, but did not place emphasis on "use value" or functionality of objects, as the Constructivists did. Malevich published his *Suprematist Manifesto* and presented his recent Suprematist works at the exhibition "0.10," held in Petrograd (formerly St Petersburg) in 1915. Following the 1917 October Revolution, however, Malevich began to explore the aesthetics of more practical objects, and by the early 1920s he was creating forms in porcelain. While working at the *State Porcelain Factory in 1923, he produced his best-known ceramics: a teapot with cups. The teapot shape, which appears to reflect the forms seen in a steam locomotive, was the ordered combination of flat and volumetric geometric shapes expressing the Suprematist preoccupation with stasis and tension within a single form. The highly conceptual nature of the other forms—half-cups which were, in fact, cups cut in half vertically—was probably more suited to inspiring thought about the artist's *modus operandi* than to drinking tea. In 1988, Robert M. Bozak and Gilles Gheerbrant of Canada reproduced the Malevich tea set in vitreous porcelain. It is faithful in form and material to the original, and was made in a limited edition of 200.

Malinowski, Arno (1899–1976). A versatile artist who worked for the *Royal Copenhagen Porcelain Factory, 1921–35, after studying sculpture, ceramics, and metalwork at the Royal Academy of Fine Arts, Copenhagen. He was awarded a silver medal at the 1925 Paris Exposition for painted and gilded decoration, but is known primarily for his figures designed and modelled for Royal Copenhagen. His figurative designs were stylish yet refined, and contrast markedly with the robust modelling of a large vase based on a form from nature, perhaps a melon or gourd. He also designed for the silversmiths, Georg Jensen.

Manship, Paul Howard (1885–1966). After studying art in his native Minnesota at the Mechanical Arts High School and later at the St Paul Art Institute, he moved to New York in 1905 to attend the Art Students League. There, during the summer, he gained technical experience as a studio assistant to Solon Borglum, the noted sculptor of subjects associated with the American West; this experience prompted his decision to become a sculptor. In 1906, he studied with Charles Grafly at the Pennsylvania Academy of Fine Arts, Philadelphia, and the following year traveled with Hunt *Diederich through Spain. After two years assisting the Viennese-born sculptor Isidor(e) Konti, he was awarded the Prix de Rome for sculpture in 1909. While based in Rome until 1912 or 1913, he traveled extensively in Greece and the Middle East, where he made a study of indigenous techniques and observed the iconographies of antiquity.

On returning to New York, he received many sculpture commissions from architects, including Welles Bosworth and Charles Platt. In addition to working on a monumental scale on public and private commissions, which included four stylized parcel-gilt bronze wall-reliefs of the Elements for the American Telephone and Telegraph Company (1930), he also made a number of bronze maquettes and figurines which were shown in museums around the country, and thus established a national reputation. One of his best-known public sculptures, the *Prometheus Fountain* commissioned in 1934, is the centerpiece of the ice-skating rink at Rockefeller Center, New York. While acknowledging his debt to Renaissance and Classical sculpture, he blended his interest in historically derived forms and mythical subjects with a thoroughly modern interest in simplification of form and truth to materials. These qualities are prevalent in his work in all materials, including clay.

Marcks, Gerhard (1889–1981). A noted sculptor and potter, who joined the *Bauhaus in 1919. He participated in the Expressionist Novembergruppe, was well known for his woodcuts and figurative sculptures, and from 1910 modelled many figures, including animals, for various ceramics firms. In 1920, he joined with the potter Max Krehan to form the *Bauhaus Pottery Workshop.

He was interested in applying his sense of sculptural form to the production of ceramics, creating unique pieces whose forms drew on local pottery traditions; often, he would paint these himself. This notion of the ceramic *objet d'art*, however, soon came into conflict with the broader Bauhaus agenda of designing for serial production. (Ironically, his students Theodor *Bogler and Otto *Lindig excelled at producing such prototypes.) When the Bauhaus moved in 1925, he became director of the ceramics workshop at Schloss Giebichenstein, near Leipzig. While there, he began designing for the *Staatliche Porzellan-Manufaktur (KPM), Berlin, producing such wares as a salad and bon-bon set (1931) in the style of laboratory petri dishes. In 1937, he was prohibited by the Nazis from working or exhibiting, though he continued to produce designs for KPM and was also awarded the Grand Prix at the International Exposition in Paris. From 1946 to 1949, he taught at the Landeskunstschule in Hamburg, before moving to Cologne, where he devoted himself to sculpture.

Martel, Joël and **Jean** (both 1896–1966). Twin brothers from Nantes who attended the École Nationale des Arts Décoratifs in Paris and collaborated in their artistic endeavors. They created objects ranging from small table-sculptures to car mascots, from architectural ornaments to massive

Mazzotti, Torido. Vase, glazed earthenware, 1930. H. 7⅛ in. (18.0 cm).

monuments. For the 1925 Paris Exposition they created concrete Cubist trees for a garden designed by their friend, the architect Robert Mallet-Stevens, with whom they often collaborated; they also made low-relief carvings for the Concorde Gate and Mallet-Stevens's Tourism Pavilion, and decorated the powder room in the Sèvres Pavilion.

In 1930, the brothers were founding members of the Union des Artistes Modernes (UAM). They were known for their distinctive stylized representations of animals, as well as for Cubist abstractions and figures. They worked in a wide range of media including terra cotta, porcelain, zinc, and bronze. From 1925 to 1938 they created designs at *Sèvres for ceramic production, and in 1937 decorated several pavilions at the Paris Exposition. They also made bas-reliefs for churches and designed a number of war memorials in France after World War II.

Massoul, Félix (1872–1942). Trained as a painter, he began his work as an artist-potter in 1900. He attended the École des Arts Décoratifs, Paris, and worked at Maisons-Alfort (Seine), collaborating with his wife in experiments using enamels and metallic glazes on earthenware. He introduced processes used by the Gallo-Romans, combining them with 18th-century soft-paste porcelain techniques. He sometimes used a siliceous clay like that of the ancient Egyptians. He made utilitarian pieces such as bowls and vases and decorated them with geometric designs in rich dark tones and gold. His simple, curvilinear forms and red, blue, and turquoise luster glazes are reminiscent of Islamic ceramics, and his glaze application created subtle, decorative effects. In 1930, while working for *Sèvres, he produced red-glazed pieces influenced by Hispano-Moresque pottery, and vases in antique style decorated with yellowish mat glazes on a light-blue ground.

Mayodon, Jean (1893–1967). A French painter and ceramist, he established a kiln at Sèvres (Hauts-de-Seine) c. 1918. From 1934 to 1939, he served as artistic consultant to the Manufacture Nationale de *Sèvres and was later appointed its artistic director (1941–42). He exhibited his first polychrome ceramics in Paris at the Musée Galliéra in 1919, and later designed pieces for the Paris retailer Georges Rouard. Inspired by Middle Eastern and Persian ceramics. He painted decoration, which incorporated stylized animals, as well as with nudes, athletes, and archers, was inspired by Middle Eastern and Persian ceramics. Some were in low-relief or painted using metallic oxides (copper, chromium, iron) highlighted with gold. In addition to vases, plates, and bowls, he designed enamelled earthenware fountains, screens, tiles, and pools, and executed commissions for the liners *France* and *Normandie*. At the 1925 Paris Exposition, he exhibited a shallow bowl decorated

with nudes on red crackle glaze with gold luster. His mythological subjects involved the use of complex glazing techniques. The visual complexity of resulting wares lends the work lasting significance.

Mazzotti, Torido (b.1895). Italian potter, who, with his younger brother Tullio *d'Albisola, is often given credit for creating the "albisolese style" of ceramics at their workshop in *Albisola. He recalled that in his early days he was responsible for the technical aspects of the pottery, while his brother brought in new ideas and sought to broaden the commercial side of the business. In 1925, a satellite company was formed at Albisola Superiore, with the aim of producing wares for a broad market. In 1936, the two parts of the company were merged, and moved to a new site in Sansobbia.

While being nominally functional, Mazzotti's ceramic designs, which combined bold forms with abstract painting, are probably of greater theoretical interest than they are actually useful. His designs fit well with those of other avant-garde Futurists, and he exhibited his wares with them in various places, including the Paris Exposition of 1937.

Melandri, Pietro (1885–1976). In 1922, the Italian industrialist Umberto Focaccia acquired production facilities for Melandri at Faenza. Melandri, who was famous for his uneven temperament, faced many problems, but was not deterred by the economic crisis of 1929, the loss of his partnership with Focaccia, or his displacement in the context of the other artistic work going on in Faenza at that time. From 1920 to 1940, his work was shown regularly in major exhibitions, including those in Paris in 1925 and 1937, at which he was awarded prizes.

Metthey, André (1871–1921). A French ceramist who worked as a painter, sculptor, and interior designer before opening a ceramics studio in Asnières (Hauts-de-Seine) in 1901. His early work in stoneware was inspired by Japanese and Korean models, which he decorated with *flambé* glazes. Later, however, he called on artist friends such as Matisse, Bonnard, Derain, Vuillard, and Redon, to decorate earthenware pieces. His own decorations included geometric patterns and stylized plants, animals, and figures. It was his custom to fire pots three or more times in order to achieve a variety of rich colors, including gold crackle. He also produced tin-glazed pieces and painted white earthenware with clear alkaline glazes in the Persian style. The use of *pâte de verre* and a return to stoneware production marked his later years.

Mintons Ltd. Established in 1793, this firm went through various incarnations before finally becoming Mintons Ltd in 1873. Under its French art director

Mintons. Group of kitchen storage jars and pitcher, c.1937.

Munari, Bruno. *Bull Dog*, glazed terra cotta. H. 7 in. (18.0 cm).

Murray, Keith. Coffee service in glazed earthenware designed by Murray for Josiah Wedgwood & Sons Ltd, c.1935. H. 7 in. (17.8 cm).

Léon Victor Solon (1872–1957) at the turn of the century, the firm was a leading producer of Art Nouveau ceramics; Solon pioneered the *pâte-sur-pâte* process and developed a sinuous style appropriate to typical Art Nouveau motifs such as peacocks, flowers, and nudes. In 1902, Solon and his assistant John William *Wadsworth (who succeeded him in 1909) introduced *Secessionist Ware*: matching water jugs and basins, *jardinières* and pedestals, plates, etc., decorated in a style heavily influenced by *Jugendstil* (German Art Nouveau). Striking color contrasts (e.g. crimson against green) and floral patterns made this ware extremely popular and assured its production until the beginning of World War I.

Mintons had been in the vanguard of Art Nouveau, but at the 1925 Paris Exposition it was evident that the firm had not kept up with the times, since it exhibited unadventurous tableware and a small collection of lusterware bowls. Hard hit by the financial crash of 1929, the company decided to mass-produce Art Deco wares. The firm's new art director, Reginald *Haggar, designed many patterns and forms, ranging from landscape motifs to various geometric shapes, from stylized flowers to cuboid vases. However, his ideas were not completely accepted, and many designs were unexecuted. He finally left Mintons in 1935 and John Wadsworth (art director 1909–14) returned to Mintons' art department, where he followed through on many of Haggar's innovations. Under Wadsworth, Mintons began producing tablewares such as the renowned *Solano* line, which appeared in 1937, at first in pastel shades like powder pink, pale blue, and celadon; often, one pastel color would be applied to a segment of a cup or teapot, while leaving the rest of the body exposed in its natural, ivory shade. Later versions were overpainted with enamel polka dots or bands, while Art Deco designs expanded to include ornamental pieces, toiletries, flower holders, and other such items. After 1939, however, earthenware production at Mintons practically ceased, and the main emphasis was then placed on making high-quality bone-china tablewares.

Moser, Koloman (1868–1918). Best known as a painter and designer, he founded the Vienna Secession in 1897 in collaboration with the architects Josef *Hoffmann and Josef Maria Olbrich and the painter Gustav Klimt. In 1900, he began teaching at the Kunstgewerbeschule in Vienna, where he had once been a student, and would remain there until the end of World War I. Moser and Hoffmann taught design courses at the special ceramics workshop (set up at the Kunstgewerbeschule in 1876) and had many of their works executed by the porcelain manufacturer Josef Böck. In 1903, professing faith in the ideas of John Ruskin and William Morris, the leading figures of the

English *Arts and Crafts Movement, Moser and Hoffmann jointly founded the *Wiener Werkstätte; Moser left in 1906, but continued working at the Kunstgewerbeschule, where he produced jars and vases with relief decoration that sometimes imitated flower-petals or was abstract.

Munari, Bruno (b. 1907). In 1927, after meeting Filippo Tommaso Marinetti, he aligned himself with the Milan Futurist Group. One of the first Futurists attracted to ceramics, he began collaborating with Tullio *d'Albisola in 1928. He drew heavily on traditional Italian fables as a source of inspiration, and much of his work is imbued with a strong sense of irony. His animal figures—extremely whimsical in comparison with the work of other Futurists— were assembled using extruded ceramic "tubes" cut into various lengths; he dubbed them his mechanical vision of nature. Although his work was not exhibited as frequently as that of some of his Futurist colleagues, he worked within the movement for nearly ten years, developing one of the more original and recognizable styles; at the same time he was active as painter whose work reflected the influence of Surrealism.

Murray, Keith (1892–1981). An architect by training, he began working at *Wedgwood in the early 1930s. He was one of the few true Modernists in England; although simple, his works convey the Modernist ethic of functionalism, while also possessing the timeless quality of Song Dynasty ceramics. While at Wedgwood he designed vases, tea and coffee sets, mugs, jugs, and bowls which were decorated with mat or semi-mat monochrome glazes in white (Moonstone), cream, green, or yellow. The plainness of the glazes enhanced his simplified forms. His last designs for ceramics were completed before World War II, and continued in production until the 1950s. In 1938 Wedgwood commissioned Murray and his partner C. S. White to design the company's new Barlaston factory.

N

Nadelman, Elie (1882–1946). After studying in Poland and serving in the Russian army, he moved to Paris in 1905 to pursue a career as a sculptor. Having made himself known to the leading representatives of the French avant-garde (Picasso, Brancusi, the Steins), he eventually left for the USA and settled in New York. Prior to 1930, he sculpted primarily large, monumental figures, but with the advent of the Depression, he lost his home and studio and turned to experimenting with materials such as plaster, papier-mâché, and clay, while simultaneously developing an ever increasing passion for folk art. He began collecting the clay figurines of

Nadelman, Elie. *Two Figures*, terra cotta, c.1935–40. H. 16¾ in. (42.5 cm). This painted form served (posthumously) as the model for a large sculpture placed in the lobby of the New York State Theater Lincoln Center, New York.

JAIS ≋
Jais Nielsen

Noritake

Faïencerie de Quimper Odetta

Tanagra and Taranto, and toys made by Central European folk artists, whose influence can be felt in his works of this period. He nearly always depicted the human figure, distorted almost to the point of abstraction; though antithetical to Art Deco's often severe geometry, the extreme stylization of his work fits with the spirit of the era.

He had experimented with terra cotta in 1912–13, and after his death a second body of terra cotta work was produced at the Inwood Potteries (where Nadelman had once worked) by his one-time assistant Julius Gargani.

Nash, Paul (1889–1946). Although best known for architectural renderings and textile designs, Nash, together with a number of his contemporaries (including Dame Laura *Knight, Duncan *Grant, Vanessa *Bell, Graham Sutherland and Sir Frank *Brangwyn,) also designed pottery. The work they did for *Foley Potteries, E. *Brain & Co., and A.J. *Wilkinson helped bolster the English ceramics market through the collaboration of artists with industry. Nash was given a free hand by Foley, and his designs, which were sometimes painted by Clarice *Cliff, were thought by some to be of better quality than hers. In all his work he was an advocate of modern design, expressed particularly well by his fabric designs, which often reflected trends in avant-garde art movements.

From 1933–34, Nash created tableware patterns for E. Brain & Co. (art director Thomas Acland Fennemore) and at A.J. Wilkinson (Clarice *Cliff). His work was shown in a 1934 exhibition, "Modern Ware for the Table." In 1940, he was appointed an official war artist. His book, *An Autobiography and Other Writings*, was published posthumously.

Nielsen, Jais (1885–1961). Originally educated in Denmark as a sculptor and ceramist, he became known for his sculptural pieces in stoneware. After working as a painter in Paris, he began as a designer at the *Royal Copenhagen Porcelain Factory in 1921. His work, with its varied subject matter and exquisite glazes on high-fired bodies, was unusual in style and was well received. It made a great impression, particularly on British visitors, at the 1925 Paris Exposition, where it earned him a Grand Prix. The strength of his work lies in expressive modelling, accentuated by the unctuousness of celadon or dramatized by *sang-de-bœuf* glaze.

Noritake (subsidiary of Morimura Brothers). The Morimura Brothers porcelain works at Nagoya in Japan witnessed the fortuitous confluence of a number of special components. The dynamic designs used for the decoration of their porcelain were conceived by an international group of artists who took their inspiration from several sources, including

popular European culture, as expressed in the periodicals of the era such as *Vogue* and in 18th-century French models, as viewed in popular illustrations by Dupas etc. Cyril Lee and Charles Kaiser were responsible for the marketing and design decisions of the company.

In 1904, Morimura Gumi (the Morimura group) founded the factory known as Nippon Toki Kabushiki Kaisha, which produced Noritake porcelain in the Art Deco style. Between 1921 and 1931, some 900 designs of so-called "fancy" wares, for which the company is known abroad, were documented. These were meant to attract customers to the firm's dinnerware, which always featured historically based, traditional designs. Although the backstamp 'Noritake' was used from 1921 to 1941, the name was officially employed only from 1977. Interest in Noritake products endures not only because of their varied, often amusing, decorative designs, but also because a great deal of the material survives in good condition and can still be acquired. The company's Art Deco porcelains also offer a lively visual record of the design trends of the era, and although some examples may appear to be no more than kitsch, others feature vibrant, imaginative, and beautiful hand-painted decoration.

Nove. The area around Nove developed as one of the principal centers of ceramics production in Italy. A notable example among the many factories which grew up there was *Ceramiche Zen.

O

Odetta, Faïencerie de Quimper. It is said that faience is an industry of place, and the area around Quimper in Brittany is best known for its production of objects that are easily recognizable as part of a long and venerable tradition, which began *c.* 1659. They satisfy a need for daily reminders of the simple things in life. The most familiar designs, which are still produced today, are hand-painted patterns *à la Bretonne*, depicting local people in traditional dress. During the 1920s, Manufacture Henriot à Quimper invited a local artist named Mathurin Méheut (1882–1958) to design dinnerware in the contemporary style. He made three groups of dishes—*La Flore* (flora), *La Forêt* (the forest), and *La Mer* (the sea)—which in both subject matter and rendering were evocations of the era; all were presented at the 1925 Exposition in Paris. At the same time, Odetta produced glazed stoneware that was consistent in form and decoration with the work of other French artist/potters.

Ohler, Willi (1888–1975). A painter, sculptor, and architect, he worked part-time at Bauerntöpferei von Rudolph Friedrich, Breitenbrunn, before assuming

Worpswede
Willi Ohler

control in 1920. In 1922, he moved to Worpswede, where Bernhard Hoetger gave him a studio in the Worpsweder Kunsthütten (artists' studios), which were part of an artists' colony; he was artist-in-residence in painting there. Together, Ohler and Hoetger established a pottery known as the Worpsweder Töpferei von Hoetger-Ohler for the production of everyday and luxury tablewares in stoneware. In 1926, other founded his own pottery (Worpsweder Töpferei), relinquishing control of it in 1959 to Gisela Meyer-Kaufmann.

P

Peche, Dagobert (1886–1923). From 1906 to 1911, he trained at the Akademie der bildenden Künste and at the Technische Hochschule, Vienna. Though known principally for metal, glass, ivory, and textile designs, starting in 1913 he also designed tableware forms and patterns for the well-known porcelain manufacturer Josef *Böck, and decorated a coffee service designed by Josef *Hoffmann. In 1915, he became manager of the Artists' Workshops of the *Wiener Werkstätte, running its Zurich branch from 1917 to 1918. In 1919, he succeeded Hoffmann as artistic director of the Wiener Werkstätte, and in that role led the workshop away from the strict geometry of the right angle to a lyrical style that drew its inspiration from Austrian Baroque and Rococo art. His flamboyant style was characterized by spindly curlicues, and in the minds of some, lacked the strength of Hoffmann's earlier vision. He was a member of the Austrian Werkbund, and examples of his work were posthumously included in the 1925 Paris Exposition.

Petri-Raben, Trude (Gertrude; 1906–68). A sculptor and painter, she learned ceramics at the *Staatliche Porzellan-Manufaktur, Berlin, under Otto Gothe, and later worked full-time there as a designer (1927–29). She was known for simple forms suited to serial production. One of her most famous designs was the *Urbino* service of 1930–31, which remained in production for 40 years. Eschewing superfluous ornament or color, it was classically modern in form and spirit, while gently evincing a Chinese influence. In 1937, she was awarded the Grand Prix at the International Exposition in Paris. She emigrated to America in 1952.

Pilkington's Tile and Pottery Co. The Pilkington pottery was opened near Manchester in 1891 by four brothers to produce architectural tiles. In 1900, they opened the Royal Lancastrian Pottery for the production of art wares. Gordon *Forsyth oversaw the design department at Royal Lancastrian, 1906–20, attracting a number of fine designers including Charles E. Cundall, Richard *Joyce, W.S. Mycock,

Petri-Raben, Trude. *Urbino* dinner service, glazed porcelain, Staatliche Porzellan-Manufaktur, Berlin, c.1930–31.

and Gwladys M. Rogers. William Burton, a chemist then researching glaze effects at *Wedgwood, was appointed manager within the first year of his employment. The chance discovery of an opalescent glaze facilitated the development of the richly colored, very popular Lancastrian Ware in 1903. Burton also developed a range of scarlet and tangerine orange glazes using uranium, which were later known as "uranium orange." That same year, a pottery wheel was installed by Pilkington's, and the factory launched its first lines of lusterware in 1906. The factory produced a wide variety of glazes ranging from pale pink to purple, with textures that mimicked orange peel to those with vellum smoothness. Some were speckled or mottled, as well. Burton's development of an iridescent luster gave rise to a new pottery line, *Royal Lancastrian*.

When William Burton retired in 1915, his brother Joseph became managing director of the company and provided outstanding leadership until his death in 1935. Gwladys Rogers's *Lapis Ware* was launched in 1928, featuring abstract patterns painted on biscuit pottery in colors created by Joseph Burton (mostly greens, blues, and grays), which reacted with the mat glaze used over them to produce a misty effect; the pattern was very successful. Though public interest in luster painting declined, and non-luster glazes were developed in the firm's later years, lusterwares remain Pilkington's most renowned output. By 1937 the design and production of the ornamental wares that had made Pilkington's reputation stopped, although some blanks were still being painted and sold in 1938. In 1948 William Barnes re-opened the art department. In 1964 Pilkington Tiles Ltd merged with Carter & Co., and in 1971, they became autonomous units within the Thomas Tilling Group.

Ponti, Gio (Giovanni; 1891–1979). A well-known Italian architect, who was also a prolific designer for ceramics, the most successful of which were done in the period 1923–30, when he was art director of *Richard-Ginori. In 1922, he founded Novecento, a group of designers whose work, in stark opposition to that produced by Futurists, was based on "being Italian, being traditional, and being modern." In addition to his design work, Ponti founded the periodical *Domus*, which is still published today; he characterized its aims as a battle "almost won, against the fake antique," and "still to be won, against the ugly modern."

His designs for tableware, ornamental vases, and monumental urns are characterized by a blending of traditional and modern values, featuring odalisques, architecture, and drapery as painted decoration. Such work was generally executed in a style exhibiting the same formal qualities as Italian neoclassical architecture, accentuated by lush decoration using

Popova, Liubov. Design for a cup and saucer.

Henry Varnum Poor

Powell, Alfred. Charger, earthenware with hand-painted decoration depicting a man-of-war, Josiah Wedgwood & Sons Ltd, c.1930.

richly colored glazes highlighted with gold. Often, his designs, which sometimes exhibit a wry sense of humor, prefigure Fornasetti's work of the 1940s and 1950s. In other instances, he was influenced by Italian folk pottery, ornamenting vases with figures of peasants clad in brightly colored costumes. His maiolica designs, which represent a conscious departure from the centuries-old traditional style, feature objects in steep perspective (which also recall Surrealist paintings by Giorgio de Chirico). After leaving Richard-Ginori to pursue a career as an architect and industrial designer, he occasionally returned to the firm in the 1930s, 1940s, and 1950s, creating designs for some of the most sumptuous modern ceramics.

Poole Pottery Ltd. Company founded in Poole, Dorset, by the Carter family: in 1873, Jesse Carter established a tile-making firm, control of which eventually passed to his sons Charles and Owen. In 1908, it became Carter & Company Ltd, and in 1921 a subsidiary company, *Carter, Stabler & Adams, was formed. Although the description "Poole Pottery" was in use from at least 1914, the name was not adopted officially until 1963.

Tiles were the company's principal product until 1901, when Jesse Carter retired. Later, Owen Carter, who had been a friend of William De Morgan and William Burton, pioneers of art pottery, sought to promote the production of art pottery and to emulate their luster-glazed ware. From 1914 to 1917, Poole produced pieces designed by Roger Fry for sale at the Omega Workshops.

After the subsidiary was formed in 1921, the parent company concentrated on the production of glazed earthenware, stoneware, garden ornaments, and tiling, while Carter, Stabler & Adams produced a range of domestic and art wares.

Poor, Henry Varnum (1888–1971). After majoring in economics and art at Stanford University, California, he attended the Slade School of Art in London, where he was introduced to Cubism, which experience prompted him to go to Paris to study at the Académie Julien. Upon his return to the USA in 1912, he taught in California, and moved to New York shortly after the end of World War I. He produced his first ceramics in the early 1920s: inspired by tribal and non-Western ceramics, and motivated partly by economic necessity, he concentrated at first on simple tableware. He liked to use sgraffito decoration before applying a glaze. Disliking the fussiness of extreme technical perfection, he sought spontaneity in his work, even finding the results of accidents in production to be generally favorable.

Although he always intended his wares to be practical and functional, he gained instant recog-

nition when his first ceramics were shown in 1923 at the Montrose Gallery in New York. He eventually turned to more profitable architectural commissions, all but abandoning ceramics after 1933. He did, however, publish *A Book of Pottery: From Mud to Immortality* (1958), in which he expressed his views on the aesthetics of working in clay.

Popova, Liubov Sergeevna (1889–1924). A prominent member of the Russian avant-garde in the first quarter of this century, who in a short career (cut short by her premature death from scarlet fever) pursued a new visual language that was initially defined by the tenets of painting, but evolved into so-called "production art." Her work progressed through: Cubo-Futurism (a strictly Russian phenomenon), 1913–15; the Suprematist and early Constructivist period of Painterly Architectonics, 1916–19; and Constructivism, 1920–22. In 1920, she began designing stage sets and costumes and in the final phase of her career, 1922–24, she called herself an "artist-constructor." In 1921, with other members of the avant-garde, she signed a proclamation renouncing easel painting. (She completed her final painting in 1922.)

She studied painting in Moscow and Paris and worked intermittently in the studio of Vladimir *Tatlin in Moscow. In 1914, she showed two Cubist paintings with the Jack of Diamonds group in Moscow, and in 1915 exhibited in "The Last Futurist Exhibition of Paintings: 0.10," in which Kasimir *Malevich revealed his new Suprematist style and Tatlin and Popova both showed reliefs. In 1918, while teaching at Svomas (Free State Art Studios, the post-Revolution Moscow art schools), she participated in the "5th State Exhibition: From Impressionism to Non-objective Art." In a group exhibition, held in Moscow, "5 × 5 = 25," five painters (Popova, Rodchenko, Stepanova, Exter, and Vesnin) each showed five paintings. From 1920 to 1923, she joined INKHUK (The Institute of Artistic Culture), which was under the leadership of the painter Vassily *Kandinsky. Her work in all media, from typography and textile design to painting on ceramics, expressed the Revolutionary creative foment of Russia.

Powell, Alfred Hoare (1865–1960) and **Ada Louise Powell** (1882–1956). Alfred Powell first worked in the field of architecture and was a member of the Society for the Protection of Ancient Buildings, before he began submitting ceramic pattern designs to *Wedgwood in 1903 (his association with the company lasted until 1940). After his marriage in 1906, his wife Louise (née *Lessore, granddaughter of Émile Lessore and sister of Thérèse), joined him in designing for Wedgwood. By this time, she was already accomplished in calligraphy, illuminating,

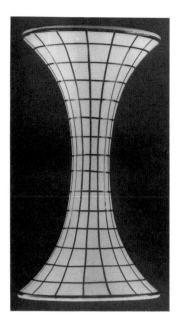

Powolny, Michael. Vase intended to hold violets, glazed earthenware, c.1906. H. 5⅛ in. (13.0 cm).

Primavera, Atelier. Globular vase with narrow opening and decorative medallions, stoneware, c.1930. H. 18 in. (45.7 cm).

Atelier Primavera

in designing for Wedgwood. By this time, she was already accomplished in calligraphy, illuminating, and embroidery, as well as having devised painted patterns for Ernest Gimson's furniture. She had trained at the Central School of Art and Design in London and was a member of the Society of Scribes and Illuminators.

Spurred on by the success of Alfred's early designs, Wedgwood's art director, John Goodwin, gave the Powells a free hand in the design and production of art wares. At the same time, he managed the mass-production, enlisting the design talents of local artists, as well as those of two Frenchmen, Marcel *Goupy and Paul Follot, on a freelance basis. At Wedgwood, the Powells' influence was profound and lasting. Together, they re-introduced freehand decorating into the industrial setting, and in the 1920s helped to establish a department for hand-painting, a move that seemed radical at the time. Their idea, which they described as "good workmanship with happy thought," was rooted in *Arts and Crafts philosophy, and required the introduction of handcraft into industry. This approach subverted entrenched hierarchies of the factory workplace, and allowed for greater expression on the part of workers. The paintress Millicent *Taplin received her training from the Powells.

The Powells' own designs were highly complex, and although some are signed by one or the other, many are collaborations. The process of using on-glaze enamels and lusters necessitated the simplification of some of their patterns before they were transferred onto ceramics. Taplin was one of the main interpreters in this process. Stylistically, the Powells' patterns echoed Arts and Crafts aesthetic content, most particularly in stylized floral borders used on Wedgwood wares. In fact, at Louise's suggestion, some 18th-century patterns were revived, including *Vine*, *Oak Leaf*, and *Crimped Ribbon and Wreath*, and proved to be popular with the public.

Louise Powell was frequently commissioned to paint decorative platters, often 20 in. (50 cm) in diameter and emblazoned with a coat-of-arms; these were referred to as "Mrs Powell's Bread and Butters," as she often presented such pieces to hosts who entertained the couple on their country estates. In the 1930s and 1940s, Alfred Powell designed plaques with views of Barlaston Hall, ships, and animals. He was still painting pots at the age of ninety.

Powolny, Michael (1871–1954). Austrian sculptor and ceramist, co-founder of the Vienna Secession in 1897. In 1906 he and Berthold *Löffler originated the Wiener Keramik, whose output of decorative ceramic objects and sculptures was sold through the *Wiener Werkstätte. His own ceramic work abounds with curlicues and putti carrying garlands of flowers, but some white earthenware compotes and other

objects for the table were decorated with the distinctive black-and-white checkerboard pattern associated with the Wiener Werkstätte. His work earned acclaim, largely for the application of his sculptor's sensibility to ceramic form.

Powolny was important not only for his designs but also as a teacher. From 1909 to 1936 he was head of the ceramics department at the Kunstgewerbeschule in Vienna, where he had once been a student. Among his best-known pupils were Susi *Singer, Vally *Wieselthier, and the Americans Russell Barnett *Aitken and Viktor *Schreckengost.

Primavera, Atelier. Established in 1912 as the design studio of the Paris department store Les Grands Magasins du Printemps, it produced objects to complete the aesthetically unified interior landscape of the home: decorative sculptural figures, tableware, inexpensive vases, and lamps embellished with popular Art Deco motifs such as stylized flowers, foliage, birds, and nudes. Many of Primavera's ceramics were made at a factory in Saint-Radegonde-en-Touraine (Indre-et-Loire). The department store also sold ceramics made at the *Longwy factory. The studio often commissioned well-known designers: Colette Gueden, Jean and Jacques *Adnet, Marcel *Renard, and Robert *Lallemant all worked there. Madeleine Sougez created vases and lamps using common Art Deco designs, sometimes collaborating with the artist Claude Lévy. (Some of the opulent, glazed ceramics which Lévy created for Primavera were shown at the 1925 Paris Exposition.) From 1923 to 1925 the studio was headed by the renowned painter and ceramist René *Buthaud.

R

Rapin, Henri (1873–1939). French painter, illustrator, decorator, and designer working in a variety of materials. By 1900, he was exhibiting regularly in Paris at the Salon d'Automne. In 1920, when Maurice Lechevallier-Chevignard, director of *Sèvres, set up a department for the production of faience under Maurice *Gensoli, Rapin was one of the well-known designers commissioned to design tableware and vases. The two men collaborated on porcelain light fixtures for the Sèvres "Salon de Lumière" at the 1925 Paris Exposition. Rapin helped Henri Patout and André Ventre with the design of the Sèvres Pavilion. His association with Sèvres also included his appointment, from 1928 to 1934, as inspector of art pieces. During this time, he worked closely with Camille Tharaud who researched glazes.

Ravilious, Eric William (1903–42). An important designer for *Wedgwood, he had earlier trained at Eastbourne, Brighton, and the Royal College of Art, London, and had experience as an artist, wood-

Red Wing Pottery. Vase, glazed earthenware, c.1936–40. H. 10¼ in. (26.0 cm)

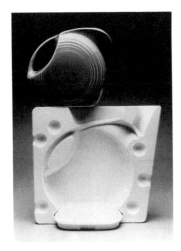

Rhead, Frederick Hurten. *Fiesta* disc pitcher (with original mold), glazed earthenware, Homer Laughlin Co., 1936. H. of pitcher 7½ in. (19.1 cm).

a number of artists (including Ravilious) to create designs for production. Using his knowledge of engraving, he made a number of commemorative pieces (featuring garden implements, fruit, fish, alphabets, and mythological figures) that revived the use of overglaze printing. His designs successfully merged traditional values, especially in his choice of forms, with Modernism. He also produced more thematic pieces, such as a Christmas tableware set and a series of patterns related to travel. He became an official war artist in 1940, and was killed in the course of fulfilling a mission.

Red Wing Pottery. The Red Wing Stoneware company was founded in 1878 in Red Wing, Minnesota; after the turn-of-the-century it became known as Red Wing Union Stoneware. Initially, the pottery produced a line of useful household items such as jugs and crocks, but as the meaning of "useful" evolved with the changing needs of the public, the company began producing art pottery, in addition to dinnerware lines. The art pottery line comprising flower pots and vases had simple decorative designs featuring flowers and birds. During the 1930s, the range was increased further with the addition of ashtrays, mugs, bowls, candlesticks, trays, and covered jars in a growing number of patterns. A colored dinnerware line, *Gypsy Trail*, was developed to compete with *Homer Laughlin's *Fiesta Ware* and Metlox's *Poppy Trail*. The air of a Mexican fiesta was communicated by the designs, featuring a series of single, bright mix-and-match colors, and in the names given to many of the dinnerware lines, seeking to evoke the spirit of magic from south of the border with Mexico.

Red Wing and Shawnee Pottery both produced molds for Rum Rill Pottery in Little Rock, Arkansas. George Rumrill designed a line of art ware that bore his backstamp but was made at Red Wing. His line featured a wide range of mat and crystalline glazes, among others, that were developed by Red Wing. From 1936 the company traded as Red Wing Potteries, Inc., and was known by this name until it closed in 1969.

Renard, Marcel. French designer who worked at Pomone, the atelier of the Paris department store Au Bon Marché. There, he created simply decorated tablewares and accessories to complement the store's stylish furnishings. From 1924 to 1935, he exhibited regularly at the Salons and Pavilions of the Société des Arts Décoratifs, and he designed bronze medallions for the 1925 Paris Exposition. In the late 1920s, he produced a number of stylized figurines of nudes, including *La Soie*.

Rhead, Charlotte (1885–1947). Although she was the sister of the noted designer Frederick Hurten

*Rhead, her work was by no means overshadowed by that of her brother. Her designs were popular with the public and manufacturers who, recognizing that the cachet of a "Charlotte Rhead" design was commercially advantageous, created a special backstamp with her name to accompany certain of her patterns. With their modulated colors and decorative motifs rooted in the *Arts and Crafts tradition, Charlotte Rhead's patterns of the 1920s contrast with those of many of her contemporaries (most notably those of Clarice *Cliff), yet somehow they blend with modern British styles. Many of her designs were executed by means of "pouncing" (in which a silhouette of the pattern is outlined on the ceramic surface); the pattern was then "tube-lined" and the resulting raised outlines served as guides in coloring the pieces. The technique of tube lining gradually replaced *pâte-sur-pâte* as a more practical method of creating relief decoration largely because it was time-saving and more cost-efficient.

Rhead, Frederick Hurten (1880–1942). A noted designer, he came from an English family prominent in ceramics, whose members included his father, Frederick Alfred Rhead (1857–1933), and his sister, Charlotte *Rhead. He himself had a prolific career, working for various factories both in England and in the USA (including *Roseville and *Weller), after he emigrated in 1902. Throughout the first decade of the century, his designs demonstrated influences ranging from neoclassicism to Art Nouveau. He taught at the University City School of Ceramics in St Louis, Missouri, and while working there wrote *Studio Pottery* (1910). He also established his own workshop in California, where he made garden ornaments and vases with sgraffito decoration. In 1916, he founded a magazine called *The Potter*.

In 1927, he became art director of the *Homer Laughlin Company, for which he designed the *Fiesta* line, mass-produced tableware free of "derivative" ornament. It was boldly modern: made in five different color editions—red, blue, green, yellow, and ivory—the unornamented pieces were formed from simple concentric bands that imitated the throwing ridges normally associated with work done on the potter's wheel. *Fiesta* proved immensely popular from its introduction in 1936, when a clever sales strategy—encouraging middle-class consumers to purchase items in various colors and then mix-and-match them at the table—helped to boost sales. The line remained in production for over 20 years and has recently been reissued in editions that use the same molds developed by Rhead in the 1930s. (Note: *Fiesta* red was originally made using uranium oxide. This practice had to be abandoned during World War II when research work on the atomic bomb project resulted in uranium being unavailable for commercial use.)

Robineau, Adelaide Alsop. Vase with excised decoration, glazed porcelain, 1928.

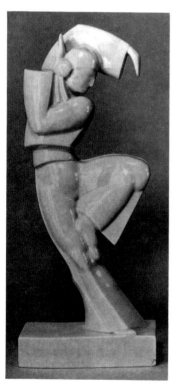

Robj. *Spanish Dancer*, glazed figurine by Marjerie, 1929. H. of figure 17⅛ in. (43.5 cm).

Richard-Ginori, Società Ceramica. Established in Doccia in the late 19th century, when several Italian ceramics manufacturers combined, Richard-Ginori first gained a reputation for producing large porcelain pieces in Art Nouveau style. In 1923, Gio *Ponti joined the firm as art director and led its aesthetic renewal. The company was awarded a Grand Prix at the 1925 Paris Exposition, where Ponti's design for a small neo-classical room was well received by the critics. His designs earned both the company and the architect great acclaim; after leaving in 1930, he occasionally designed pieces for it throughout the next two decades. Under the art direction of Giovanni Garibaldi, the firm continued to make useful table-wares and decorative wares (employing industrial production methods) in addition to what Ponti himself described as "great pieces of art for museums and collectors."

Rix(-Tichacek), Kitty (Katharina; *c.* 1890s–?). After attending the Wienerberger Werkstättenschule, she was, together with her sister Felice (1893–1967), a member of the *Wiener Werkstätte. There, she created over 800 textile patterns and was one of 58 distinguished designers of ceramics. In 1925, her work was exhibited at the Paris Exposition and in the Deutsche Frauenkunst. In the case of objects produced in the same medium it is often difficult to distinguish the work of the two sisters.

Robineau, Adelaide Alsop (1865–1929). After studying painting in New York with William Merritt Chase, she returned to Minnesota and taught china painting at St Mary's Hall, Fairbault (where she had previously been a student), and in 1899 married Samuel Robineau, a Parisian. (Many women of her era began their careers as potters with china painting.) Together, they founded the Keramic Studio Publishing Company, which produced the influential magazine *Keramic Studio* (later called simply *Design*), edited by her.

After moving to Syracuse, N.Y., in 1901, she and her husband established the Robineau Pottery and began experimenting with porcelain and glazes. (Besides her unique pieces, the pottery produced, between 1905 and 1910, signed porcelain doorknobs which provided a steady source of income.) Using as her guide the experiments published by the great French art potter Taxile Doat in his treatise on *grand feu* (high-fired) ceramics, she started on a journey of discovery, making complex vessels of excised and carved porcelain with multicolored crystalline, mat, and semi-mat glazes. She also sought technical advice from Charles Fergus *Binns. During this period, she perfected the technique of excising and also developed a semi-opaque glaze, which enhanced her complex designs. *The Apotheosis of the Toiler*, known as the *Scarab Vase* (1910), was considered her

greatest accomplishment; its complexity, which exemplified her high artistic standards, was indicative of her small output totalling only about 600 pieces in twenty-five years.

Although she was known as one of the leading American art potters whose work was sympathetic to the American *Arts and Crafts Movement, in fact, her ceramic decoration was a hybrid, combining many diverse influences. Early in her career, she derived many ideas from *Art et Décoration*, the French magazine which featured the work of Art Nouveau artists such as Gallé, Edmond *Lachenal, and Guimard. Later, she incorporated Mayan and Oriental motifs, which lent her work an affinity to Art Deco ceramics of the same period. Although she never received great financial rewards for her work, she did win several major prizes. In 1930, the Metropolitan Museum of Art, New York, held a memorial exhibition of her work.

Robj. A French company, based in Paris, that sold a wide range of high-style objects during the late 1920s and the 1930s. Many well-known artists and designers worked for Robj, designing statuettes, lamps, inkwells, bookends, ashtrays, cocktail shakers, glass jars, liquor bottles, cigarette boxes, etc. The atelier was known particularly for its *bibelots* (knick-knacks), although it made functional wares as well. Humorous caricatures having wide popular appeal included figures of various nationalities in "native" costumes, workers of various types in their respective outfits, and so on. The humor of these pieces emerged largely from the contrast between the intended function and the figure chosen to embody it, e.g. five corpulent figures for a *pot de crème* service, or heads shaped like apples, cherries, and pears for the lids of *confitures*.

In addition to this popular line, Robj made purely decorative porcelain figures that represented the cubistic style of Art Deco. In 1927, as a means of attracting artists to design for the company, Robj sponsored a competition which was judged by accomplished ceramists. A number of well-known artists submitted clay models, and Henri Martin won the prize with a statuette consisting of two figures designed to hold a clock. Robj continued to sponsor the annual contest until 1931 and had several of the prize-winning designs manufactured in exclusive limited editions by *Sèvres. The results were well received both on the Continent and elsewhere, and illustrations of Robj figures occur regularly in French periodicals and *The Studio: Yearbook of Decorative Arts* throughout the late 1920s and early 1930s.

Rookwood Pottery. The name of this Ohio pottery was adopted from that of the Longworth family estate; it was founded in 1880 by Maria Longworth Nichols (Storer) with financial support from her

Rossi, Bartolomeo. Covered container, tin-glazed terra cotta, 1930. H. 10 ⅝ in. (27.0 cm).

BAVARIA

Rosenthal

Royal Copenhagen Porcelain. *Fairy Tale*, glazed porcelain with gilt decoration, Gerhard Henning, 1921.

father. The pottery made a major contribution to the field now called "American art pottery," creating extraordinary decoration showing the influence of Japonisme and European Art Nouveau. Tiles and tile murals in this style can still be seen in New York City subway stations. Charles (Carl) Schmidt, Matthew Andrew Daly, Sara Sax, Sadie Markland, Fred Rothenbusch, Timothy Hurley, Sturgis Lawrence, and Kataro Shirayamadani were among the leading Rookwood decorators. During the late 1920s, some shapes were decorated with stylized flowers by Lorinda* Epply in the Art Deco style. The pottery closed in 1967.

Rörstrand Porslins Fabriker. In 1726 this factory was founded in Lidköping with the patronage of the Swedish Royal family. It subsequently competed directly with the *Gustavsberg factory. Early on, Rörstrand copied the styles of other well-known factories including the enamel work of *Limoges, Palissy ware, and *Mintons' majolica. In 1874, the company attempted to tap the vast Russian market for ceramics by establishing a factory in Helsinki. By 1916 that factory, named *Arabia, had become independent.

Edward *Hald and Louise Adelberg created patterns for Rörstrand in the style dubbed "Swedish Grace." The style exhibited the functionalist qualities that were so important to the Scandinavian consumer, combined with a chic classicism, perhaps in the form of stylized floral decoration. Gunnar Nyland was another important designer; he made powerful figurative sculptures in stoneware. He was director of Rörstrand from 1931 until the late 1950s.

Rosenthal. Phillip Rosenthal (1855–1937) founded a decorating studio at the end of the 19th century, but the business soon grew to include the production of white ware, and eventually became a porcelain manufacturer. Early in the 20th century, the factory in Selb produced three well-known services— *Darmstadt* (1905), *Donatello* (1907), and *Isolde* (1910)—which consisted of open, low vessels decorated with narrow, colored and gilded bands. During the 1920s, the firm created many wares for the burgeoning department-store trade, including figures, vases, and decorative items. Male figures were commonly styled as Pierrot, from the Italian *commedia dell'arte*, and females were *à la mode* in contemporary dress. Such pieces were often designed by Ferdinand Liebermann. The Rosenthal factory has a history of engaging artists as designers. Limited-edition wares were created by such cultural luminaries as Raymond Loewy, Walter Gropius, Henry Moore, and Salvador Dalí.

Roseville Pottery (active 1892–1954). Located in Zanesville, Ohio, this company originally produced utilitarian stoneware, subsequently expanding to include four factories for the production of special stoneware, art ware, and cooking ware. *Rozane*, a popular line hand-decorated with portraits, animals, and flowers on a golden-brown ground, was derivative of *Rookwood's Standard ware. Under Frederick Hurten *Rhead, art director 1904–8, more artistically advanced lines were introduced. *Woodland* (1905) and *Fudji* (1906) were designed by Gazo Fujiyama, a Japanese artist previously employed at the *Weller Pottery. These wares featured Japanese-style or Art Nouveau-inspired flowers, applied in colored slip on incised bisque backgrounds. Rhead himself designed *Della Robbia* (1906), a line executed by a time-consuming process that involved carving designs into moist clay, either by hand or using a stencil, then applying colored slips. Designs ranged from naturalistic depictions of flowers and landscapes to stark abstractions reminiscent of the work of Charles Rennie Mackintosh and the Vienna Secession. These lines were expensive to produce, hence unprofitable. After Rhead's departure (he was replaced by his brother, Harry), Roseville concentrated on producing molded art ware in simple, conservative shapes, spray-glazed or decorated using stencils or decals.

The most innovative of the later lines was *Futura*, designed by Harry Rhead's successor, Frank Ferrell. Introduced in 1928, it featured bold Art Deco shapes, many of them molded in angular and geometric forms. The line was variously decorated with colored leaves in mat or high-gloss glazes in startling combinations of pink and steel-grey, brown blending to gold, and a high-gloss emerald green. *Futura* was the most perfectly realized Art Deco line produced by an American pottery. The company also produced more conservative "modern" ware, including: *Rosecraft Hexagon* (1924); *Baneda* (1933), which featured a band of molded, stylized flowers that was a simplified version of *Della Robbia*; and *Topeo* (1934), which featured graduated beads projecting from the necks of vases. During the 1940s, the company specialized in the production of gaudy, widely popular molded floral lines. Roseville suffered in the postwar recession, closing in 1954.

Rossi, Bartolomeo. Founder of Bartolomeo Rossi e figlio in Savona in 1864. The firm's original purpose of producing toys and terra cotta pipes was transformed in 1919, when the company began to make art wares in the "Savonese" style, and became known as C.A.S. Although most of the wares reflected local pottery tradition, C.A.S. produced other work that was decidedly modern both in form and in decoration.

Royal Copenhagen Porcelain Factory. The factory was supported by the Danish royal family from 1775

Royal Doulton. *Tango* tea service, cream-colored soft-paste porcelain with rim-banded gilt decoration, *c.*1932.

Royal Copenhagen

to 1867, since when it has been in private hands. The extremely high quality of the factory's hard-paste porcelain has always made its wares desirable. Its outstanding dinner service, *Flora Danica*, was originally commissioned by Christian VII of Denmark, possibly intended as a gift for Catherine the Great of Russia. In the late 19th-century, Arnold Krog took over as art director and developed a technique of underglaze painting which creates the distinctive soft white and pastel shades for which Copenhagen wares are still known. From 1909 to 1914 and 1920 to 1925, Gerhard Henning, one of Denmark's best-known sculptors, modelled figures that were produced in creamy-white porcelain.

Royal Doulton. The original firm, Doulton & Co., was established in 1815 to produce stoneware drain-pipes and conduits; towards the end of the century, it began producing art wares at its renowned Lambeth Studio. In 1901, it was granted a Royal Warrant by King Edward VII, and was thereafter called Royal Doulton. The firm became well known for table-wares, which often attested to the stunning results of its researches into glazes. The Chinese-influenced *Flambé* ware, popular in the early part of the 20th century and marketed as *Sung* after 1919, featured the use of high-temperature glazes that produced arresting effects. The iridescent reds and streaked blues of *Flambé* earned high praise from Gordon *Forsyth in his review of the British exhibits at the Paris Exposition of 1925.

By the 1930s, mass-produced tablewares and ornaments were the mainstay of Doulton's business. Under the art direction of Charles Noke and his son

Cecil Jack Noke, the firm produced a number of fashionable Art Deco tablewares alongside its more traditional designs. In 1932, it introduced *Casino*, a simple, streamlined shape decorated with patterns such as *Lynn* (a stylized Paisley design) and *Bella* (a floral design). Another shape—*Tango*—relied for its effect on an elegant, gently curvilinear outline and highly stylized decoration reminiscent of a sunburst.

Throughout the Art Deco period, Doulton produced a variety of new patterns in a wide range of styles, as well as garden ornaments by Gilbert *Bayes. Following the opening of Tutankhamen's tomb in 1922, some wares were decorated with ancient Egyptian designs. The company pioneered a "total design" aesthetic, matching tableware to tablecloths, and manifested an experimental tendency rare among manufacturers of the period. However, a series of decorations depicting nude bathers, issued in 1924, were considered too *outré* and as a result the offending parts were soon overpainted.

Royal Lancastrian Pottery. See under Pilkington's Tile and Pottery Co.

Ruhlmann, Jacques-Emile (1879–1933). One of the best-known French Art Deco furniture designers, he established his own atelier, called Etablissements Ruhlmann et Laurent, shortly after World War I. He first achieved international acclaim at the 1925 Paris Exposition with his "Pavillon d'un Collectionneur" (residence for a rich [art] collector). He eschewed contemporary artistic influences in favor of 18th-century neoclassical aesthetics. He preferred to create forms that were elegant, clean, and simple,

Schliepstein, Gerhard. *Woman with Fawn*, figural group, Rosenthal, 1920s. H. (approx.) 18 in. (45.7 cm).

Schreckengost, Viktor. *Air* (one of four masks depicting the Elements commissioned for the New York World's Fair, 1939); terra cotta glazed in red, turquoise, black, and white.

using luxurious, rare materials (including exotic woods). When the use of metal mounts became popular after 1925, he added plaques of silver and bronze to his furniture. He sought to develop a modern style under the patronage of wealthy clients, thanks to which he was able to lavish many months of handwork on any given object. This held true for his ceramics as well. In the late 1920s, he began working for *Sèvres, where he produced designs for porcelain as neoclassical in inspiration as his furniture designs had been. A palette of pale blues, browns, and beiges—all highlighted by gold—evinced the luxury and quality that his patrons expected, and the monumental scale of his ceramics likewise suggested that they were intended primarily for display. Many of his designs, however, were first displayed posthumously at the retrospective in the Louvre in 1934.

S

Sandoz, Edouard-Marcel (1881–1971). Originally from Basle, where his father had founded a chemical company, he attended the École des Beaux-Arts in Paris, where he studied sculpture with Antonin Mercié and painting with Ferdinand Cormon. Like his contemporary Paul Jouve (1878–1973), Sandoz specialized as an *animalier*, producing sleek, highly stylized sculptural representations in wood, bronze, stone, and ceramic. His proto-Art Deco porcelain tea and coffee sets (1916–17), shaped like birds, brought him international recognition. These were produced by Théodore *Haviland & Cie of Limoges and marketed by Charles Haviland Frères in Paris.

The teapots, creamers, and covered boxes are whimsical representations of such subjects as mandarin ducks and penguins. Their sophisticated, cubistic modelling and inherent geometry are infused with Sandoz's wit. Although in their own day Sandoz's animal forms gained great popularity, they retain a timeless quality that does not date. In 1921, he designed an animal series for Porcelaine de Paris. Two pieces, *Vase Poisson-Chat* and *Chat Debout*, were exhibited at the 1925 Paris Exposition, and thereafter he exerted considerable influence in the field of ceramic design. Haviland continued to execute his designs until 1952, and he also worked with *Sèvres from 1927 to 1936, as well as for the Italian company *Richard-Ginori.

Sandoz exhibited his work at the Salon of the Société Nationale des Beaux-Arts in Paris, and in Barcelona and Brussels. He succeeded the Polish pianist and composer Paderewski as a member of the Beaux-Arts section of the Institut de France.

Schliepstein, Gerhard (b. 1886). After studying briefly at the Academy of Applied Arts in Berlin, he abandoned academic life to work independently. He pioneered a new relationship between art and the tradition of the modelled porcelain figure. His elongated forms of real and mythical figures raised the design of the porcelain figurine to the level of fine art. Many of his forms portray an ideal of aristocratic svelteness, projecting cultivation and nobility. Their refinement has a subtlety in common with Chinese Tê-hua representations.

Schliepstein worked for *Rosenthal in Selb, where the company's high-fired porcelain body provided a perfect vehicle for his stylized forms. While at Rosenthal, he sometimes made stunning lamp bases, transforming an everyday functional object into a work of art. He also worked at the *Staatliche Porzellan-Manufaktur, Berlin.

Schreckengost, Viktor (b. 1906). A leading representative of the fourth generation of a family of potters, he studied at the Cleveland Art Institute before going to Vienna in 1929 to train with Michael *Powolny. Upon his return to the United States in 1930, he began teaching at the Cleveland School of Art and worked for R. Guy *Cowan. At the Cowan Pottery Studios he designed twenty punch bowls, one of which was ordered by Eleanor Roosevelt for a party given by her husband, then governor of New York State. Decorated in a sgraffito technique using a bright-blue slip, the bowls featured bold juxtapositions of words and images: cocktail glasses, dancers, skyscrapers, and electric lamps collided with words such as "stop," "go," "follies," and "jazz." Though produced at the outset of the Depression, the bowls reflected a Jazz Age spirit that ensured success when a trade version was marketed in a range of sizes and colors.

After Cowan closed in 1931, Schreckengost designed for a number of ceramic firms and continued to teach at the Cleveland Art Institute, where he was eventually ran the Industrial Design Department. In 1933, he designed a dinner service for the American Limoges Ceramics Company. Its sleek lines and unadorned surfaces represented a move toward an Art Moderne style, and the ware proved so popular that the company had to expand production in order to meet demand. He received over fifty awards for his ceramic works, sculptures, and paintings, including a gold medal from the American Institute of Architects in 1958.

Serré, Georges (1889–1956). A french ceramist who was apprenticed in the *Sèvres factory 1903–14, In the course of military service during World War I he was sent to Saigon, where he became familiar with Chinese and Khmer ceramics. In 1920 he set up his own studio in Sèvres, and while his Khmer-inspired work remained rugged in character, some of his porcelain and stoneware pieces were influenced by his mentors Emile *Decœur and Emile *Lenoble, revealing a refinement that contrasted

Serré, Georges. Stoneware vessel with relief decoration, 1933. H. (approx.) 10 in. (25.5 cm).

Sèvres, Manufacture Nationale de. Polar bear, red-glazed porcelain figure in the style of François Pompon, c.1925. H. 14½ in. (37.0 cm).

ENGLAND

R⁢756533

Shelley Potteries Ltd

with his earlier output. Many of his simple forms feature carved or incised decoration in low relief. His work was sold by the Paris retailer Georges Rouard.

Sèvres, Manufacture Nationale de. Established in the 18th century under French royal patronage, this porcelain factory produced Art Deco ceramics designed by well-known contemporary artists. Jean *Luce was a technical advisor, and Henri *Rapin, in addition to designing, was the factory's director 1920–34. Maurice *Gensoli, who began as a decorator, 1921–27, was instrumental in leading the style of decoration away from floral motifs toward the use of figurative and animal subjects. For the 1925 Paris Exposition, Sèvres commissioned artists including Raoul *Dufy, Jacques-Emile *Ruhlmann, Robert *Bonfils, Jean *Dupas, and the *Martel brothers to design vases, fountains, and tablewares. The factory also exhibited a wide range of monumental ceramics (decorative panels and richly enamelled sculptures), as well as new items such as pipes, chess sets, buttons, and flagons.

Shearwater Pottery. This pottery was in operation by 1935 in Ocean Springs, Mississippi, under the management of G.W. Anderson and his wife, who had trained at Newcomb College Pottery. Later, the Andersons were joined by their sons: James, Peter (who studied at Alfred University), and Walter (who attended the Pennsylvania Academy of Fine Arts). Shearwater is essentially a studio pottery, focusing on one-of-a-kind pieces made from local clays, with the three brothers acting as the main designers. Their preferred subjects included fish and pelicans—themes inspired by the pottery's close proximity to water—and members of the local population. These were modelled as bookends or used as painted decoration on vases.

Shelley Potteries Ltd. In 1872, James Wileman, who owned the Foley China Works at Fenton in Staffordshire, formed a partnership with Joseph Ball Shelley to manufacture porcelain. The venture was called Wileman & Co. Following Wileman's retirement in 1892, Shelley, who had been joined by his son Percy (who took over the company in 1896 when his father died), continued to produce porce-

lain for the American market, which was exported from 1896 using the trade name "Foley China." That year, Percy built a factory to produce earthenware, the first production being an art ware line, *Intarsio*, designed by Frederick Alfred Rhead. In 1910, Wileman & Co. had to replace the Foley backstamp with "Shelley," because "Foley China" was registered as a trademark by E. *Brain & Co. The firm changed its name to Shelleys in 1925, becoming Shelley Potteries in 1929.

Beginning in the late 1920s, Shelley Potteries and A.J. *Wilkinson became the only two English producers to adopt aggressive marketing techniques. Shelley created a public identity in 1926 with the introduction of the "Shelley Girl," an *à la mode* woman rendered in Art Deco style, sipping tea from a Shelley teacup. The company issued a newsletter, *Shelley Standard*, from 1927 to 1931, also with marketing in mind. In 1928, Eric *Slater took over from his father Walter as design director, plunging the company's design program into the modern era. His *Queen Anne* shape of 1926, which proved to be the most popular, was more traditionally based than his Art Deco designs *Vogue*, *Mode*, *Eve*, and *Regent*, all introduced between 1930 and 1932.

In 1929, Shelley also engaged the illustrator Hilda Cowham, who produced one of the company's most successful products, a line of nursery ware called *Playtime*. The following year Shelley commissioned the children's book illustrator Mabel Lucie *Attwell to design a new line. She produced a tea set series with pieces shaped like animals (e.g. duck teapot, chicken sugar bowl) for children and, for the child in the adult buyer, a line with illustrations recalling the sweeter moments of childhood.

In 1965, the company changed its name to Shelley China Ltd, and in 1966 it became part of Allied English Potteries, which merged with the Doulton Group in 1971.

Simmen, Henri (1880–1969). A Flemish architect and ceramist, he studied with Edmond *Lachenal before opening his own studio in France at Meudon (a suburb of Paris). He produced salt-glazed stoneware, often painted in brown with gilded highlights, and experimented with *flambé* glazes. After World War I, he travelled through China, Korea, and Japan to study oriental ceramic styles and techniques. He modelled his pieces entirely by hand, often relying on subtly colored or crackle glazes in red, white, sea-green, and imperial yellow. His forms, frequently decorated in low relief or engraved with geometric motifs, were often inspired by nature. His Japanese wife created finials, lids, and stands carved from precious woods or ivory for his ceramics.

Singer, Susi (1895–1949). Studied in Vienna at the Kunstschule für Frauen und Mädchen and then at

Skeaping, John. *Lion and Prey*, glazed earthenware figure, Josiah Wedgwood & Sons Ltd, *c*.1930.

Lavenia
S. 122

Società Ceramica Italiana di Laveno

Séraphin Soudbinine

the Kunstgewerbeschule with Michael *Powolny. She is best remembered for her figurines made while at the *Wiener Werkstätte and the Wiener Keramik. In fact, when the Wiener Keramik began production in 1906, it followed the earlier trend of Powolny and Berthold *Löffler in making unique figurative pieces. Singer's figures, which sometimes had an undulant quality like those of Vally *Wieselthier and Gudrun *Baudisch-Wittke, were expressively modelled. Examples were shown at the 1925 Paris Exposition, and earned awards at later international exhibitions. In the late 1930s, she emigrated to the USA.

Skeaping, John Rattenbury (1901–80). A designer and sculptor, he was first recognized in the field of ceramics for his series of fourteen stylized animal figures modelled for *Wedgwood in 1926. After the 1929 Stock Market crash, Wedgwood had the idea of commissioning Skeaping and several other artists to create innovative products to attract new customers in spite of the recession. Skeaping chose to make a series of animals including bison, kangaroos, sealions, deer, and polar bears that were made in glazed Queen's ware (creamware) or black basalt. His choice of animals reflected a predilection during the period for exotic subject matter. In 1930 his vase design won a competition held to commemorate the 200th anniversary of Josiah Wedgwood's birth.

Skellern, Victor (1908–66). After training at the Potteries art schools, he studied under Gordon *Forsyth at the Burslem School of Art, as well as at the Royal College of Art in London. He became one of the principal designers, along with Millicent *Taplin and Star *Wedgwood, at Josiah *Wedgwood & Sons Ltd, where he started working in the design department in 1923. In 1934, he was appointed art director and increased the company's commitment to experimentation and originality, later instituting technical advances such as overglaze lithographic transfer-printing. These innovations eventually replaced hand-painting and allowed Wedgwood to produce less expensive wares and gain a greater market share. His work included designs for commemorative pieces, characters from Shakespeare, Gilbert and Sullivan, and *The Canterbury Tales*. In 1935, his work was included in the exhibition "British Art in Industry" at the Royal Academy in London, as well as being shown in Brussels and Paris. His collaborative design with Millicent Taplin, *Strawberry Fields* (1957), won the Design of the Year Award from the Council of Industrial Design.

Slater, Eric (b. 1902). Son of the artist Walter Slater, he is best known for his work at *Shelley Potteries, where he began working in 1919. Although he originally intended to become an engineer, he trained in design at the Burslem and Hanley art schools. At

Shelley he began by designing patterns in traditional styles, for example, *Archway of Roses* for the octagonal *Queen Anne* shape which was popular during the 1920s, showing off the delicate translucency of Shelley's fine bone china.

Realizing the limitations of working with existing forms, Slater created *Vogue* and *Mode* in 1930, both clearly reflecting the influence of Cubism and the severe geometry of Art Deco. As well as being *au courant*, these forms emphasized the innate qualities of thin-bodied bone china. There were, however, customer complaints about *Mode*'s solid triangular handle. Slater then created the more practical shape of *Regent* in 1932. That year, he chanced on a glazing technique using powdered pigments suspended in turpentine which, when allowed to dry at different rates, created a swirling, random effect. Called *Dripware*, it rapidly gained public approval.

Società Ceramica Italiana di Laveno (Lavenia). This Italian ceramic company, founded in 1856 in Laveno, merged in 1924 with Franco Revelli's company Società Ceramica Revelli. The new operation continued to produce earthenware table settings and porcelain plates. Eventually, another factory was opened in Verbano, producing technical ceramic products, as well as tableware. When the architect Guido Andlovitz was appointed artistic consultant to Società Ceramica Italiana in 1923, he brought with him the influence of many concurrent art movements, particularly those of France and the *Wiener Werkstätte. Some of his late work showed the influence of Japonisme and revealed a knowledge of Asian art. His openness to many styles affected the production of the factory during his long association with it, lasting for almost 40 years.

Soudbinine, Séraphin (1870–1944). A native of Russia, he first planned a career as an opera singer, but when he moved to Paris, he was so impressed by the work of Auguste Rodin that he gave up singing in order to work with the sculptor. Later, on a trip to New York, he saw the Far Eastern ceramics at the Metropolitan Museum of Art and was persuaded to devote his talents to exploring the high technical and aesthetic standards he observed in the Japanese and Chinese wares. Many of his forms are simple, such as low, open bowls. Others are characterized by sculptural qualities, which sometimes took the form of distinctive, stylized animals. He liked to contrast thick, mat, dark glazes with white crackle glaze, and also mat and glossy surface treatments. His distinctive cipher is a six-winged seraph's head. After the death of his wife, he would often add the words "*En souvenir de ma femme*" to his pieces.

Speck, Paul (1896–1966). Swiss-born artist. In 1914, he began studying painting in Munich under

S. Stückgold. After World War I, he took up ceramics at Debschitz-Schule, completing the state exams in ceramics, which were geared to proficiency in making pipes and stove pipes. He was apprenticed at Münchner-Werkstätte, Munich, 1919–24, and began working in the architectural ceramics department of the Grossherzogliche Majolika-Manufaktur and as a designer for the *Staatliche Majolika-Manufaktur Karlsruhe. There, he designed various functional pieces inspired by Cubism, in addition to architectural ceramics. At the same time, he became an instructor at the Landeskunstschule, and from 1929 to 1933 was Professor of Sculpture there. In 1933, he was dismissed for political reasons.

Staatliche Majolika-Manufaktur Karlsruhe. This factory's history is a complex one involving aristocratic, state, and private management. Initially, the factory resulted from the merger in 1901 of two existing studios, one of which operated in Grand Duke Friedrich I's pottery in Baden. One of the pre-existing studios had produced wares similar to Italian Renaissance-style maiolica. The court controlled the pottery until 1913, and from 1914 to 1920 *Villeroy & Boch leased it. It was owned by the state but privately administered from 1919 to 1927. In 1927, the state assumed control of the pottery in order to prevent its failure.

During the 1920s, Karlsruhe employed a number of respected artists and designers, including Max Laeuger, Martha Katzer, Ludwig König, Paul *Speck, and Paul Scheurich. Their work during the 1920s and 1930s reflected many of the current stylistic trends in ceramic design. Some of the painted wares showed an awareness of ethnographic art. Others had banded and aerographed decoration and forms made with ridges that imitated throwing marks (used entirely for decorative effect). These conventions of form and decoration were similar to ones seen at the *Bauhaus and in some English potteries.

Staatliche Porzellan-Manufaktur, Berlin. This former royal porcelain factory was established as the Königliche Porzellan-Manufaktur (KPM) by Frederick the Great of Prussia in 1763, and became the Staatliche Porzellan-Manufaktur in 1918. Since then it has continued to use the KPM abbreviation. The factory was directed by Nicola Moufang (1925–28) and Count Günther von Pechmann (1928–38), both of whom promoted modern design ideas as exemplified by the work of the Deutscher Werkbund and the *Bauhaus. Using designs from the School of Applied Arts in Halle, the factory produced porcelain in the modern spirit designed by Marguerite *Friedländer-Wildenhain and Hubert Griemert. KPM also made Trude *Petri-Raben's *Urbino* service and figurative works by Ludwig Gies. Recently, the factory has returned to producing styles of an earlier era to meet public demand. Marks from the interwar period include a printed blue scepter, along with that of the individual designer.

Stabler, Harold (1872–1944). A designer, jeweler, and silversmith, he studied cabinetmaking and metalwork in the late 1890s at the Keswick School of Art, which was supported by John Ruskin. He taught in London from 1907 to 1937. After visiting the Deutscher Werkbund exhibition in Cologne in 1914, he helped to found the Design and Industries Association, which recalled the *Arts and Crafts Movement in its antipathy to the machine.

He and his wife Phoebe *Stabler established a studio in London, where they produced distinctive figural groups. In 1921, the two joined John *Adams and Charles Carter to form *Carter, Stabler & Adams Ltd. There, Stabler worked primarily as an artistic consultant and painter, designing coffee ware and tiles, while his wife modelled figures. His tiles often depicted hunting or sporting motifs.

Stabler, Phoebe (d. 1955). A trained sculptor, modeller, and designer, she shared a studio with her husband Harold *Stabler in London. The two made many ceramic sculptures together, and a saltglazed figure of a seated boy earned particular praise for Phoebe. Her *Picardy Peasants* of 1911 were produced by both *Royal Doulton and Carter & Co. Ltd, where she and her husband worked from 1913 onward. In addition, the two worked on architectural commissions; their war memorial for Rugby School (1922) was subsequently cast by *Carter, Stabler & Adams for the 1925 Paris Exposition.

State Porcelain Factory, Leningrad (after 1925 Lomonosov Porcelain Factory). Factory founded in St Petersburg in the mid-18th century as the Imperial Porcelain Manufactory to supply fine porcelain for the Tsar, the court, and Imperial gift-giving occasions. During World War I, output was expanded in order to produce items for army hospitals. However, the October Revolution of 1917 completely transformed the purpose of the factory, which was nationalized and renamed the State Porcelain Factory. Workers appropriated existing stocks of green and biscuit wares and painted blanks with Communist emblems, such as the hammer and sickle. *Agitprop* slogans such as "Down with the Bourgeoisie!" and "Away with Capital!" adorned the new products, though ironically the cost of hand-painting these wares still made them too expensive for the average worker. Mikhail *Adamovich, Sergei *Chekhonin, and Nikolai *Suetin were all porcelain painters during this time, and Kasimir *Malevich was also active there. By 1925, the factory was exhibiting avant-garde wares, some of which were shown at the Paris Exposition.

Taplin, Millicent. *Falling Leaves* table ware ("Bond" shape), glazed bone china, with detail showing hand-painted decoration, Josiah Wedgwood & Sons Ltd, c.1930.

Tatlin, Vladimir. Set of porcelain feeding bottles with rack; bottles designed by Tatlin and made by Alexei Sotnikov, Dulevo Factory, 1930–31.

Suetin, Nikolai Mikhailovich (1897–1954). A Russian painter, graphic artist, designer, and porcelain decorator, he was one of the leading exponents of Suprematism, pioneered by Kasimir *Malevich. The Suprematist aesthetic formed the basis for Suetin's designs produced at the *State (Lomonosov) Porcelain Factory, where he was chief artist from 1932. Among his most notable designs were a coffee service, an inkstand, rectangular ceramic vases, and a Suprematist tea service (with a chart painted on the back of the tray to specify how the service ought to be laid out when not in use) which was shown at the 1925 Paris Exposition.

T

Taplin, Millicent Jane (Millie; 1902–80). A noted designer, decorator, and freehand paintress, she was one of the few English women with a working-class background to be promoted to designer in the pottery industry. Like many of her contemporaries, she left school at 13 to work and help support her family. Thanks to a scholarship, she was able to attend Stoke School of Art in the evenings. After working at Greens in Fenton as a liner (painting gold lines on wares) and at *Mintons, she moved to *Wedgwood in 1917. There, she trained with Alfred and Louise *Powell and was soon adapting their designs to suit the skills of the paintresses. In 1928, when the separate hand-craft and hand-painting studios were merged, she was promoted to designer and became manager of the department.

Her designs, which showed the influence of 18th-century patterns in their restraint and delicacy, were frequently accentuated by the addition of platinum luster, as in *Falling Leaves* and *Winter Mornings*, both based on natural forms. In contrast, *Sunlit* and *Moonlight* reflected the geometric and abstract designs commonly thought of as Art Deco, which had become increasingly popular since the 1925 Paris Exposition. The bold modernity of these patterns was aimed at a larger public with—in the words of Victor *Skellern—"some taste and no money." With the world recession of the early 1930s, streamlined production techniques were called for to produce wares with wide market appeal. Nevertheless, while complementing the body shapes in use at the time, Taplin's hand-painted designs continued Wedgwood's long tradition of high quality, while reflecting contemporary design trends. She became head of the hand-painting department in 1956, and retired in 1962.

Tatlin, Vladimir (1885–1953). After studying at the Moscow School of Painting, Sculpture, and Architecture, Tatlin was appointed as an administrator at NARKOMPROS (the Commission for Public Education), in charge of "monumental propaganda."

In the early 1920s, he taught at various studios in Moscow and Petrograd (St Petersburg) and worked to create new types of furniture, textiles, and ceramics for the fledgling Soviet state. His famous *Monument for the Third International*, shown at the 1925 Paris Exposition, earned him a gold medal and wide acclaim. Subsequently, he taught at the Kiev Art Institute and at VKhUTEIN in Moscow, where he began working with Alexei Sotnikov (a trained artist who eventually worked as a porcelain modeller at the *Dulevo factory and was awarded prizes at several international exhibitions.) The two men collaborated on projects such as the ceramic baby feeders 1930–31: as objects, these are beautifully abstracted, organic forms that appear to mimic a woman's breast. A special wicker-covered wire rack was required to hold the "bottles" when not in use.

Taylor, William Howson (1876–1935). A joint founder (with his father Edward R. Taylor) in 1898 of the Ruskin Pottery as a small, independent business interested in combining craft and industry. (The new pottery was named after the champion of the *Arts and Crafts Movement, John Ruskin; the use of the name was formally sanctioned by the Ruskin family in 1909.) Though the workshop produced a range of decorated wares (vases, bowls, jugs, trays, candlesticks, and cufflinks), it was noteworthy particularly for Taylor's experiments with *soufflé*, *flambé*, and luster glazes. Using a local clay, he developed a white body for use in his high-temperature experiments, producing a variety of textures, colors, and patterns. For the production of *flambé* and *sang-de-bœuf* pieces, a special kiln known as the "Secret Red Kiln" was used, but the secret recipes for Taylor's various glazes perished when he retired, destroying all his notes.

Teco Pottery. In 1886, William Day Gates founded the American Terra Cotta and Ceramic Company in Terra Cotta, Illinois, to make architectural terra cotta, bricks, and sewer pipes. The acronym Teco, derived from the first letters of "terra" and "cotta," was given to the art pottery line, which was made experimentally starting in 1895. The first artwares were glazed in mute browns and reds. Wares decorated with a mat green glaze similar to one popularized by Grueby Pottery were also sold commercially. Successful experiments soon led to the introduction of crystalline and aventurine glazes. At the 1904 St Louis Exposition, Teco became the first American art pottery to work with such glazes, but critics thought that the quality was inferior to that of several European makers, including *Sèvres, *Royal Copenhagen, and *Rörstand. Gates's early forms were Gates's early forms were elaborately detailed, often using vegetation, such as flower petals and ears of corn, as structural elements, though other

Villeroy & Boch. Teapot by Rudolf Mezger, glazed earthenware ("Haag" pattern), c.1935. H. 5⅛ in. (13.0 cm).

Teco wares had no corollary in nature and were quite abstract in appearance. Some shapes were designed by local Prairie School architects such as Louis Sullivan and George Grant Elmslie, making Teco wares art pottery *by architects, for architects.* (Frank Lloyd *Wright is reputed to have designed at least one piece—an umbrella stand—for Teco.)

As production demands increased, design complexity was reduced, and in the early 20th century most of the innovative glazing effects were replaced by "Teco green," a mat glaze (similar to one made by Grueby Pottery) which created a mossy, crystalline effect on the characteristic stoneware-like body. The art line was abandoned *c.* 1922, but the company continued to produce garden ornaments, tea sets, and relief-decorated tiles. The business was eventually sold in 1930.

V

Vacchetti, Sandro. After developing a reputation as director of *Lenci, he formed a partnership in 1934 with the ceramist Nello Franchini. The company, named Essevi, was located in Turin. During the 1930s, it produced a line of hand-painted figurines that expressed some of the thematic preoccupations of the era, such as Barbier-style ladies in formal dress and truly exotic female, chimerical animal combinations. These were made in glazed terra cotta with painted decoration, and showed-off nicely the high degree of technical mastery achieved at Essevi.

Velten-Vordamm. During the 1920s, under the direction of Hermann Harkort, this German factory used the talents of established designers, from whom tableware designs were commissioned on a freelance basis. It had a series of distinguished art directors, two of whom had been associated with the *Bauhaus: Theodor *Bogler from 1925 to 1926, followed by Werner *Burri, who stayed until 1931. Gerhard *Marcks, also from the Bauhaus, contributed models for animal figures. In both form and decoration, the output of the factory reflected contemporary aesthetic trends. Around a hundred decorators painted simplified floral and figurative patterns, each requiring only one or two strokes. Hedwig *Bollhagen followed Bogler's lead in designing patterns with banded, linear decoration that was intended to emphasize the formal qualities of the wares. Bogler's designs were more austere than the work he produced at the Bauhaus.

Villeroy & Boch. The result of a consolidation of the potteries of N. Villeroy and Jean-François Boch in the early 19th century, this firm has become one of the leading producers of earthenware in Germany. Employing the best Art Nouveau designers at the turn-of-the-century, it sought to create earthenware products that would rival the aesthetic richness of porcelain. However, the firm accomplished this not by setting the pace in design, but by following stylistic trends; this strategy had the advantage of assuring the success of many wares, which were produced in line with public taste. For instance, when designs by artists like Henry van de Velde, Peter Behrens, Josef Maria Olbrich, and Adelbert Niemeyer became marketable, the company adapted the style for its own products, such as the *Budapester Form* of 1905.

Although Villeroy & Boch may not have been in the vanguard of design, the firm was consistently innovative in the realms of science, business, and marketing. Throughout the 1920s and 1930s, the company worked on methods of incorporating aesthetic ideals into mass-production techniques. In 1928, the firm opened a research institute in Dresden, which led to certain technical developments, such as the perfection of serial production of slipware. In 1932, Villeroy & Boch engaged Hermann *Gretsch, creator of functional Modernist ceramics whose designs did not hinder their manufacture. Another important development was the concept of the modular unit: a seemingly endless number of lines could be mass-produced by using a single, basic form with variations of functional parts like spouts and handles (the *Kugelform* or "bullet-shaped" service was the most successful example). *Kugelform* was also marketed in an innovative fashion that anticipated Homer *Laughlin's *Fiesta Ware*: purchasers could buy individual pieces, available in a range of colors, rather than complete sets.

Volkmar, Leon (1879–1959). Son of the distinguished American potter Charles Volkmar (1841–1917), he was born in France where his father was employed. He studied there from 1898 to 1900. After he returned to the USA, he helped his father set up the Volkmar Kilns in New Jersey in 1902. He was head of pottery at the newly formed Pennsylvania Museum School of Industrial Art. In 1910 he helped a former student, Jean Durant Rice, to set up a pottery in Bedford Village, New York; it made domestic wares, accessories, and art pottery. Volkmar formulated the glazes – aubergine, copper reds and blues, brown, yellow – and like the French potters Edmond and Raoul *Lachenal, he developed an Egyptian blue glaze which enhanced his simple forms. When Mrs Rice died, Volkmar inherited a share of the pottery, and by 1924 was able to purchase the remaining portion; he changed the name to Durant Kilns (1911–30), which was consistent with the backstamp and trade name. (Durant was Mrs Rice's maiden name.)

Volkmar won a bronze medal at the 1937 Paris Exposition for his cream-colored earthenware. Like earlier forms produced at the Durant Kilns, his work showed the influence of Near and Far Eastern wares.

Vyse, Charles. *Amphitrite astride a Hippocampus,* figural group, 1930. H. 7⅞ in. (20.0 cm).

Wadsworth, John. Vase (with related watercolor design), bone china with stylized lotus decoration, Mintons, c.1937.

Vyse, Charles (d. 1968). An academic sculptor and potter, he often collaborated with his wife, Nell, in making figurines or figural groups such as *The Tulip Girl* or *The Balloon Seller.* Vyse trained at the Hanley School of Art and in the Staffordshire Potteries.

Although the Vyses worked mostly in a naturalistic style using life models, some of their subjects reflected the contemporary taste for the exotic, as in the case of mythical female figures juxtaposed with exotic animal forms, such as a hippocampus or seahorse; Nell did the modelling and decorating, while her husband handled the technical aspects such as mold-making, casting, and firing. His interest in techniques was wide-ranging and he carried out many glaze experiments, including, in the late 1920s, duplicating Chinese Song-dynasty glazes. Thereafter he copied many Song and T'ang wares, but surprisingly decorated them with a range of modern subjects some derived from Vorticist painting.

W

Wächtersbacher Steingutfabrik. A German pottery near Frankfurt, founded in 1832 by Count Adolf zu Ysenburg und Büdingen and a group of local residents following the discovery of clay deposits in the region. At the outset the factory had only a dozen workers, but by 1883 the number had risen to 350, and by 1903 to 738. At first the factory produced only simple, utilitarian objects, such as cups, bowls, plates, and—most surprisingly—blood-letting bowls. The only concession to luxury was a group of vases in the Biedermeier-style. (This style was abandoned after the founding of the German Empire in 1870.) The first boom in sales and production took place under Max Roesler, director of the factory from 1874 to 1890. During this period a program of profit-sharing was established, with the owner taking half, the remainder being divided among the administrative staff and clay workers.

During the *Art Nouveau period, the factory's importance began to grow due to its association with an artists' colony in nearby Darmstadt, whose residents provided creative input. Pieces made in the Art Nouveau style continued to be produced until the 1920s. The influence of Josef Maria Olbrich is reflected in the factory's use of geometricized designs, and demonstrate the impact of the prevailing Art Deco style.

In 1921, the art wares department was closed due to poor sales, and the firm again concentrated on producing domestic wares. Ursula Fesca, who had previously been employed at *Velten-Vordamm, joined the firm as a designer in 1931. Her teapot called *Harlem,* created in 1932, helped contribute to the factory's reputation as artistically important. By the 1930s, its production included a vast range of domestic wares, garden ornaments, jardinières, desk

sets, bread boxes, cake plates, etc. It is one of the few factories of the period that survives today.

Wadsworth, John William (1879–1955). After studying at the Stockport Schools of Art, in 1898 he gained a scholarship to the Royal College of Art, London. There, he encountered the work of two men who profoundly influenced him: the illustrator and designer Walter Crane and the *Arts and Crafts idealist W.R. Lethaby. He began work at *Mintons in 1901 as assistant art director under Léon Victor Solon. Together, they designed *Secessionist Ware,* a popular line which was inspired by contemporary Viennese design. In 1915, he went to the Royal Worcester factory as art director, but returned to Mintons in 1935. At that time Wadsworth **was** able to accomplish what Reginald *Haggar could not: he designed tableware with modern styling, specifically Art Deco. In difficult economic times, the management accepted his modern designs more readily than they had done during Haggar's directorship.

Wain, Louis (1860–1939). A popular illustrator of the Edwardian period, best known for his humorous anthropomorphic cats, which were featured on postcards, posters, and in magazines. His illustrations were naturalistic, sometimes even sentimental. He also created the first animated cartoon cat, *Pussyfoot,* in 1918. During the 1920s, he designed figures of cats which were produced by an as yet unidentified British pottery. For his ceramic figures, he preferred brightly painted Cubist and stylized cat shapes. One such model was called *Felix, the Lucky Futuristic Cat.* In 1924, he was placed in a mental hospital, where he remained for the rest of his life; while there, he executed a series of dazzlingly colored and patterned "psychotic" cat drawings.

Walters, Carl (1883–1955). An American ceramist who first studied painting in New York under Robert Henri. His first ceramics were made when he was nearly 40 years old, after he had built a studio and kiln at his home; they included candlesticks, bowls, vases, and plates covered with calligraphic designs inspired by the ancient Near East. Throughout the 1920s, he concentrated on ceramic sculpture: he generally produced colorful, witty animal figures that were strongly modelled, drawing on sources ranging from American folk art to ancient Egyptian, Persian, and Chinese ceramic models. He was also known for his work with glazes; he once spent two years experimenting with an Egyptian blue glaze. His early training as a painter often emerges in his surface decoration, in which patterns of colors and shapes tend to take on an independent quality not linked to the ceramic form. His work was shown at various museums in the United States; his entries in the 1933–34 Century of Progress Exposition in

Wedgwood, Josiah, & Sons Ltd. Plate designed by Eric Ravilious, Queen's Ware with transfer-printed decoration depicting Piccadilly Circus, London, 1938.

Wedgwood, Star. *Stars* tea set, handmade bone china with hand-painted decoration, Josiah Wedgwood & Sons Ltd, 1930s.

Chicago—humorous decorative ceramics of a bull and a warthog—brought him much acclaim. He was awarded Guggenheim fellowships in 1936 and 1937, and thereafter he established the Norton School of Art in Florida.

Wedgwood, Josiah, & Sons Ltd. Although the company's origins, dating from 1759, are far removed from the modern period, a knowledge of its founder, Josiah Wedgwood I (1730–95), provides the key to understanding its history. The company was based in Burslem, Staffordshire, until 1769, when it moved to the Etruria factory; it was eventually transferred to Barlaston in 1940, and remained in family hands until 1967. Josiah Wedgwood was not only a gifted ceramist (he developed jasper, one of the distinctive clay bodies for which the company is famous), but was also a socially aware businessman who believed that the work environment should be a healthy place for employees. He pressed the government to build a canal linking Staffordshire with London, so guaranteeing the viability of the area around Stoke-on-Trent for ceramics production. (Initially wares had been transported overland, resulting in a high percentage of loss due to breakage.)

In 1902, Wedgwood established a showroom in Paris and began developing a business relationship with the retailer Georges Rouard. John Goodwin oversaw the production of dinnerware, leaving all decisions concerning art wares to Alfred and Louise *Powell. This talented pair, steeped in *Arts and Crafts philosophy, instilled a little of it into commercial production by reviving freehand painting in industry. To this end, Alfred started a school for freehand painting at Etruria in 1914. One of his students was Millicent *Taplin.

In 1915, Daisy *Makeig-Jones's *Fairyland Lustre* was introduced, with great success. The complex, varied pattern was hand-painted with lusters, which were being reintroduced into commercial ceramics. Her patterns helped establish Wedgwood in the ornamental bone china market, and her influence on Wedgwood's production continued until 1929, parallel to the period when lusters enjoyed general popularity. By 1931, many of her wares, for which up to six firings were required, were withdrawn due to the overall downturn in demand. Wedgwood asked for her resignation in 1930.

In 1923 Victor *Skellern joined Wedgwood and was art director from 1934 to 1965. He sometimes collaborated with the technician/designer Norman Wilson, who developed the mat straw and green glazes for Keith *Murray's designs *c.* 1935. Skellern's personal design philosophy reflected the modern ethos to "interpret fundamentals in a humane manner." During his tenure at Wedgwood, designers who contributed to its output included the well-known Bloomsbury Group artists Duncan *Grant

and Vanessa *Bell, the artist/ engraver Eric *Ravilious and John *Skeaping, who was responsible for a series of animal figures. From 1933 to 1939, Murray made his mark as a Modernist; his distinctive designs remained in production until the late 1950s and are currently considered highly collectible.

Wedgwood, Star (Cicely; b. 1903). The daughter of Major Frank Wedgwood, chairman and managing director of *Wedgwood 1916–30, she studied briefly at the Royal College of Art in London in 1923, and while there admired the Chinese ceramics at the Victoria and Albert Museum; she went on to study at the Burslem College of Art. Her primary ceramics training, however, was under Alfred and Louise *Powell at Wedgwood's Etruria factory. The Powells, who espoused learning by doing, taught her the technique of underglaze painting. At a Grafton Galleries exhibition of new Wedgwood wares in 1936, six of her designs were featured (she was listed in the catalogue as one of the firm's principal designers, although her position there was never formalized). Her best-known designs include: *Stars*, white stars and gold on a dark-blue ground; *Lady Jane Grey*, a floral design in white and silver on grey; and *Eurydice*, with a hand-painted border of silver and green on a green ground.

Weller Pottery. Founded by Samuel Weller in 1882, this company originally produced flower pots and jardinières decorated with house paint before its entry into the art pottery field. With the acquisition of the Lohunda Pottery, Steubenville, Ohio, in 1895, three separate plants produced art pottery, garden ware, and utility ware. By 1910, Weller claimed that his pottery was the largest in the world, occupying 300,000 sq ft and employing 600 workers; 20 trained decorators were present during its peak in the 1920s. The company was the biggest competitor of *Roseville Pottery of Zanesville, Ohio. Its first popular artware line, *Louwelsa*, was slip-painted with backgrounds sometimes applied using an atomizer. Hand-decoration included fruits, flowers, or portraits (frequently of American Indians), and was derivative of *Rookwood Standard ware.

Art pottery production was expanded with the introduction of several prestige lines, such as *Dickens' Wares* or *III Dickens*, *Jap Birdimal* and *L'Art Nouveau*, which were designed by Frederick Hurten *Rhead: *III Dickens* replaced *II Dickens*, a more complex design, produced with high-gloss and light-mat grounds with portraits of Dickens characters (or other subjects) etched sgraffito-style in outline and filled in with bright colors. Rhead's more economical design featured an overall clear glaze, with the head of a Dickens character in white on a black cameo-type disc and a quotation from Dickens inscribed in white on another disc.

874

|

Wiener Werkstätte

In 1901, in order to compete with Roseville and J.B. Owens Pottery Co., another leading art pottery in Zanesville, Weller employed Jacques Sicard, a French potter, who created *Sicardo*, or *Sicardo Weller*, a line characterized by metallic luster designs on iridescent backgrounds. In 1904, *Aurelian*, a variant form of *Louwelsa*, was produced, the background color being applied by brush instead of an atomizer. *Aurelian*'s decoration was highly derivative of Rookwood Pottery's *Sea Green* ware. Weller also recruited the Japanese designer Gazo Fujiyama in 1906, and manufactured his *Fudzi* ware, (Fujiyama was also employed by Roseville, where his line was produced as *Fudji*).

Weller Pottery continued to introduce new lines, but after 1910 most were mass-produced. Yet, under John Lessell, art director from 1920 until 1924, two hand-decorated lines were introduced: *LaSa*, with an overglaze tree motif on a luster background of sky, water and land; and *Lamar*, an overglaze decorated ware with black trees on a deep-red ground. With the departure of Lessell and the death of Samuel Weller in 1925, development of art pottery ceased. The firm finally closed in 1949.

Wiener Werkstätte. Founded in 1903 by Josef *Hoffmann and Koloman *Moser, these artists' collaborative workshops evolved from the desire among artists of the Vienna Secession (founded, 1897, in revolt against tradition) to create modern forms that revealed existential truth. To accomplish their goal of *Gesamtkunstwerk*, integrating all the fine and applied arts into a single aesthetic statement within an architectural context, the members of the Wiener Werkstätte created everything from furniture and textiles, ceramics and glass, to costumes and bookbinding. A business associate, Fritz Waerndorfer, provided the financial backing for the workshops from 1903 to 1913. In the beginning, Hoffmann refused to accept artistic compromises in designing, which often meant that production costs bore no relationship to the realities of the marketplace.

Early on, overall production reflected contradictory viewpoints namely purist vs ornamental, the former manifested in a "severe," geometric style influenced by the ideas of Hoffmann. From 1910 until 1923 the workshops came under the directorship of Dagobert *Peche, whose flowing style was more overtly decorative and market driven. (Later, Hoffmann's style also evolved in a more ornamental way.) The second period, which coincides with the increased involvement of Peche is considered by some to be the decadent phase of the workshops, although many enduring objects were produced during this time.

At one time the workshops employed about 100 artists, mostly women, many of whom had attended the Vienna Kunstgewerbeschule. The proliferation of women throughout the workshops was partly due to the dearth of men available in the aftermath of World War I, but probably also resulted from the tradition of women working in the applied arts. In the workshops, all designers were afforded a great deal of artistic freedom. Chinaware was produced for the Wiener Werkstätte at the Josef Böck porcelain factory and glass by Bohemian glass manufacturers. Products of the Wiener Keramik, which was founded in 1906 by Michael *Powolny and Berthold *Löffler, were marketed through the Wiener Werkstätte. The Wiener Keramik merged in 1912/13 with Gmundner Keramik (founded in 1908 by Franz Schleiss) and Vereinigte Wiener Werkstätte, becoming Vereinigte Wiener und Gmundner Keramik. (In 1918 the firm became Gmundner Keramik GmbH.) There was a fertile exchange of personnel between the Vienna Kunstgewerbeschule and the various ceramic workshops associated with the Wiener Werkstätte.

The Austrian idea of *Gesamtkunstwerk*, which engendered many innovative designs by architects, artists, and designers became a model for many other groups and individuals around the world. A range of creative practitioners—from the *Czech Cubists, who produced a full range of useful objects, including ceramics, to the French couturier Paul Poiret, who opened his Atelier Martine in Paris after a visit to Vienna—were inspired by the example of the Wiener Werkstätte.

Wieselthier, Vally (Valerie; 1895–1945). At the Kunstgewerbeschule in Vienna during World War I, she was able to study with such eminent artists and designers as Josef *Hoffmann, Koloman *Moser, and Michael *Powolny. At the *Wiener Werkstätte, she was also influenced by Dagobert *Peche, creating designs for ceramics, glass, wallpaper, and textiles. In 1925, when she participated in the Paris Exposition, she won gold and silver medals. She developed a colorful, spontaneous style for figurative ceramics notable for their expressive modelling and painterly glaze effects. When a Wiener Werkstätte exhibition toured the USA in 1928, her ceramics were much admired. In 1932, she moved to the USA, where she was associated with the Contempora Gallery, New York, and designed for General Ceramics, New York, and Sebring Pottery Company, Ohio.

Though most of her work in America became rather sentimental, she will be remembered for her audacious, oversized "garden figures" composed of multiple, stacked parts. Characterized by a witty inventiveness, these were clearly conveyed the intention of their creator to be considered alongside other sculptors of her era.

Wilkinson, A.J., Ltd. The company was founded in Staffordshire by A.J. Wilkinson. After his death in 1894, his brother-in-law Arthur Shorter acquired

Winter, Thelma Frazier. *Night with Young Moon*, allegorical glazed earthenware group, 1938. H. 18½ in. (47.0 cm).

control. At that time, the company was known for producing glazed earthenware and traditionally designed tableware which showed the influence of *Art Nouveau. However, by the 1920s the taste for such traditional wares had waned, and the firm, then under the direction of Shorter's sons, began to experiment with new shapes and glazes. In 1929, the firm introduced *Bizarre* ware designed by Clarice *Cliff and produced at Newport Pottery, Burslem. This quickly became a household favorite, and an entire workshop was devoted exclusively to its production. In 1930, Cliff took over the firm's art direction, but demand for extravagant lines such as *Bizarre* waned with the Depression. By 1941, the *Bizarre* workshop had closed, and Wilkinson reverted to producing ceramics based on more traditional models.

Winter, Thelma Frazier (1903–77). One of the artists associated with R. Guy *Cowan, whose Pottery Studio was dedicated to the production of artistically praiseworthy, reasonably priced ceramics. Some of her work shows the influence of Viennese ceramics, which she came to by way of her husband Edward Winter and Viktor *Schreckengost (fellow Cowan artists who had studied in Vienna). Some of her expressively modelled heads and figures of the late 1930s have much in common with those of Vally *Wieselthier and Susi *Singer. During the 1940s, her imagery, which remained stylized, became highly colored with decorative subjects based on medieval court jesters, exemplified by *The Performers* (1949).

Wood & Sons. An English company with a history that dates back to the 18th century, when Ralph, Aaron, and Moses Wood joined forces to create Toby jugs and Staffordshire figures. The business became Wood & Son in 1865, producing primarily earthenware and ironstone bodies. (In 1907, the name was changed to Wood & Sons.) Feeling the pressure from Japanese and Czechoslovakian products during the 1920s and 1930s, the company began to employ in-house and freelance designers to introduce ideas. In 1920, it acquired the Crown Works, Burslem, to produce art wares, and next year added the Ellgreave Pottery to produce Charlotte *Rhead's designs.

Around 1931, Susie *Cooper became closely linked with the company. (Up to this point she had only acquired their ceramic blanks to decorate and sell under her own name.) In exchange for contemporary pattern designs, Harry Wood of H.J. Wood Ltd, a related family-owned company, agreed to produce four of Cooper's shapes in an ivory-bodied earthenware: *Kestrel* and *Curlew* (1932) and *Falcon* and *Spiral* (1937).

Charlotte Rhead, whose father Frederick Alfred Rhead (1857–1933) was art director of Wood & Sons from 1913 until his death, was employed to design a line of ornamental wares. Between 1913 and 1926, she designed a great variety of highly individual and influential patterns that used the technique known as tube-lining.

In 1954, the company began trading as Wood & Sons (Holdings) Ltd; during the 1980s, it passed out of family control, but the name was retained.

Wright, Frank Lloyd (1867–1959). As one of the leading architects in America, Wright was able to synthesize a variety of influences—the *Arts and Crafts Movement, Japonisme, Modernism—into an individualized style. He believed that every element of an interior should resonate with the whole, and thus he designed complementary furniture, lights, fittings for his buildings. He attempted ceramic design on only a few occasions. In fact, he wrote in 1928 that "We have little or nothing to say in the clay figure or pottery as a concrete expression of the ideal of beauty that is our own…The life that flowed into this channel in ancient times apparently now goes somewhere else." Wright is said to have produced at least one model for *Teco, and may have designed ceramic pieces for the Larkin Building in New York, but perhaps his most noted ceramics were porcelain dishes (designed in 1916) for the Imperial Hotel in Tokyo. The compass-drawn motif chosen by Wright as decoration for his hotel dinnerware—clean circles in red, yellow, and green outlined in black—evinced his freshly modern aesthetic.

Wright, Russel (1904–76). A noted American designer who had not only an aesthetic, but a purposeful philosophy that encompassed the rapid social changes of the interwar years, he believed that designs for tableware served the dual function of highlighting food and creating a mood for a meal. For him tableware was also part of an integrated environment that synthesized design with the concept of "modern living." Finally, he considered that tableware should be well designed, yet made in a cost-efficient manner, thus enabling it to be mass produced. He believed that good design was intertwined with a good "lifestyle." This kind of thinking ran parallel to the ideal of "social engineering" through design that had begun with the English *Arts and Crafts Movement. However, Machine Age designers saw technology and mass-production as useful allies and they readily embraced them to further their goals.

After earning a reputation during the 1930s with his innovative products, e.g. spun aluminum "stove-to-table wares", Wright conceived the design for *American Modern* tableware in 1937; this represented the practical fulfillment of his ideas about design and manufacturing, but another two years were to elapse before he found a manufacturer willing to produce the line. Finally, the near-bankrupt Steubenville Pottery brought out *American Modern*, which would

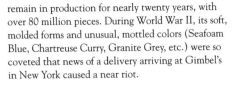

Wright, Russel. *American Modern* teapot, glazed earthenware, 1937. H. 7 in. (17.8 cm).

remain in production for nearly twenty years, with over 80 million pieces. During World War II, its soft, molded forms and unusual, mottled colors (Seafoam Blue, Chartreuse Curry, Granite Grey, etc.) were so coveted that news of a delivery arriving at Gimbel's in New York caused a near riot.

Z

Zaccagnini, Ugo (1868–1937). After working for *Richard-Ginori, he opened his own factory in Florence in the late 1880s. Until 1936, his company was called Ugo Zaccagnini e Figli, but in a reorganization the name was changed to Ceramiche Zaccagnini S.A. The business was run by Zaccagnini and members of his family, including his children Urbano, Pietro, Prisco, Adele, and Enrichetta. As a public company, Ceramiche Zaccagnini grew and began to export to the USA on a grand scale. During the 1920s, Gio *Ponti designed a number of pieces for the factory. In the 1940s, the firm was granted rights to make ceramic reproductions of *Disney cartoon characters. Fosco Martini, one of the better-known employees, was noted for his animal figures. Urbano Zaccagnini, besides helping to manage the business, produced terra cotta pieces. These sometimes appeared to be wrapped in rope, a *trompe-l'œil* effect made possible by clay's plastic nature.

Zeisel, Eva (*née* Polanyi Stricker; b. 1906). A precocious, prolific, and inspired Hungarian designer for industry active from the 1920s to the 1960s. Her work, taken as a whole, sets high standards for factory-made ceramics. Starting out as a painter, she quickly devoted herself to ceramics. After a brief apprenticeship with a Budapest potter, she opened her own pottery in 1925. Her earliest hand-thrown work reveals the influence of Hungarian folk pottery along with the witty stylization of *Wiener Werkstätte work. While managing her own studio, she also became a freelance designer for the Kispester Pottery in Budapest, producing tea sets and novelties which reflected the work of Viennese contemporaries. In 1927, she became a journeyman potter and designer, working briefly at the Hansa Kunstkeramik in Hamburg before moving to the Schramberger Majolika-Fabrik where, despite lack of experience, she was appointed designer.

She learned drafting on the spot, which she supplemented by making paper cutouts of her designs. (She continued this working method throughout her career.) Some of her early, austere work for Schramberg acknowledges the ideas of the Deutscher Werkbund and the *Bauhaus. Having attended the 1925 Paris Exposition, she was also aware of design trends in avant-garde movements. But her approach neither followed the latest fashion nor was it based on a strictly doctrinaire outlook. Zeisel allowed the

human experience to imbue her designs, which took into account both the consumer and the manufacturer, allowing human and animal contours to play an active role.

By 1930, she had moved to Berlin, where she designed for the conglomerate Christian Carstens Kommerz Gesellschaft. She abruptly left in 1932 to work as a "foreign expert" in the Soviet Union. Here, as Director of the China and Glass Industry of the Russian Republic, she designed everything from tableware to electric sockets and ceramic irons. She left the USSR in 1937 for Vienna, and married Hans Zeisel, a lawyer. In 1938, she emigrated to New York, where the focus of her career changed.

In 1939, she began teaching at Pratt Institute in Brooklyn, applying her prodigious talents to transforming the ceramics department from one that was craft-minded to one focused on the principles of design. Zeisel designed into the 1960s, primarily creating dinnerware patterns for Castleton, *Hall and *Red Wing. She returned to Hungary to design for Kispester Granit Porcelain Factory and for *Zsolnay in the 1980s. In 1992, a retrospective was organized by the Smithsonian Institution Traveling Exhibition Service and Le Château Dufresne, Musée des Arts Décoratifs de Montréal, the catalogue for which provides the basis for this biographical sketch.

Zell-Harmersbach, Steingutfabrik Georg Schmider. In 1820, Georg Schmider founded this company to produce tablewares in stoneware and porcelain, but the latter was discontinued in 1940. In the 1920s and 1930s, the factory produced stylish wares, some aerographed with varied, brightly colored concentric bands. This provided a less expensive means of decorating than hand-painting, which was popular at some other factories. Body shapes conformed to contemporary models, which displaced historical forms in favor of those based on aerodynamics or resulting from the combination of geometric shapes, particularly the half-circle and half-sphere.

Zen, Ceramiche. *See* Ceramiche Zen.

Zsolnay. Hungarian factory, renowned for its complex glazes, founded by Ignaz Zsolnay in 1862 in Pécs. By 1865 his brother, Vilmos, controlled the factory. Zsolnay made traditional domestic pottery, along with decorative pieces based on Persian and Turkish models. From 1893 to 1910, Vinsce Wartha (1844–1914) ran an experimental studio devoted to glazes. He developed a high-fired, iridescent red glaze, *Eosin*, which was first exhibited in Vienna in 1899–1900. Sometimes the glaze was applied over etched decorative motifs, and then further highlighted with gold luster. Some of the complex *Eosin*-decorated pieces are similar to Hispano-Moresque lusterwares. The factory is still in operation.

Zsolnay

LIST OF COLOR PLATES AND PHOTOGRAPHIC SOURCES

Abbreviations: D. = diameter; H. = height; L. = length; W. = width.

1. Floor vase, Gustav Heinkel, 1930; inscribed "GH". H. 27 in. (68.5 cm).
2. Teapot, Margarete Friedländer-Wildenhain, 1930. H. 5 in. (12.7 cm).
3. Teapot, sugar bowl, and creamer, Eva Stricker, late 1920s. H. of teapot 5¾ in. (14.8 cm).
4. Teapot, Grete Heymann-Marks, 1930. D. 6¾ in. (17.1 cm).
5. *Korean Dancer*, Constantin Holzer-Defanti, Rosenthal, 1919. H. 15½ in. (40.0 cm).
6. "Madeleine" coffee service, Rosenthal, c.1927–34. H. of pot 9½ in. (24.0 cm).
7. Coffee service, Germany, n.d. H. of pot 7 in. (17.8 cm).
8. Tea caddy, Paul Speck, c.1926. H. 5 in. (12.7 cm).
9. Collared vessel, Grete Heymann-Marks, 1920s. H. 4⅞ in. (12.4 cm).
10. Plate with decoration by Willi Ohler, c.1920s; D. 6⅞ in. (17.5 cm).
11. Footed box, decoration by Hermann Volmar, 1920s/30s. H. 3¾ in. (9.5 cm).
12. Bottle vase, Germany, n.d. H. 8½ in. (21.6 cm).
13. Pitcher, Werner Burri, c.1927–30. H. 11 in. (27.9 cm).
14. Small pitcher, Theodor Bogler, c.1925–26. H. 5½ in. (14.0 cm).
15. Tea caddy, Paul Speck, c.1926.
16. Coffee pot, Ursula Fesca, 1935.
17. Tea set, Rosenthal, 1930s. H. of teapot 5⅝ in. (14.3 cm).
18. Flared vase attributed to Carstens, 1920s/30s. H. 5⅝ in. (14.3 cm).
19. Small luster-decorated vase, 1920s; stamped (in green) "Weimar Germany" with shield. H. 4½ in. (11.4 cm).
20. Vase, Gustav Heinkel, c.1925–30. H. 16 in. (40.7 cm).
21. Head, Gerhard Marcks, c.1923.
22. Stoneware vases, Reinhold & Co., Bunzlau, 1930.
23. Bread box, Villeroy & Boch. H. 6 in. (15.2 cm).
24. Pot-pourri vase, Vally Wieselthier, Wiener Werkstätte, c.1922–28. H. 14 in. (35.6 cm).
25. Vase designed by Koloman Moser, 1900. H. 8¾ in. (22.1 cm).
26. Vase, Hilda Jesser, Wiener Werkstätte. H. 9¼ in. (23.5 cm).
27. Tea service designed by Josef Hoffmann, Wiener Porzellan-Manufaktur Augarten, c.1928.
28. Design for a coffee pot, Vally Wieselthier, before 1929.
29. Box and vase, F. von Zülow, Wiener Porzellan-Manufaktur Augarten, 1925.
30. Hand-painted figures, Berthold Löffler, Wiener Keramik, c.1905. H of gnome 5⅛ in. (13.0 cm).
32. Bookend, 1930s; impressed "Bimini" with potted plant. H. 7 in. (17.8 cm).
33, 34. Seated and kneeling figures, Susi Singer, 1920s. H. 7¼ and 7 in. (18.4 and 17.8 cm).
35. Bottle vase with luster decoration, Zsolnay, 1920s. H. 18 in. (46.0 cm).
36, 37. Plates with decoration designed by M.M. Adamovich, State Porcelain Factory, Petrograd, 1919 and 1922.
38. Plate decorated with slogan, probably State Porcelain Factory, Petrograd, 1919. D. 9⅝ in. (24.5 cm).
39. Vase, Czechoslavakia, n.d. H. 8¾ in. (21.6 cm).
40. Coffee set, after 1918; marks (stamped) "M, Z, Czechoslovakia" and birdman device. H. of pot 9 in. (22.9 cm).
41. Coffee set, after 1922; marks (stamped) "Pulz, Luna Made in Czechoslovakia." H. of pot 8⅝ in. (21.9 cm).
42. Fish, c.1930, maker unknown.
43. Covered box, designed by Pavel Janák, decorated by František Kysela, 1914. H. 4½ in. (11.6 cm).
44. Cup and saucer, c.1925–40; stamped "Shelley, England." D. of saucer 5½ in. (14.0 cm).
45. "Tea-for-two" set, c.1930; marks (on teapot) "SHELLEY/ENGLAND/11742e/RD2." W. of teapot 8¼ in. (20.9 cm).
46. Demitasse set, c.1929–39; (black decal) "Bizarre by Clarice Cliff, hand painted, Newport Pottery, England." H. of coffee pot 6¾ in. (17.2 cm).
47. Globular jug, 1930s; marks (gold decal) "Jewel Ware, British Made" and (impressed) "No. 222 Made in England." H. 7⅛ in. (18.1 cm).
48, 50. Animal figures modelled by John Skeaping, 1927 and later; (printed in blue) "WEDGWOOD ETRURIA ENGLAND, MADE IN ENGLAND." H. of polar bear 7⅛ in. (18.4 cm).
49. "Toucans," Adrian Paul Allison, c.1930. H. 11¼ in. (28.6 cm).
51. Drawing by Louis Wain, n.d.
52. Figures based on designs by Louis Wain, date and maker unknown.
53. Vases designed by Keith Murray, Wedgwood, 1930s.
54. Plate, creamer, and teapot, A.J. Wilkinson Ltd, c.1930.
55. Cup, saucer, and plate, Shelley Potteries, 1930.
56, 57. "Kestrel" coffee set and teapot, Susie Cooper, 1930s.
58. Group of hand-painted *Bizarre*/"Fantasque" pieces by Clarice Cliff, c.1930. D. of plate 9½ in. (23.8 cm).
59. Milk jug by Clarice Cliff, c.1925–35; "Fantasque"/*Bizarre* logo.
60. Nursery teapot designed by Mabel Lucie Attwell, 1926; stamped "Shelley England." H. 5 in. (12.7 cm).
61. Vase with flanged handles, Royal Art Pottery, 1930s. H. 9⅛ in. (23.5 cm).
62. "Moon and Mountain" tea set, Susie Cooper, c.1930. D. of plate 7⅛ in. (17.8 cm).
63. "Machine Age" toast rack, c.1925 or later; stamp "Carlton Ware, Made in England, 'trademark'." L. 6¼ in. (15.9 cm).
64. "Casino" casserole, Royal Doulton, 1932 or later. D. 10½ in. (26.7 cm).
65. Pyramidal jug, c.1934–50; stamped "Royal Winton, Grimwades, England." H. 9½ in. (24.2 cm).
66. Cube tea set, R.C. Johnson, George Clews & Co., designed 1916.
67. Pieces by Charlotte Rhead, A.E. Richardson & Co., 1930s.
68. Charger, Charlotte Rhead, 1930s.
69. "Circus" plate, designed by Dame Laura Knight, c.1932–34. D. 10¾ in. (27.5 cm).
70. "Harvest" vase with decoration after Frank Brangwyn, Royal Doulton, c.1935. H. 7 in. (17.8 cm).
71. Vases by William Howson Taylor, Ruskin Pottery Workshop, 1924/1933.
72. Footed bowl, Claude Lévy, 1920s; marks "Primavera France" and artist's signature. H. 7½ in. (17.1 cm).
73. Bulbous bottle, Jean Mayodon, n.d. H. 13½ in. (27.3 cm).
74. Melon-shaped vase, Raoul Lachenal, 1920s. H. 10¾ in. (27.3 cm).
75. Tapering vase, Félix Massoul, c.1920–25. H. 11¼ in. (28.6 cm).
76. Teapot, Raoul Lachenal, 1920s/30s. H. 5½ in. (13.3 cm).
77. Group of vases, Raoul Lachenal, 1920s/40s. H. (yellow, blue) 9⅛ in. (23.2 cm), (red) 7¼ in. (18.4 cm).
78. Charger, Raoul Lachenal, 1920s/30s; signed "Lachenal unique." D. 17¾ in. (37.5 cm).
79, 80. Design for bowl by Jacques-Emile Ruhlmann, and bowl, Sèvres, 1932. H. of vase 8 in. (20.5 cm).
81. Monumental vase, Sèvres, 1929; signed "L. Trager d'après Beaumont." H. 24 in. (61 cm).
82. Footed bowl, Jean Mayodon, Sèvres, n.d.; mark "JM, Sèvres." H. 11½ in. (28.8 cm).
83. Stoneware vase, Edouard Cazaux, c.1925. H. 26¾ in. (68.0 cm).
84. Bottle, René Buthaud, c.1918–25. H. 11 in. (28.0 cm).
85. Vase with lug handles, René Buthaud, 1925. H. 11⅜ in. (29.0 cm).
86. *L'Adieu au Voyageur*, designed 1930 by Jean Debarre, Sèvres, 1933. H. 19⅝ in. (49.8 cm).
87. Candelabrum, Robert Lallemant, 1920s; signed. H. 7⅞ in. (20.0 cm).
88. *St George and the Dragon*, Fau & Gaillard, c.1924.
89. Plates with decoration designed by Jean Luce, 1937.

90. Molded vase, Robert Lallemant, c.1925–30. H. 8½ in. (21.6 cm).

91. Charger, Anne-Marie Fontaine, Sèvres, 1927. D. 16⅛ in. (41.0 cm).

92. Large charger, R. Chevallier, Longwy, 1920s. D. 27 in. (68.2 cm).

93. Plates, Jean Luce, 1923. D. 8⅛ in. (20.5 cm).

94. Large charger, André Metthey, c.1917–19. D. 23⅛ in. (59.0 cm).

95. Footed vase, Frédéric Kiefer, 1930s. H. 8¾ in. (22.3 cm).

96. Plate, Emile Decœur, 1920s/30s. D. 10⅛ in. (25.8 cm).

97. Globular vessel, Auguste Delaherche, n.d. H. 7 in. (17.7 cm).

98. Small vase, Georges Serré, 1932; signed "GS." H. 6⅞ in. (17.2 cm).

99. Bowl, Maurice Gensoli, n.d. D. 14 in. (35.6 cm).

100. Vase, Odetta, n.d.; mark "HB, Quimper, Odetta." H. 11½ in. (29.1 cm).

101. Shallow bowl, Séraphin Soud-binine, 1930s. D. 9 in. (22.9 cm).

102. Lidded box, Marcel Guillemard, c.1930. H. 8 in. (20.3 cm).

103. Globular vase, René Buthaud, c.1925–29. H. 5 in. (12.9 cm).

104. Tea set, France, 1930s. Marks: cup and saucer stamped "Walt Disney," sugar bowl with decals "Mickey Mouse" and "Marque Déposée, Walt Disney SA."

105. Pair of vases, Longwy, n.d.

106. Consommé cup and saucer, Gien (Loiret), after 1928.

107. Creamer and teapot, 1920s; teapot stamped "Robj, Paris, importé du Luxembourg, E55."

108. Stoneware charger, Charles Catteau, Boch Frères Keramis (design no. 2282), 1937–39; signed "B.F.K. Ch. Catteau" and stamped "Keramis. Made in Belgium" with logo. D. 14 in. (21.6 cm).

109. Stoneware vase, Charles Catteau, Boch Frères Keramis, 1920s/30s. H. 8½ in. (21.6 cm).

110. Stoneware vase, Charles Catteau, Boch Frères Keramis (design no. 1056), c.1925–26. Marks: (painted) "B.F.K. Ch. Catteau" and (incised) 'Grès, 961, Keram." H. 16 in. (40.7 cm).

111. Earthenware vase by Charles Catteau, Boch Frères Keramis, 1925. Marks "1023" and "Keramis. Made in Belgium." H. 10¼ in. (25.6 cm).

112. Three-tiered vessel, Charles Catteau, Boch Frères Keramis, n.d. Marks: (impressed) "1086," (painted) "D1301," and stamped logo "Keramis. Made in Belgium." H. 9 in. (22.9 cm).

113. Earthenware vase with floral decoration, Charles Catteau, 1928. Marks: "908"[?] and "D.1208" and logo stamped in green "Boch Frères. Made in Belgium." H. 11½ in. (28.8 cm).

114. Group of decorated vases, Charles Catteau, Boch Frères Keramis, 1920s. H. of middle vase 16⅛ in. (40.3 cm).

115. Earthenware pitcher, N.V. Kennemer Pottery, c.1930. H. 6½ in. (16.5 cm).

116. Pieces from "Thea" tea service, G.M.E. Bellefroid, De Sphinx, 1935. H. of teapot 5 in. (12.7 cm).

117. *Argenta* urn, W. Kåge, Gustavsberg, c.1928–30. H. 12 in. (30.4 cm).

118. *Argenta* chimerical figure, Wilhelm Kåge, Gustavsberg, c.1939; impressed factory mark incorporates the name Kåge. H. 9 in. (22.9 cm).

119. Large urn, Kähler Keramik, before 1917. H. (approx.) 19 in. (48.2 cm).

120. Porcelain centerpiece, Royal Copenhagen, 1930. L. 17¼ in. (43.7 cm).

121. Male head with mount, Jais Nielsen, Royal Copenhagen, 1930. Marks: "Jais" and factory "waves." H. of head 8¾ in. (22.2 cm).

122. Stoneware covered jug, Jais Nielsen, Royal Copenhagen, 1925. Marks: "Jais" with factory mark and "20101." H. 6½ in. (16.5 cm).

123. Earthenware vase, Friedl Kjellberg, Arabia, 1933. H. 9 in. (23.0 cm).

124. Porcelain bowl, Friedl Kjellberg, Arabia, 1930s. H. 5 in. (12.5 cm).

125. Covered jar, Kähler Keramik, before 1917. H. 9⅞ in. (25.0 cm).

126. Covered jar with fish finial, Greta-Lisa Jäderholm-Snellman, Arabia, 1930s.

127. Globular vase designed by Gio Ponti, made by Ugo Zaccagnini, 1927. H. 8½ in. (21.5 cm).

128, 129. Monumental maiolica urns, designed by Gio Ponti, Richard-Ginori, c.1923–30. H. 31⅞ in. (81.0 cm).

130. Pair of lamp-bases, designed by Gio Ponti, Richard-Ginori, 1920s. H. 8¼ in. (21.0 cm).

131. Covered box, designed by Gio Ponti, Richard-Ginori, 1920s.

132. Footed vase, designed by Gio Ponti, Richard-Ginori, 1923. H. 13½ in. (34.3 cm).

133. Globular vase, Antonio Zen, Nove, 1920s. H. 9⅜ in. (28.8 cm).

134. Maiolica plate, Amerigo Lunghi, U. Grazia, Deruta, 1924; signed and dated. D. 9 in. (23.0 cm).

135. Maiolica vase, Gabriele Bicchioni, Maioliche Deruta e CIMA, 1935. H. 11¾ in. (30.0 cm).

136. Maiolica vase, Ezio Cocchioni, Maioliche Deruta e CIMA, 1935. H. 19 in. (48.0 cm).

137. Coffee service, B.M.C., c.1932–34. H. of coffee pot 3½ in. (8.9 cm).

138. Terra cotta decanter, designed by N. Diulgheroff, made by Torido Mazzotti, c.1935–37. H. 7½ in. (19.0 cm).

139. *Aerovaso*, Fillia, c.1932. H. 7 in. (18.0 cm).

140. Vase, Farfa/Tullio d'Albisola, c.1931–32. H. 10½ in. (26.0 cm).

141. *Bullovaso*, Farfa/G. Mazzotti, c.1931–32. H. 10¾ in. (27.5 cm).

142. Teapot, Tullio d'Albisola, c.1930. H. 4⅜ in. (11.0 cm).

143. Figures of the Magi, Dino Gambetti and Tullio d'Albisola, 1930. H. (approx.) 8¼ in. (21.0 cm).

144. Vase in the form of a cyclist, G.M. Anselmo, c.1937–38.

145. Figure with cat, Sandro Vacchetti, Essevi, 1936. H. 16¼ in. (41.0 cm).

146. Figure of a clown, A.C.J. Gaudenzi, 1928. H. 5 in. (12.7 cm).

147. Earthenware pig, Carl Walters, c.1934. H. 8⅛ in. (20.6 cm).

148. Earthenware vessel, Henry Varnum Poor, 1920s; signed. H. 4½ in. (11.4 cm).

149. Plate with still-life decoration, Henry Varnum Poor, 1933. D. (approx.) 12 in. (30.5 cm).

150. Footed vessel, Henry Varnum Poor, 1920s; mark "HVP." H. 9½ in. (24.0 cm).

151. Three-handled urn, Fulper Pottery Co., 1920s. H. 13⅛ in. (33.3 cm).

152. Vase, Lorinda Epply, Rookwood Pottery, 1931; signed with monogram. H. 7 in. (17.2 cm).

153. Hunt plate, Viktor Schreckengost, c.1930–35. D. 11⅜ in. (29.0 cm).

154, 155. Globular vase, Waylande Gregory, 1920s. H. 8¼ in. (21.0 cm).

156. Tea service designed by J. Martin Stangl, Fulper Pottery Co., c.1928–29. H. of teapot 7⅞ in. (20.0 cm).

157. Plate and cup, Viktor Schreckengost, 1934.

158. *American Modern* dinnerware, Russel Wright, Steubenville Pottery, from 1939. D. of plate 10 in. (25.5 cm).

159. *Circle Vase*, Trenton Potteries, 1930s. H. 8⅜ in. (21.3 cm).

160. *Automobile* teapot, Hall China Co., c.1940. H. 5 in. (12.7 cm).

161. Examples of *Fiesta Ware*, Frederick H. Rhead, Homer Laughlin Co., 1936.

162. Slip-cast pitcher, Hall China Co., c.1923–39. H. 7½ in. (19.1 cm).

163. *Cubist Cat*, Shearwater Pottery, 1928. H. 12¼ in. (31.1 cm).

164. *Ruffle pot*, J.A. Bauer Pottery, 1930s. H. 5⅞ in. (14.6 cm).

165. *Futura* vase, Roseville Pottery, 1928.

166. Earthenware vase, R. Guy Cowan, c.1917. H. 7½ in. (18.7 cm).

167. Ziggurat vase, USA, 1930s. H. 9 in. (22.9 cm).

168. Stoneware vase, Maija Grotell, c.1939. H. 14 in. (35.6 cm).

169. Globular vase, Richard O. Hummel, 1930. H. 8 in. (20.3 cm).

170. Turquoise vessel, Arthur E. Baggs, 1935. H. 7⅝ in. (19.4 cm).

171. Footed bowl, Leon Volkmar, 1920s. H. (approx.) 6½ in. (16.5 cm).

172. "Jazz Age" punch bowl, Viktor Schreckengost, 1931. H. 8 in. (20.5 cm).

173. *Bird and Wave*, Alexander Blazys, c.1929. H. 15 in. (38.1 cm).

174. *Mother and Child*, Karoly Fülöp, 1930s; signed. H. 24 in. (61 cm).

175. Plate, Thelma Frazier Winter, 1931.

176. Charger, Wilhelm Hunt Diederich, 1920s. D. (approx.) 15 in. (38.0 cm).

177. Plate, Henry Varnum Poor, 1931. D. 12 in. (30.5 cm).

178. Charger, Viktor Schreckengost, 1931. D. 16¾ in. (42.5 cm).

179. Boudoir lamp/vase, Frank Graham Holmes, Lenox China Co., c.1928.

180. *Madonna*, Margaret Postgate, 1929. H. 7⅛ in. (18.1 cm).

181. *Europa*, Paul Manship, c.1930. H. 17 in. (44.4 cm).

182. *Sailing Ship*, Fulper Pottery Co., c.1920–25. H. 12¾ in. (32.5 cm).

183, 184. *Antinea* and *Introspection*, A. Drexel Jacobson, c.1929. H. 13¼ in. (33.7 cm) and 8⅜ in. (21.2 cm).

185. Head, Waylande Gregory, 1928; (incised on neck) "W Gregory." H. 14½ in. (37.0 cm).

186. Salt and pepper shakers, creamer, and sugar bowl, Japan, 1920s/30s. H. of creamer and bowl 3 in. (7.8 cm).

187. Creamer, sugar bowl, tray, Japan, after 1921. L. of tray 7½ in. (19.0 cm).

188. Owl pitcher, Japan, after 1921. H. 4⅛ in. (10.5 cm).

189. Bird pitcher, Japan, after 1921. H. 4½ in. (11.5 cm).

190. Vases, Japan, 1920s/30s. H. 6⅞ in. (17.5 cm) and 4 in. (10.1 cm).

191. Novelty cat teapot, Japan, c.1935. H. 5 in. (12.7 cm).

192. "Jewels" bowl, Noritake, c.1922–29. D. 8½ in. (21.6 cm).

193. "Alexandra Pierret" figure, Noritake, 1920s/30s.

194. "Arabella" covered box, Noritake, c.1922–29. H. 4¾ in. (12.1 cm).

195. Sugar bowl and creamer, Noritake, 1920s. H. of bowl 3¼ in. (8.3 cm).

196. Tea set with tray, Japan, 1930s. W. of tray 8¾ in. (22.1 cm).

197. Seven-chambered vase, Japan, after 1921. H. 6¼ in. (15.9 cm).

198. Footed plates, Japan, 1920s/30s. D. 7¼ in. (18.1 cm).

199. Rectangular vase, Kent Art Ware, after 1921. H. 8½ in. (21.6 cm).

200. Tableware for the Imperial Hotel, Tokyo, Frank Lloyd Wright, c.1922.

201. "White Cap" plate, Noritake, c.1922–29. D. 6¼ in. (15.8 cm).

Photographic sources

Courtesy, Arabia Museum, Helsinki, Finland: pls. 123, 124, 126.

Courtesy, Galerie L'Arc en Seine, Paris: pl. 83.

Art Resource, New York (photo Erich Lessing): pl. 29.

Bandol Collection, Merion, PA (photos John White): pls. 74, 76, 77, 78, 105.

Courtesy, Chris Beetles Ltd, London: pls. 51, 52.

Collection of Dawn Bennett and Martin Davidson, New York City (photos John White): pls. 108, 110.

Courtesy, Carole Berk, Bethesda, MD: pls. 53, 67, 68.

Courtesy, Bröhan-Museum, Berlin: pls. 16, 22; pages 2, 138, 170 (below), 178.

Brooklyn Museum, New York: pls. 158 (gifts of Russel Wright, Paul F. Walter, and Ina and Andrew Feuerstein; photo Schecter Lee), 169 (H. Randolph Lever Fund, 72.40.25).

Collection of Michael Cardew: page 27 (above; photo Garth Clark).

Collection Cardinaël-Morel, Paris: page 143.

Courtesy, Ceramic Arts Foundation (formerly ICH), New York City: pls. 42, 50, 54, 55, 66 (photo John White), 70, 99, 115, 139, 142, 143, 144, 146, 154, 149 (above), 165, 168; pages 18 (photo Rose Krebs), 130, 135 (below), 141 (above and below), 168 (below), 175, 183.

Courtesy, Linda Cheverton Art & Antiques, Colebrook, CT: pl. 56.

Courtesy, Christie's, New York: pls. 131, 200; pages 156, 172.

Garth Clark Gallery, New York: pl. 177 (photo John White).

Cleveland Institute of Art, Cleveland, OH: page 144, 148 (reproducd by courtesy of Edris Eckhardt).

Cooper-Hewitt, National Design Museum, Smithsonian Inst./Art Resource, New York: pls. 88 (Gift of Stanley Siegel, 1975-32-4), 89 (Gift of James M. Osborn, 1969-97-14; photo John Parnell).

Courtesy, Cowan Pottery Museum, Rocky River Public Library, OH: pls. 166, 172, 173, 180, 181, 183/184 (photo Larry L. Peltz); page 137 (below).

Cranbrook Academy of Art Museum: page 152 (below).

Courtesy, Richard Dennis Publications: pl. 48; pages 160 (above), 167 (below).

Detroit Institute of Arts: pl. 149.

Collection of R.A. Ellison (photos John White): pls. 71, 73, 84, 95, 97, 101, 150, 151, 155, 170, 171, 182.

Courtesy, Elvehjem Museum of Art, (Ludmilla M. Shapiro Collection), Madison, WI: page 17.

Everson Museum of Art, Syracuse, N.Y.: pages 152 (above), 170 (above; photo Garth Clark), 182 (photo Garth Clark).

Courtesy, Barry Friedman Ltd, New York: pls. 14, 15; pages 134, 159, 167 (above).

Courtesy, U. Grazia, Deruta, Italy: pls. 134, 135, 136.

Courtesy, Edward Hallam, Epsom, Surrey: page 133.

Courtesy, Homer Laughlin Company (photos Michael Keller): pl. 161; page 169 (below).

Collection of John Innes (photos Billy Cunningham): pls. 111, 112, 113, 114.

Courtesy, Michael Kizhner Fine Art, Los Angeles, CA: pl. 174.

Courtesy, Ken Kolski: pl. 152.

Lenox China and Crystal, Lawrenceville, N.J.: pl. 179.

Courtesy, Lomonosov Porcelain Factory Museum, St Petersburg: page 16 (below).

Collection of John Loring, New York (photos Billy Cunningham): pls. 58, 62, 82, 98, 133, 148.

Collection of Todd Marks (photos John White): pls. 4, 8, 9, 10, 11, 18.

Collection of Esa Mazzotti, Albisola Marina, Italy: pls. 140, 141; page 164 (above).

Courtesy, Giuseppe Mazzotti, Albisola Marina, Italy: page 163 (above).

Courtesy, Galerie Metropol, Vienna: pls. 25, 27 (collection of Dr E.P.), 30, 31.

The Metropolitan Museum of Art, New York: pages 136 (Purchase 1929, Edward C. Moore, Jr, Gift), 146, 168 (above; Purchase, Emilio Ambasz Gift, 1990), 171 (below; Edward C. Moore, Jr, Gift, 1923).

Courtesy, Minton Museum, Royal Doulton Tableware Ltd, Stoke-on-Trent: page 153 (bottom), 163 (below), 179 (below).

Courtesy, Dr Erwin Müller: page 173 (above).

Musée des Arts Décoratifs, Paris: pls. 85, 93, 106; pages 14 (top), 161 (below), 174 (above).

Museo delle Porcellane di Doccia, Sesto Fiorentino, Florence (photos Jan Axel): pls. 128, 129.

Museum of Decorative Arts, Moscow: page 177 (below).

Museum of Decorative Arts, Prague: pl. 43.

The Museum of Modern Art, New York: page 129.

Museum voor Hedendaagse Kunst, Het Kruithuis, 's-Hertogenbosch, The Netherlands: pl. 116.

Courtesy, Musumeci Editore, Quart (Aosta), Italy: pls. 137, 145; page 171 (above).

Courtesy, Lillian Nassau Ltd, New York (photos John White): pls. 24, 26, 35, 72, 100, 120, 153, 185.

Newark Museum of Art, Newark, N.J. (photos Sarah Wells): pages 149 (below; purchase 1980, Sophronia Anderson Bequest Fund), 169 (above; purchase 1971, Thomas L. Raymond Bequest Fund).

Collection of Norwest Corporation, Minneapolis, MN: pls. 1, 2, 45, 64, 80, 90, 102; pages 13 (above and below), 158 (above), 158.

Courtesy, Österreichisches Museum für angewandte Kunst, Vienna: pl. 28; pages 14 (center; photo Ludwig Neustifter), 15.

Courtesy, Le Pavillon de Sèvres, London; pls. 79, 81, 91.

Private collections: (photo Dennis Buck) page 173 (below); pl. 61 (photo courtesy, Ceramic Arts Foundation); page 154 (photo Jane Courtney Frisse); pls. 191, 198 (photos John White).

Private collection, New York (photos John White): pls. 3, 17, 19, 39, 40, 41, 44, 46, 47, 57, 59, 63, 65, 87, 107, 167, 186, 187, 188, 189, 190, 195, 197, 199.

Private collection, Ohio (photo Christina Corsiglia): pl. 175.

Courtesy, Rosenthal AG, Selb, Germany: pls. 5, 6.

Collection of Charles Sanna, New York; courtesy, Cynthia Beneduce and Brian Windsor (photo John White): pl. 104.

By permission of Viktor Schreckengost: pls. 157, 178 (photo courtesy, Christina Corsiglia).

Collection of Judith and Martin Schwartz, New York: pls. 192, 193, 194, 201.

Collection of Jerome and Patricia Shaw, Southfield, Michigan: pls. 13, 21, 32, 69, 75, 117, 118, 147; (photos Joseph Somers and Anna Lopez-Somers) pls. 20, 23, 132, 138, 176; pages 137 (above), 140.

Courtesy, Fred Silberman & Co., New York City: pls, 7, 33.

Collection of Roy Silverman, New York City (photos John White): pls. 92, 94, 96, 103, 121, 122, 127.

Courtesy, Sotheby's, London: pl. 86.

Courtesy, Sotheby's Belgravia, London: pages 150, 161 (above), 174 (below), 179 (above).

Courtesy, Sotheby's, New York: page 20 (above).

Courtesy, Staatliche Porzellan-Manufaktur, Berlin: page 166.

Courtesy, State Historical Museum, Moscow: pl. 38.

Collection of William Strauss (photo John White): pl. 160.

SÚPPO Archive, Štenc Collection, Prague: page 157.

Collection of Edward Thorp, New York (photos John White): pls. 34, 109, 119, 125, 130.

Courtesy of the Board of Trustees of the Victoria and Albert Museum, London: pages 16 (above), 20 (below), 22, 131 (below), 135 (above), 151 (above; photo Garth Clark), 153 (top).

Walker Art Gallery, Liverpool: page 27 (below).

Collection of Arnold and Susan Wechsler, New York City (photos John White): pls. 12, 60, 159, 162, 164, 196.

Courtesy, the Trustees of the Wedgwood Museum, Barlaston, Staffordshire: pages 177 (above), 180 (above and below), 181.

Courtesy, the Wolfsonian Foundation, Miami Beach, Florida, and Genoa, Italy: pls. 49, 156; (the Mitchell Wolfson, Jr, Collection) 36, 37, 163; page 29.

Courtesy, Zabriskie Gallery, New York City: pages 131, 165 (photo William Suttle).

GLOSSARY

This glossary includes definitions of terms relating to ceramics in general, as well as techniques, materials, etc. which are of particular interest in the context of the interwar years. Descriptive information, when appropriate for illuminating the definitions, refers to designers or makers in the A–Z reference section; such references are indicated by an asterisk, as are terms of special interest which are defined in the glossary itself.

aerographing Applying color to ceramic wares by means of an airbrush or spray gun, sometimes employed with stencils cut in decorative patterns. The Italian Futurists employed *aeropittura* ("air painting") to convey the sensation of speed— the by-product of new technologies developed during the first decades of the 20th century. The technique was used by Giuseppe *Galvani to depict a leaping deer, and by Gio *Ponti to show an early propeller-driven plane looping-the-loop.

banding A technique by which concentric bands or stripes of color are applied by centering *blanks on a banding wheel (turntable) while holding against it a natural bristle brush (known in Great Britain as a "pencil") previously dipped in glaze; bands may be wide or narrow, shaded or flat, or wash banded. In England skilled exponents were called "banders." Many of Susie *Cooper's designs used banded decoration. Theodor *Bogler of the Bauhaus also used decorative stripes and bands.

blanks Undecorated, unglazed wares. In Soviet Russia, blanks from the former Imperial Porcelain Factory were painted with *agitprop* slogans promoting socialist ideals. In England, they were bought in quantity by firms such as A.E. *Gray & Co. of Stoke-on-Trent, which specialized in decoration, but had no production facilities.

body The central portion of a ceramic vessel, as distinct from ancillary parts such as its foot, neck, collar, spout, or handle. See also *clay body*.

bone china (*china*) During the search for true, Oriental porcelain in Europe, a clay body fritted with animal bone ash, was used to permit a lower temperature for firing than that required for porcelain. Although bone ash is burned out during firing, it lends bone china the translucent quality of porcelain. Because the clay is not plastic enough to be hand-thrown or modelled, bone china is most often slip-cast (*casting).

casting, slip-casting A technique used to form wares by filling plaster molds with *slip. The highly porous molds draw excess water from the slip, thereby "setting-up" or hardening it into the shape imposed by the mold. Slip-casting is one of the principal techniques used in the mass-production of ceramics; it makes possible serial repetition of forms and the production of uniform parts such as handles and spouts that cannot be formed on a wheel.

ceramic (adj.) Made of formed and hardened clay (in its broadest meaning, the term describes any nonmetallic mineral, including clay, glass, brick, and vitreous enamels, which can be hardened by exposure to high temperatures).

ceramics A generic term incorporating a seemingly infinite range of domestic, ornamental, sculptural, architectural, sanitary, and technical wares made from fired clay.

china see *bone china*

clay body (*body*) A homogeneous blend of clays and other constituents from which *ceramics are formed, principally *earthenware, *stoneware, and *porcelain.

crackle, craquelure (French) A decorative treatment characterized by all-over hairline cracks in a *glaze surface. Probably originating as a chance firing defect, and exported as early as the Song Dynasty (960–1280) by combining a *clay body and a *glaze with different rates of thermal expansion and contraction during firing and cooling, thereby causing a "bad fit." The resulting random hairline cracks were accentuated by rubbing ink or pigment into them, the excess being wiped away. (When unintended, the same effect is called "crazing," and is considered an undesirable feature.) René *Buthaud used *craquelure* to great effect in both figurative and abstract decoration.

earthenware A low-fired (under 1100° C), porous clay body that is impervious to liquids only if glazed; common examples are *terra cotta and *whiteware.

enamel (*China paint*), *émail* (French) Pigments derived from metallic oxides which are applied as decoration over a fired *glaze, the object then being refired to fix the colors. The lush, varied palette available using enamels facilitates the creation of intricate designs which sometimes mimic *cloisonné* enamelling on metal. Enamels remain on the glaze surface as they are not fired at a temperature high enough to fuse with it. Charles *Catteau, who was artistic director of *Böch Frères Keramis, created a seemingly infinite number of imaginative designs using polychrome enamel decoration.

engine-turned decoration, guillochage (French) Incised patterns made on unfired, *leather-hard ceramics, by using an engine-turning lathe. The technique was developed by Josiah *Wedgwood in Staffordshire from 1763, when he acquired an engine-turning lathe, capable of producing many patterns. Keith *Murray revived the visual effect of such decoration in some of his molded and wheel-thrown designs for *Wedgwood during the 1930s, using concentric, incised lines and graduated bands or steps as symbols of the machine age and modernity.

faience, faïence (French), *Fayence* (German) Decorated tin-glazed *earthenware. The English term, which is derived from the French, probably refers to the Italian town of Faenza, and includes not only French wares but also Delftware, as well as German and Scandinavian varieties. Italian wares of this type are known as *maiolica. Currently, "faience" simply means glazed earthenware, and is used as such in this book. The term always refers to decorated wares.

firing The process of rendering preformed clay objects permanently hard by heating them usually in a *kiln, though *ceramics can be fired in a pit covered with wood or dung. The various *clay bodies require different firing temperatures, which bring out the inherent characteristics of *earthenware, *stoneware, and *porcelain.

freehand painting Hand-painted patterns applied to *ceramic wares by skilled workers. In the factory environment this practice was the legacy of the British *Arts and Crafts Movement; it made possible the application of artistic designs to mass-produced wares. During the interwar years, in particular, the proliferation of hand-decorated wares in factories was the result of manufacturers both large and small seeking to increase their market share by improving their products. In general, such wares are considered to have greater value and status than their transfer-printed or dipped counterparts.

Freehand painting was exclusively done by women who, it was assumed, had a special talent for such work. At *Wedgwood, Louise and Alfred *Powell and Daisy *Makeig-Jones exerted a strong influence on production through their many designs specifically created for freehand painting. In her designs, Susie *Cooper took into account the special skills of *paintresses, having been one herself. In Japan, the Morimura Brothers of *Noritake created thousands of hand-painted wares for sale in the USA.

glaze A glassy coating. Glazes, which are mineral oxides (for color), powdered rocks, or clays suspended in water, are applied to porous *clay bodies to render them impervious to liquids, and also to increase the strength and durability of *earthenware. In the case of *stoneware and *porcelain, which become vitreous when fired, glazes are used simply to enhance their inherent characteristics and for decorative purposes. Such decoration can be applied with a brush or a spray gun, by pouring, or by dipping an object in the glaze.

hard-paste porcelain True, high-fired *porcelain, as opposed to artificial porcelains such as *soft-paste and *bone china.

kiln An oven specially designed for *firing ceramic wares or for fixing *enamel decoration.

leather-hard Any partially hardened, unfired *clay body. As its moisture content evaporates, a clay body hardens to a state resembling leather, into which decoration can be carved, incised, scratched or lathe-turned.

luster, lustre A thin coating of metallic oxide applied on the *glaze, resulting in an iridescent gloss or shiny metallic finish. During the interwar years, lusterware was produced universally. The Czechoslovakian ceramics industry probably learned the technique from German factories, and it was subsequently copied in Japan by *Noritake. The thinness of the metallic coating and low firing range (luster is fired to a temperature equal to that used for overglaze enamels) gives it little long-term durability; hence, few dinner plates are decorated in this way, though luster surfaces are often found on dessert sets and decorative accessories.

maiolica (Italian) Decorated tin-glazed *earthenware made in Italy. See also faience; Majolica.

Majolica The trade name given to highly decorated, lead-glazed *earthenware developed by Léon Arnoux at *Mintons between 1848 and 1851 in a style inspired by that typical of *maiolica of the Renaissance era.

mat (matt, matte) Dull, non-reflective, as in certain *glazes. Keith *Murray used a series of mat glazes, such as Moonstone, to enhance his Modernist designs for *Wedgwood during the 1930s.

paintress A specialist woman decorator in the British pottery industry. These employees decorated ceramic wares with over-glaze or under-glaze patterns created by designers such as Susie *Cooper and Clarice *Cliff. Girls would often leave school as early as twelve or thirteen years old to become paintresses. With the job, which had a superior status in the potteries, came better working conditions, a certain degree of autonomy in the workplace, and higher pay commanded by skilled labor. With talent and determina-

tion a paintress could sometimes become a designer, as in the case of Millicent *Taplin, but in practice it was unusual for a working-class woman to be promoted.

porcelain, porcelaine (French), Porzellan (German) Porcelain is composed of white refractory clay (kaolin) and feldspathic rock (petuntse) which fuses to form a glassy substance when subjected to high-temperature *firing (1450º C). A porcelain *clay body can be modelled, wheel-thrown, jiggered, or molded. The fired clay is characterized by its whiteness, translucency (when thinly formed), resonance, and tensile strength. See also hard-paste porcelain; soft-paste porcelain.

pouncing A technique for transferring intricate patterns to ceramic wares in preparation for hand-painting. A pricked paper pattern applied to the surface to be decorated is dusted with powdered charcoal which is tapped through it, providing an outline of the design for the painter to follow. (Powdered charcoal is used because it is clearly visible, but it leaves no lasting mark.) The technique, popular during the 18th century and again during the 1920s and 1930s in Europe, is still used for hand-painted designs. Many of Louise *Powell's complicated designs for *Wedgwood were transferred by this method.

press mold A porous plaster-of-Paris mold into which wet clay is pressed by hand. Excess water in the clay is absorbed by the mold, allowing the formed ceramic object to retain its shape when unmolded. Currently, the ceramics industry is being transformed by the introduction of dry-pressure molding, a process restricted to wares in uncomplicated shapes. Because of massive tooling costs, it could limit the future mass-production of ceramics to shapes with sales potential measured in millions of units.

serial production Industrial mass-production in which a succession of logical steps are performed by a number of different workers. Serial production necessitated a new specialization, that of the industrial designer, whose job it was to reconcile the dichotomy between aesthetic/design concerns and execution/production methods. Although the concept of serial production is readily associated with sleek

Modernist designs such as those of *Bauhaus ceramists and the architect Keith *Murray, tradition-based ceramics were produced in the same manner in England and elsewhere.

sgraffito A decorative technique of scratching a design on leather-hard ceramics, sometimes through a coating of *glaze or *slip to reveal the contrasting colour of the *clay body beneath.

shagreen, sharkskin, galucha (French) A luxurious decorative finish used on some Art Deco furniture by the ébéniste Jacques-Emile *Ruhlmann. A similar surface effect was created with *glaze on *porcelain.

slip Liquid clay with a creamy consistency, used for *casting, luting, trailing, sprigging, or decorating. It is also used as an overall coating in a color different from that of the *clay body.

slip-casting, see casting

soft-paste porcelain, pâte tendre (French) A porcelain *clay body containing a fluxing agent which allows for vitrification at 1200º C instead of the 1450º C required for *hard-paste porcelain. Most English porcelain and, in France, that of Vincennes and Sèvres (called porcelaine de France) is of the soft-paste type.

stoneware, grès (French), Steinzeug (German) A *clay body ranging in texture from smooth to pebbly or coarse, consisting of clay and fusible stone and fired to vitrification at 1250º C or above. Stoneware bodies come in a variety of colors, ranging from off-white to earthy brown shades to brown-black.

terra cotta, Terrakotta (German) A red *earthenware body, usually unglazed. The ubiquitous flower pot is made of terra cotta, which is also used in making architectural ceramics, such as decorative tiles and brick.

throwing rings/marks Surface ridges that result from the pressure of the potter's fingers on the clay when it is formed using a wheel; these are easily "smoothed out" if the effect is thought to be undesirable in a finished work. However, in the industrial production some designs, such as the *Homer Laughlin Company's Fiesta pattern, mimic throwing marks, thereby

linking the mass-made ware with earlier hand-made pots.

transfer printing A method—developed in Staffordshire, England, in 1756—of transferring engraved images onto ceramics. Printed transfers, also called decals, allow detailed decorations to be applied to ceramics in a less expensive manner than hand-painting. A pattern is etched on a stone or copper plate (later screen printing was also used for this purpose), an individual matrix being used for each color, and then transferred to a thin sheet of paper. To transfer the image from the paper to a glazed surface, it is first soaked in water, so softening the film holding the images, allowing it to slide from the paper onto the ceramic ware, which is then fired. The image fuses with the *glaze surface, becoming somewhat permanent. (Transfer prints are vulnerable to scratching.) Susie *Cooper created some designs in the 1930s which combined transfer-printed motifs with *freehand painting. Often, *enamel decoration, requiring a separate *firing, is used to enhance monochromatic transfer-printed designs.

tube-lining Thin, extruded or trailed outlines of *slip applied to wares to hold patterns of polychrome *glazes and prevent them from running together. The technique was first developed in the late 1890s and was popularized by William Moorcroft (1872–1945). Decorators such as Charlotte *Rhead used this method to create complicated floral designs, which were popular during the 1920s and 1930s.

volcanic glaze A *glaze that bubbles, blisters, and/or craters during firing, due to the addition of ingredients which boil, such as silicon carbide powder. Volcanic glazes, so named because the result resembled molten lava, were used by Raoul *Lachenal. His signature color was Egyptian blue; he also used clear red and yellow to enhance his Oriental-style pots.

whiteware (white earthenware), Steingut (German) White *earthenware, mostly associated with industrial production. Like *porcelain, whiteware (which is most often *slip cast and is much used in industry) provides a neutral background for all forms of decoration. It is often used in manufacturing dinnerware, such as Russel *Wright's American Modern.

BIBLIOGRAPHY

Albis, Jean d', *Haviland*, Paris, 1988.

Anderson, Ross and Perry, Barbara, *The Diversions of Keramos: American Clay Sculpture 1925–1950*, Syracuse, N.Y.: Everson Museum of Art, 1983.

Les Années '25: Art Déco/Bauhaus/Stijl/Esprit Nouveau, Paris: Musée des Arts Décoratifs, March–May 1966.

Anscombe, Isabelle, *Omega and After: Bloomsbury and the Decorative Arts*, London and New York, 1991.

Anscombe, Isabelle and Gere, Charlotte, *Arts and Crafts in Britain and America*, New York, 1978;

——, *A Woman's Touch: Women in Design from 1860 to the Present Day*, London and New York 1984.

Applegate, Judith, *Art Deco*, New York: Finch College Museum of Art, 1970.

Art de la Poterie en France: De Rodin à Dufy, L', Sèvres: Musée National de Céramique, June–October 1971.

Art Déco en Europe: Tendances décoratives dans les arts appliqués vers 1925; Brussels: Société des Expositions du Palais des Beaux-Arts, 1989.

Arwas, Victor, *Art Deco*, New York, 1980.

Atelier Robert Lallemant (1902–1954), sale catalogue (Ader Picard Tajan), Paris, April 1983.

Atherton, Carlton, "Early American Stoneware Craftsmanship," *Design*, December 1934.

Atterbury, Paul and Batkin, Maureen, *The Dictionary of Minton*, Woodbridge, Suffolk, 1990.

Atterbury, Paul and Irvine, Louise, *The Doulton Story*, Royal Doulton Tableware Ltd for the Victoria and Albert Museum, London, 1979.

Bach, Richard, "Contemporary Industrial Arts," *Design*, December 1934.

Banham, Reyner, *Theory and Design in the First Machine Age*, London, 1960.

Bartlett, John A., *British Ceramic Art 1870–1940*, Atglen, PA, 1993;

——, *English Decorative Ceramics*, London, 1989.

Batkin, Maureen, *Good Workmanship with Happy Thought: The Work of Alfred and Louise Powell*, Cheltenham Art Gallery and Museum, 1992.

Battersby, Martin, *The Decorative Thirties*, London, 1971, and *The Decorative Twenties*, London, 1969; both reprinted New York, 1989.

Bayer, Herbert and Gropius, Walter, *Bauhaus 1919–1928*, New York: The Museum of Modern Art, 1938.

Bayer, Patricia, *Art Deco Source Book: A Visual Reference to a Decorative Style, 1920–1940*, Secaucus, N.J., 1988.

Bayley, Stephen, *Twentieth-Century Style and Design* (with Philippe Garner and Deyan Sudjic), New York, 1986.

Bel Geddes, Norman, *Horizons in Industrial Design*, Boston, MA, 1932.

Bernstein, Melvin H., *Art and Design at Alfred: A Chronicle of a Ceramics College*, London and Toronto, 1986.

Bogaers, Marie-Rose, *Made in Holland: Domestic Pottery 1945–1988*, 's-Hertogenbosch, The Netherlands, 1988.

Bojani, Gian Carlo, *Ceramiche umbre 1900–1940*, Perugia, 1992.

Bolliger, Barbara E. Messerli, "Paul-Ami Bonifas: The Necessity of Unity", in Pamela Johnson (ed.), *The Journal of Decorative and Propaganda Arts 1875–1945*: Swiss Theme Issue, no. 19 (1993), pp. 42–53.

Bordeaux Art Déco, Musée des Arts Décoratifs de la Ville de Bordeaux, 1979.

Bray, Hazel V., *The Potter's Art in California 1885–1955*, Oakland, CA: The Oakland Museum, 1980.

Brinckmann-Rostock, A.E., "Neue Laeuger-Keramik," *Deutsche Kunst und Dekoration*, April–September 1920.

British Art and Design 1900–1960, London: Victoria and Albert Museum, 1984.

Bröhan, Karl H., *Berliner Porzellan vom Jugendstil zum Funktionalismus 1889–1939*, Berlin: Bröhan-Museum (n.d.).

Bröhan, Karl H. and Högerman, Dieter, *Neuerwerbungen für das Bröhan-Museum*, Berlin: Bröhan-Museum, 1986;

——, *Gemälde Skulpturen Kunsthandwerk Industriedesign*, Berlin, 1985.

Brunhammer, Yvonne, *The Art Deco Style*, London, 1983.

Brunhammer, Yvonne and Tise, Suzanne, *The Decorative Arts in France, 1900–1942*, Paris, 1990.

Buckley, Cheryl, *Potters and Paintresses: Women Designers in the Pottery Industry, 1870 to 1955*, London, 1990.

Buddensieg, Tilmann, *Ceramiche della Repubblica di Weimar*, Milan, 1984.

Burckhardt, Lucius (ed.), *The Werkbund. History and Ideology 1907–1933*, New York, 1980.

Bush, Donald, *The Streamlined Decade*, New York, 1975.

Cabanne, Pierre, *Encyclopédie Art Déco*, Paris, 1986.

Cameron, Elisabeth, *Encyclopedia of Pottery and Porcelain: 1880 to 1960*, New York and Oxford, 1986.

Casey, Andrew, *Susie Cooper Ceramics, A Collector's Guide*, Stratford-on-Avon, 1992.

"Ceramica Orvietana degli Anni Venti, La," Faenza: Museo Internazionale delle Ceramiche, 1983.

Ceramiche del Museo Artistico Industriale di Napoli: 1920–1950, Florence, 1985.

Cerutti, Carla, *Les Arts Décoratifs: Art Déco*, Paris, 1986.

Chavance, René, "Une Exposition Internationale de Dessins de Bijouterie et d'Orfèvrerie," *Art et Décoration*, Paris, March 1929;

——, "Le XIXe Salon des Artistes Décorateurs," ibid., July 1929;

——, "Faïences Récentes de la Manufacture de Sèvres," ibid., May 1931.

Cheronnet, Louis, "XXIe Salon des Artistes Décorateurs, 1931," *Art et Décoration*, Paris, July 1931.

Cinquantenaire de L'Exposition de 1925 (essays by Yvonne Brunhammer, Chantal Bizot, Marie-Noëlle de Gray, Nadine Gasc, Odile Nouvel, Alain Weill), Paris: Musée des Arts Décoratifs, 1977.

Clark, Garth, *American Ceramics: 1876 to the Present*, New York, 1987;

——, *The Potter's Art. A Complete History of Pottery in Britain*, Oxford, 1995.

Clark, Robert Judson, *The Arts and Crafts Movements in America 1876–1916*, Princeton, N.J., 1972.

Coddington, Barbara; Sanford Sivitz Shaman; & Patricia Grieve Watkinson (eds.), *Noritake Art Deco Porcelains: Collection of Howard Kottler*, Pullman, WA: Museum of Art, Washington State University, 1982.

Collins, Judith, *The Omega Workshops*, Chicago, 1984.

Contemporary Swedish Decorative Arts, The Metropolitan Museum of Art, New York, 1926.

Corrieras, Dominique, *L'Homme de Keramis: Charles Catteau*, Paris, 1991.

Crispolti, Enrico, *La Ceramica Futurista da Balla a Tullio D'Albisola* (Museo Internazionale delle Ceramiche, Faenza: Strumenti di studio per la ceramica del XIX e XX secolo), Florence, 1982.

Csenkey, Eva, *La Ceramica Ungherese della Secessione*, Florence, 1985.

Cumming, Elizabeth and Kaplan, Wendy, *The Arts and Crafts Movement*, London and New York, 1991.

Cunningham, Jo, *The Collector's Encyclopedia of American Dinnerware*, Paducah, KY, 1982.

Dale, Rodney, *Louis Wain, The Man Who Drew Cats*, London, 1991.

Dale, Sharon, *Frederick Hurten Rhead, An English Potter in America*, Erie, PA: Erie Art Museum, 1986.

Darton, Mike (ed.), *Art Deco: An Illustrated Guide to the Decorative Style, 1920 to 1940*, Secaucus, N.J., 1989.

Davies, Karen, *At Home in Manhattan: Modern Decorative Arts, 1925 to the Depression*, New Haven, CT: Yale University Art Gallery 1983.

Dervaux, Adolfe, *L'Architecture Étrangère à l'Exposition Internationale des Arts Décoratifs et Industriels Modernes*, Paris, 1925.

Deshairs, Léon, "Le Mobilier et les Arts Décoratifs au Salon d'Automne," *Art et Décoration*, Paris, December 1929.

Dietz, Ulysses G., *The Newark Museum Collection of American Art Pottery*, Newark, N.J.: The Newark Museum of Art, 1984.

Drew, Joanna and Strong, Roy, *Thirties: British Art and Design before the War*, London: Hayward Gallery, 1980.

Drexler, Arthur and Daniel, Greta, *Introduction to Twentieth Century Design from the Collection of The Museum of Modern Art New York*, Garden City, N.Y., 1959.

Duke, Harvey, *Hall 2*, Brooklyn, N.Y., 1985;

——, *Superior Quality Hall China: A Guide for Collectors*, Brooklyn, N.Y., 1977;
——, *Stangl Pottery*, Radnor, PA, 1993.
Duncan, Alastair, *American Art Deco*, London and New York, 1986;
——, *Art Deco*, London and New York, 1986;
——, *Art Deco Furniture*, London and New York, 1992;
——, *The Encyclopedia of Art Deco: An Illustrated Guide to a Decorative Style from 1920 to 1939*, London and New York, 1988.

Eatwell, Ann, *Susie Cooper Productions*, London: Victoria and Albert Museum, 1987.
Eidelberg, Martin (ed.), *Design 1935–1965: What Modern Was. Selections from the Liliane and David M. Stewart Collection, Le Musée des Arts Décoratifs de Montréal*, New York, 1991;
——, *Eva Zeisel: Designer for Industry*. Montreal: Musée des Arts Décoratifs de Montréal, and Chicago, IL, 1984.
Elisel, Visconti, *E. A. Arte Decorative:Una Exposicao*, Rio de Janeiro: PUC Funarte, 1982.
Elliott, D., *Art Into Production: Soviet Textiles, Fashion, and Ceramics, 1917–1935*, Oxford: Museum of Modern Art, 1984.
Ellis, Anita J., *Rookwood Pottery, The Glorious Gamble*, The Cincinnati Art Museum and New York, 1992.
Ercoli, Giuliano, *Art Deco Prints*, Oxford, 1989.
Evans, Paul, *Art Pottery of the United States. An Encyclopedia of Producers and Their Marks*, New York, 1987.
Exposition Internationale des Arts Décoratifs et Industriels Modernes, 1925, New York, 1977 (facsimile of a copy of the catalogue in the Metropolitan Museum of Art).
Fierens, Paul, "La Peinture et la Tapisserie à l'Exposition des Arts Décoratifs Modernes," *Gazette des Beaux-Arts*, Paris, Sept.–Oct. 1967.
Fleming, John and Honour, Hugh, *Dictionary of the Decorative Arts*, New York, 1977.
Frankl, Paul T., *Form and Re-Form: A Practical Handbook of Modern Interiors*, New York, 1930.
Frelinghuysen, Alice Cooney, *American Porcelain: 1770–1920*, New York: The Metropolitan Museum of Art, 1989.
Friedl, Hans, "Goldbrokat: eine neue Porzellan-Dekoration," *Die Kunst*, vol. 78, Oct. 1937–Sept. 1938.
Fuchs, H. and Burkhardt, F., *Product, Design, History: German Design from 1920 to the Present Era*, Stuttgart, 1985.

Functional Glamour: Utility in Contemporary American Ceramics, 's-Hertogenbosch: Museum Het Kruithuis, 1987.
Fusco, Tony, *Art Deco Identification and Price Guide*, New York, 1993.

Gallotti, Jean, "Les Arts Indigènes à l'Exposition Coloniale," *Art et Décoration*, Sept. 1931.
Garner, Philippe (ed.), *Phaidon Encyclopedia of Decorative Arts, 1890–1940*, Oxford, 1978.
Gaston, Mary Frank, *Collector's Guide to Art Deco*, Paducah, KY, 1969.
Gauthier, Maximilien, "La Céramique. Exposition Internationale des Arts Décoratifs," *L'Art Vivant*, November 1925.
Gloag, John, *Industrial Art Explained*, London, 1934.
Godden, G.A., *British Pottery*, London, 1974.
Goissaud, A., "La Manufacture Nationale de Sèvres," *L'Art Vivant*, Paris, 1925.
Greif, Martin, *Depression Modern: The Thirties Style in America*, New York, 1975.
Greenberg, Cara, *New York Art Deco Exposition at Radio City Music Hall*, New York: Big Apple Events, 1975.

Hallam, Edward, *Ashtead Potters Ltd in Surrey 1923–1935*, Epsom, Surrey, 1980.
Hand-Painted Gray's Pottery: Made in Stoke-on-Trent, England, Stoke-on-Trent: City Museum and Art Gallery, 1982.
Hannah, Frances, *Ceramics: Twentieth Century Design*, London, 1986.
Harrison, Helen A., *Dawn of a New Day: The New York World's Fair, 1939–40*, New York and London, 1980.
Hars, Eva, *Zsolnay Ceramia*, Pécs, 1982.
Hautecœur, Louis, "Les Pavillons Étrangers à l'Exposition des Arts Décoratifs," *Architecture*, Paris, 1925.
Hawley, Henry Houston, "Cowan Pottery," *The Bulletin of the Cleveland Museum of Art*, vol. 76, no. 7, September 1989.
Heide, Robert and Gilman, John, *Popular Art Deco: Depression Era Style and Design*, New York, 1991.
Hennessey, William J., *Russel Wright: American Designer*, Cambridge, MA, 1985.
Heskett, John, *Design in Germany, 1870 to 1918*, London, 1986.
Hillier, Bevis, *Art Deco*, London, 1968;
——, *The World of Art Deco*, The Minneapolis Institute of Arts and New York, 1971.
Horsham, Michael, *'20s and '30s Style*, Secaucus, N.J., 1989.

Hostache, Elloe H., "Reflections on the Exposition des Arts Décoratifs," *Architectural Forum*. New York, 1926, vol. 44.
Huxford, Sharon and Bob, *The Collector's Encyclopedia of Roseville Pottery*, Paducah, KY, 1976;
——, *The Collector's Encyclopedia of Fiesta with Harlequin and Riviera*, Paducah, KY, 1981.

Jaffe, H., *De Stijl 1917–31: Visions of Utopia*. Oxford, 1982.
Janneau, Guillaume, "Introduction à l'Exposition des Arts Décoratifs; Considérations sur L'Esprit Moderne," *Art et Décoration*, 1925.
Jarchow, Margarete, *Berliner Porzellan im 20. Jahrhundert*, Berlin, 1988.
Jones, Joan, *Minton: The First Two Hundred Years of Design and Production*, Shrewsbury, 1993.
Joze, Pierre and Vautier, Dominique, *Art Déco Belgique 1920–1940*, Brussels: Musée des Beaux-Arts d'Ixelles, 1988.
"Jugendstil/Art Nouveau/Art Déco: 57. Auction," Munich: Galerie Wolfgang Ketterer, 1982.

Kallir, Jane, *Viennese Design and the Wiener Werkstätte*, New York, 1986.
Kholmogorova, O.V., Bubchikova, M.A., & Fomichyova, T.V., *Art Born of the October Revolution: Placards, Porcelain, Textiles*, Moscow: The State Order of Lenin History Museum, n.d.
Klein, Dan, *All Colour Book of Art Deco*, London, 1974;
——, *L'Esprit Art Deco* (with Nancy A. McClelland and Malcolm Haslam), London, 1987;
——, *In the Deco Style*, London and New York, 1986.
Knopf Collector's Guide to Pottery and Porcelain, The, New York, 1983.
Koch, Alexander, *Deutsche Kunst und Dekoration*, Darmstadt, 1987.
Kogchlin, Raymond, "L'Exposition des Arts Décoratifs: Les Premiers Efforts de Rénovation 1885–1914," *Gazette des Beaux-Arts*, May 1925.
Kovel, Ralph and Terry, *Kovel's New Dictionary of Marks: Pottery and Porcelain 1850 to the Present*, New York, 1985.
Kraft, Leonh., "Wiener Kunstschau 1920," *Deutsche Kunst und Dekoration*, vol. XLVII (October 1920–March 1921).

Lajoix, Anne, *La Céramique en France 1925–1947*, Paris, 1983.
Langseth-Christensen, Lillian, *A Design for Living*, New York, 1987.

Le Corbusier (trans. James Dunnett), *The Decorative Art of Today*, Cambridge, MA, 1987
Lesieutre, Alain, *The Spirit and Splendour of Art Deco*, London, 1975, and Secaucus, N.J., 1978.
Lobanov-Rostovsky, Nina, *Revolutionary Ceramics: Soviet Porcelain 1917–1927*, New York, 1990.
Loggia, Marianne, "Death and Life in Tradition: Gio Ponti's Ceramics," *American Ceramics*, vol. 10, no. 2.
Loring, John, "American Deco," *The Connoisseur*, January 1979, pp. 48–53.

Maenz, Paul, *Art Deco: 1920–1940*, Cologne, 1974 (reprinted 1980).
Magyar Art Deco = Hungarian Art Deco, Budapest: Iparművészeti Múzeum, 1985.
Manners, Errol, *Ceramics Source Book*, Secaucus, N.J., 1990.
Marchard, R., *Advertising the American Dream: Making Way for Modernity 1920–40*, Berkeley, CA, 1985.
Meikle, J.L., *Twentieth Century Limited: Industrial Design in America*, Philadelphia, PA, 1975.
Meister der Deutschen Keramik 1900–1950, Cologne: Kunstgewerbemuseum, 1978.
Menten, T., *The Art Deco Style in Household Objects, Architecture, Sculpture and Jewelry*, New York, 1972.
Miller, Judith and Martin, *Miller's World Encyclopedia of Antiques*, New York, 1989.
"Modelli di Ceramiche Stoffe, Mobilized Intarsi dell' Artiganato," *Domus*, September 1933.
Morgan, Sarah, *Art Deco: The European Style*, New York, 1990.
Mourey, Gabriel, "The Paris International Exhibition, 1925," *The Studio*, London, July 1925;
——, "Le XXVIIIe Salon de la Société des Artistes Décorateurs," *Mobilier et Décoration*, June 1938.
Müller, Erwin, *Die Wiedergeburt des Porzellans*, Munich, 1930.
Muncher, Bredt, "Die Wiener Porzellan-Manufaktur Augarten," *Decorative Kunst*, 1927.
Mundt, Barbara, *40 Jahre Porzellan*, Berlin, 1986.

Naylor, Blanche, "Industrial Art Exhibit," *Design*, June 1935.
Naylor, G., *The Bauhaus Re-Assessed: Sources and Design Theory*, London, 1985.
Neuwirth, Waltraud, *Die Keramik der Wiener Werkstätte*, Vienna: Österreichisches Museum für angewandte Kunst, 1981;

——, *Wiener Porzellan vom Spätbarock zum Art Déco*, Vienna, 1990;

——, *Wiener Werkstätte: Avantgarde, Art Déco, Industrial Design*, Vienna: Österreichisches Museum für angewandte Kunst, 1984.

Objecten Glas en Ceramiek vit Tsjechoslouakije, Rotterdam: Museum Boymans-Van Beuningen, 1970.

O'Neill, Amanda, *Introduction to the Decorative Arts: 1890 to the Present Day*, London, 1990.

Opie, Jennifer Hawkins, *Scandinavia: Ceramics and Glass in the Twentieth Century: The Collection of the Victoria and Albert Museum*, London: Victoria and Albert Museum, 1989.

Ostergard, Derek, *Art Deco Masterpieces*, New York, 1991.

Österreichische Keramik, 1900–1980, Linz: Stadtmuseum, 1981.

Peck, Herbert, *The Book of Rookwood Pottery*, Tucson, AR, 1986.

Pedersen, Roy and Wolanin, Barbara A., *New Hope Modernists 1917–1950*, New Hope, PA, 1991.

Pélichet, Edgar, *La Céramique Art Déco*, Lausanne, 1988.

Perry, Barbara (ed.), *American Ceramics: The Collection of the Everson Museum of Art* (essays by William C. Ketchum, Jr., Richard G. Case, Ulysses G. Dietz, Barbara Perry, and Garth Clark), New York, 1989.

Pickel, Susan E., *From Kiln to Kitchen: American Ceramic Design in Tableware*, Springfield, IL: Illinois State Museum, 1980.

Pincus-Witten, Robert, "Art Deco: Finch College Reviews the History of the Style," *Artforum*, December 1970.

Ponti, Gio, "L'Arredamento alla Triennale. Le Ceramiche alla Triennale," *Domus*, May 1933;

——, "Le Ceramiche Italiane alla Triennale," *Domus*, August 1935;

——, "Ceramiche Moderne Italiane al Jeu de Paume," *Domus*, June 1935;

——, "Industrie Italiane d'Arte Ceramica alla Triennale," *Domus*, June 1933.

Ponti, Lisa Licitra, *Gio Ponti: The Complete Work 1923–1978*, Cambridge, MA, 1990.

Poor, Henry Varnum, *Arts and Crafts in Detroit, 1906–1976: The Movement, The Society, The School*, Detroit: The Detroit Institute of Arts, 1976.

Porzellan-Kunst: Sammlung Karl H. Bröhan, Berlin: Schloss Charlottenburg, 1969.

Poulain-Caese, Georgette and Norbert, *Art Déco-Keramik*, Ghent, Keramisches Museum Mettlach, Schloss Ziegelberg, 1981.

Préaud, Tamara and Gauthier, Serge, *Ceramics of the 20th Century*, New York, 1982.

Ravilious and Wedgwood: the Complete Wedgwood Designs of Eric Ravilious (catalogue), London, 1986.

Read, Helen Appleton, "Twentieth Century Decoration," *Vogue*, 71 (1 April 1928).

Read, Herbert, *Art and Industry: The Principles of Industrial Design*, London, 1953, and New York, 1954.

Rémor, Georges, "Le Pavillon de la Ville de Paris," *L'Art Vivant*, 1925.

Robinson, C. and Bletter, R.H., *Skyscraper Style: Art Deco New York*, New York, 1975.

Rosenthal, Rudolph, "Applied Art of Today," *Design*, January 1935.

Rosenthal, Rudolph and Ratzka, Helena L., *The Story of Modern Applied Art*, New York, 1948.

Rosso, Fulvio M., *Per virtù del fuoco: Uomini e ceramiche del Novecento Italiano*, Aosta, 1983.

Scarlett, Frank and Townley, Marjorie, *Arts Décoratifs 1925: A Personal Recollection of the Paris Exhibition*, London, 1975.

Schedig, W., *Crafts of the Weimar Bauhaus*, London, 1967.

Schweiger, Werner J., *Wiener Werkstätte: Design in Vienna 1903–1932*, New York, 1982, and London, 1984.

Sembach, Klaus-Jürgen, *Style 1930: Elegance and Sophistication in Architecture, Design, Fashion, Graphics, and Photography*, New York, 1986;

——, *Into the Thirties: Style and Design, 1927 to 1934*, London, 1972.

Siepen, Bernhard, "Ein Neues Porzellan-Geschirr," *Die Kunst*, Oct. 1937–Sept. 1938.

Spours, Judy, *Art Deco Tableware: British Domestic Ceramics 1925–1939*, New York, 1988.

Trapp, Kenneth R., *Toward the Modern Style: Rookwood Pottery, The Carr Years 1915–1950*, New York, 1983.

Troy, Nancy J., *Modernism and the Decorative Arts in France: Art Nouveau to Le Corbusier*, New Haven, CT, 1991.

Uncommon Clay: The Mitchell Wolfson Jr. Collection of Decorative and Propaganda Arts, Miami, FL, 1985.

Valotaire, M., *Céramique Française Moderne*, Paris, 1930.

Varenne, Gaston and Chavance, René, "L'Exposition des Arts Décoratifs," *Art et Décoration*, 1925.

Vegesack, Alexander von (ed.), *Czech Cubism: Architecture, Furniture, Decorative Arts*, Princeton, N.J., 1992.

Veronesi, Giulia, *Into the Twenties. Style and Design, 1909–1929*, London, 1958; U.S. ed. *Style and Design 1909–1929*, New York, 1968.

Vienna 1913: Josef Hoffmann's Gallia Apartment, Melbourne: National Gallery of Victoria, 1984.

Villechenon, Marie-Noëlle Pinot de, *Sèvres, Une collection de porcelaines, 1740–1992*, Paris: Musée National de Céramique, 1993.

Watson, Howard and Pat, *Collecting Art Deco Ceramics*, London, 1993.

Weber, Eva, *American Art Deco*, London, 1992.

Weber, Peter, *Keramik und Bauhaus*, Bauhaus Archiv, Berlin (West), Gerhard-Marcks-Haus, Bremen and Hetjens-Museum, Düsseldorf, 1989.

Weiser, Armand, "Die Schweden auf der Pariser Kunstgewerbeausstellung," *Decorative Kunst*, October 1925.

Weiss, Peg, *Adelaide Alsop Robineau, Glory in Porcelain*, Syracuse, N.Y., 1981;

——, *The Art Deco Environment*, Syracuse, N.Y.: Everson Museum of Art, 1976.

Wentworth-Sheilds, Peter and Johnson, Kay, *Clarice Cliff*, London, 1976.

Wersin, W., "Vasen," *Die Kunst*, Oct. 1935–Sept. 1936, pp. 84–87.

Whitford, Frank, *Bauhaus*, London and New York, 1984.

Whitmyer, Margaret and Kenn, *The Collector's Encyclopedia of Hall China*, Paducah, KY, 1989.

Wiener Werkstätte and their Associates, 1903–1932, The, London: Fischer Fine Art Ltd, 1982.

Wills, Geoffrey, *Wedgwood*, London, 1988.

Wilson, Richard Guy, Pilgrim, Dianne H., and Tashjian, Dickran., *The Machine Age in America 1918–1941*, New York, 1986.

Wingler, H.M., *The Bauhaus: Weimar, Dessau, Berlin, Chicago*, Cambridge, MA, 1969.

Woodham, Jonathan M., *Twentieth-Century Ornament*, New York, 1990.

Wright, Frank Lloyd, *Frank Lloyd Wright: Architectural Drawings and Decorative Art* (Introduction by David A. Hanks and Jennifer Toher), London: Fischer Fine Art Ltd, 1986.

Wurts, R., *The New York World's Fair, 1939–1940*, New York, 1977.

Zoellner, A., "Neue Arbeiten der Porzellanfabrik Rosenthal," *Die Kunst*, Oct. 1937–Sept. 1938, pp. 21–24.

INDEX